Competitiveness and Growth
in Brazilian Cities

Competitiveness and Growth in Brazilian Cities

Local Policies and Actions for Innovation

Ming Zhang, Editor

THE WORLD BANK
Washington, D.C.

Contents

Boxes

Acknowledgments

This report has been prepared by a team led by Ming Zhang, Lead Urban Economist in the Latin America and the Caribbean Region of the World Bank. The main authors are Ming Zhang (chapters 1, 2, 5, and Executive Summary); Mark Roberts, consultant and Lecturer at the University of Cambridge (chapter 1); Fernanda Ruiz Nuñez, Young Professional at the World Bank (chapter 3); Daniel da Mata, consultant and Researcher at the Brazil Institute of Applied Economic Research (chapters 4 and 5); Monica Amorim, consultant and Professor at the Federal University of Ceará (chapter 4); Alec Hansen, consultant and President of the Economic Competitiveness Group, Inc.; Enrique Asturizaga, consultant; and Kim Cuenco, Senior Operations Officer at the World Bank Institute (chapter 5).

The original study, "Competitiveness and Growth in Brazilian Cities," was initiated by Mila Freire and Jóse Guillerme Reis, who led the concept stage of the study and continued to provide guidance and advice throughout the process. Overall direction was provided by John Briscoe and Makhtar Diop, Country Directors for Brazil; Laura Tuck, Sector Director of Sustainable Development; and Guang Zhe Chen, Sector Manager for Urban, Water, and Disaster Management in the Latin America and the Caribbean Region. Pamela Cox is the Vice President of the Region.

Jennifer Sara, Sector Leader for Brazil, provided detailed advice and comments throughout the study. Somik Lall, Tito Yepes, Sarah Anthony, and Emil de Quiros also provided valuable contributions to the study at different stages. Jonathan Aspin was the editor for the report.

The team is grateful for the detailed and helpful comments from peer reviewers Christine Kessides, Abhas Jha, Kate Kuper, Stephen Karam, and Deepali Tewari, as well as for comments from Ronald MacLean-Abaroa, Giorgio Romano Schutte, and Paula Pini. We also benefited from the valuable feedback on the presentations of the initial results of the study from the participants at a number of events in Brazil, including the World Conference of City Development in Porto Alegre in February 2008, the Seminar on the Role of Cities in National Economic Development in Brasilia in June 2007, and workshops in São Luís, Maranhão, and in Cariri, Ceará, in January 2008. The team would like to acknowledge the financial support of the United Kingdom's Department for International Development through the Markets and Governance for Poverty Reduction Fund for the Latin America and the Caribbean Region.

Finally, for their collaborative and cooperative efforts, we would like to thank the state government of Ceará, especially Secretary Joaquim Cartaxo and Executive Secretary Vania Araripe; and from the municipal government of São Luís, Mayors João Castelo and Tadeu Palácio. Their determination to promote economic development by enhancing competitiveness provided the inspiration for the team, and we hope this report can be useful to them and other Brazilian policy makers at the municipal, state, and federal levels.

Abbreviations

ABRASEL	Brazilian Association of Bars and Restaurants
AFABRICAL	Associação dos Fabricantes de Calçados (Footware Makers' Association)
BNB	Banco do Nordeste do Brasil (Northeast Development Bank)
BNDES	Banco Nacional de Desenvolvimento Econômico e Social (National Bank for Economic and Social Development)
CAD	Computer-aided design
CAM	Computer-aided manufacturing
CDC	Community development corporation
CDFI	Community development financial institution
CENTEC	Instituto Centro de Tecnologia do Ceará (Technology Center Institute of Cariri)
CIAP	Center for Information and Support for Plastics Technologies
CITEs	Centros de Innovación Tecnológica (Technology Centers)
CNAE	Classificação Nacional de Atividades Econômicas (National Classification of Economic Activities)

EU	European Union
FDI	Foreign direct investment
FETECC	Ceará Footwear Technology Trade Fair
FIMEC	International Fair of Leather, Chemicals, Components, and Equipments for Footwear and Tanneries
G-8	Group of Eight
GDP	Gross domestic product
IADB	Inter-American Development Bank
IBGE	Instituto Brasileiro de Geografia e Estatistica (Brazilian Institute of Geography and Statistics)
ICOMOS	International Council on Monuments and Sites
ICT	Information and communication technology
IPEA	Instituto de Pesquisa Econômica Aplicada (Institute of Applied Economic Research)
IPHAN	Instituto do Patrimônio Histórico e Artístico Nacional (Brazilian National Historical and Artistic Heritage Institute)
LQ	Location quotient
MCA	Minimum comparable area
MIT	Massachusetts Institute of Technology
OECD	Organisation for Economic Co-operation and Development
PCA	Principal component analysis
R&D	Research and development
RAIS	Relação Anual de Informações Sociais (Annual Records of Social Information)
SAGED	Sub-Secretary of Sustainable Development
SEBRAE	Serviço Brasileiro de Apoio às Micro e Pequenas Empresas (Brazil Micro and Small Business Services)
SENAI	Serviço Nacional de Aprendizagem Industrial (National Industrial Training Service)
SEPLAN	Secretary of Planning and Development
SINDCALC	Sindicato da Indústria de Calçados de Crato (Crato Footwear Association)
SINDHORBS	Association of Hotels, Restaurants, and Bars
SINDINDUSTRIA	Cariri Footwear Industry Association
SME	Small and microenterprise

UNESCO	United Nations Educational, Scientific and Cultural Organization
UNICAMP	Universidade Estadual de Campinas (State University of Campinas)
URCA	Universidade Regional do Cariri (Regional University of Cariri)
WEN	Wisconsin Entrepreneurs Network

Currency Equivalents

(Exchange Rate Effective December 1, 2008)
Currency unit = R$
R$$2.3 = US$1
US$0.43 = R$1.00

Fiscal Year
January 1–December 31

Executive Summary

Why City Competitiveness?

Given the Brazilian federal government's high priority on economic growth, competitiveness is at the top of the economic agenda. While economic policies at the national level are important to this agenda, more than 75 percent of people live in urban areas, which produce more than 90 percent of the gross domestic product (GDP). "What can cities do to improve economic performance and create jobs?" Mayors, governors, and federal government officials have frequently asked this question. For cities, economic competition has become more intense with globalization. Many municipal officials have been striving to enhance municipal infrastructure and services, while others have also been working on reducing the cost of doing businesses to make their areas more attractive for private investment. On the other hand, promoting local economic growth without considering local context and market conditions does not always achieve expectations. The challenge for both local and national policy makers is to understand how to promote city competitiveness. "What would work? What would not work? What are the conditions necessary for policies to be effective?" These are the main questions that this report tackles.

What Is Competitiveness?

Following similar definitions by the World Economic Forum (Porter, Sala-i-Martin, and Schwab 2007), this report defines competitiveness as *the set of institutions, policies, and factors that determine the level of productivity* of a city or region. With productivity as a basic measure, competitiveness thus encompasses connotations that include both the level of economic growth and the potential for sustained growth. Competitive local economies not only produce higher income for their cities, but are also more likely to grow faster over the medium to long term.

The concept of city competitiveness is not without its controversies. Some economists, most notably Nobel laureate Paul Krugman, have questioned the extent to which it is meaningful to even apply the term "competitiveness" to entities other than firms. It is true that cities do not compete with each other as private businesses do; in fact, in most cases, the wealth of cities is created by the private sector, and it is private businesses that need to compete, locally, nationally, and globally.

Yet location matters, and some cities provide better locations than others for private businesses to be more competitive. To become more competitive, businesses rely on a favorable local environment (one that nurtures competition and innovation). Local governments therefore can, and do, pursue policies to improve the local business environment, which in turn raises the income level of residents. Cities thus compete against each other in the sense that those cities able to provide a better business environment are likely to have more competitive private businesses. If cities are to provide this better business environment, decision makers need to understand the factors that private businesses regard as important, and the proper role of local governments.

The policies discussed in this report are essentially about promoting local economic development. However, we believe that the term competitiveness, as a dynamic concept, is helpful for local policy makers as it implies two essential aspects of promoting local economic development in today's environment: (a) cities not only need to provide a *good* business environment—they need to strive to provide a *better* one than others, at least in certain aspects (or niches); and (b) cities need to continually upgrade and innovate to achieve sustained growth.

Why Is City Competitiveness Important for Brazil?

For many mayors and governors, economic growth at the city level is important simply because raising incomes and creating jobs is their top priority. Even more, they have found that for the private sector to generate more jobs, they are competing not only with Brazilian cities but with other locations globally. So it is imperative for cities to become economically competitive. For policy makers at the federal level, because Brazil is a large country with considerable regional disparities, city-level factors and policies for growth are inevitably critical. In the past, competition among cities has focused on destructive "fiscal wars"[1]; are there better ways to encourage cities to compete? More fundamentally, to strengthen overall national economic competitiveness, what kind of economic policy role for municipal and state governments should the federal government promote?

Brazil indeed has been a global leader in many ways, including government policies for promoting local economic competitiveness. For instance, the Serviço Brasileiro de Apoio às Micro e Pequenas Empresas (Brazil Micro and Small Business Services, or SEBRAE) has been leading the efforts in fostering cluster activities (*arranjos produtivos locais* or local productive arrangements) in different sectors across the country, with a focus on essential small and microenterprises. Similarly, the Serviço Nacional de Aprendizagem Industrial (National Industrial Training Service, or SENAI) has been instrumental in enhancing the level of skills for local industrial growth. Brazilian business incubators have been noted worldwide for their innovations and success.

At the same time, city economic growth and competitiveness have generally not yet been put high on the national or local development agenda in Brazil. While many cities have given them much importance, in most cases there is a lack of high-level, citywide, coherent policies and efforts to pursue a viable strategy. At the national level, there are as yet no consistent policies and guidance on local economic development.

Other countries, however, in both the developed and developing world, have been reviewing and reconsidering their local development policies. For example, the United Kingdom set out a subnational economic development and regeneration reform agenda in July 2007 (HM Treasury 2007). In the United States, the Brookings Institution issued a report in 2008 urging that "America and its federal government must put the prosperity of the U.S. cities and suburban areas—the nation's crucial metropolitan hubs—at the center of a broad new effort to renovate American governance" (Brookings Institution 2008). In China, the dynamics of cities and other local governments have been instrumental in its rapid economic growth, and successive national medium-term policy plans have ensured them a prominent role in the national development agenda. With its profound decentralization, and the dynamics displayed by its municipalities, it is perhaps time for Brazil to develop a national policy on economic growth and competitiveness at the city level.

The Study and Outputs

This report presents the main results of the study, "Competitiveness and Growth in Brazilian Cities." The objective of the study is to contribute to answering the questions raised by mayors, governors, and central governments: "What can cities do to improve economic performance and create jobs?" The question is approached through a review of theories and policy options, preliminary benchmarking of Brazilian cities, and case studies of two specific urban areas in northeast Brazil—the Cariri region, Ceará, and São Luís, Maranhão. We believe that there is no unique approach to a strategy for city competitiveness that is applicable to all cities, and the essence of a competitiveness strategy is for each city to define a niche and its own approach. To be able to do this, local policy makers need to understand what the *factors* are that make cities competitive, and what *types* of policies may work. These two topics are therefore the focus of the study and report.

Initial results of the study were presented in several forums in Brazil, including the World Conference of City Development in Porto Alegre held February 13–16, 2008, and the Seminar on the Role of Cities in National Economic Development in Brasilia held June 18–19, 2007. Valuable feedback from these seminars and other occasions was incorporated into this report.

The following sections present an outline of the chapters and the main conclusions.

Chapter 1. What Makes Cities Competitive? Local Determinants of Competitiveness

Myriad factors contribute to economic growth and competitiveness at the city level (figure 1). The most often cited include macroeconomic environment, natural endowments, physical capital and infrastructure, and local business regulation (or cost of doing business). Less widely recognized are some local factors that are related to the dynamics of spatial concentration and innovation—the most important factors for economic vitality at the city level, which is the focus of this chapter's selective review of the local determinants of competitiveness.

Figure 1.   Key Drivers of City Competitiveness and Their Interlinkages

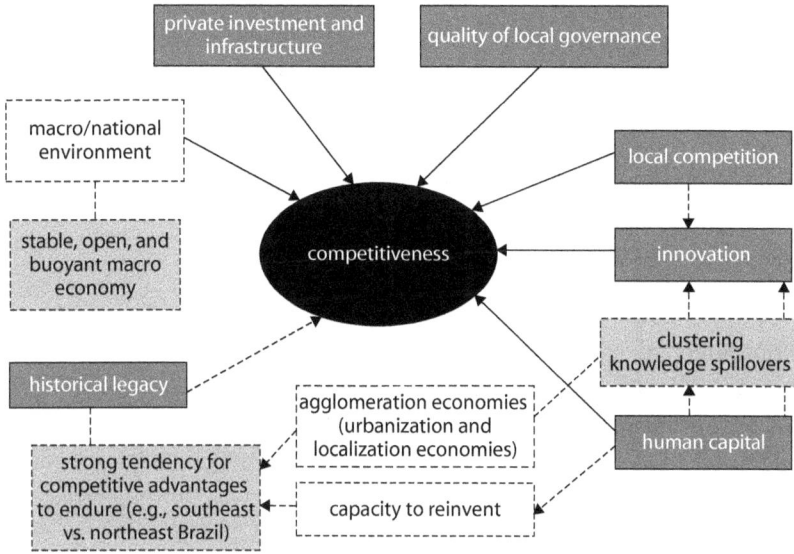

Sources: Authors, based on various sources.

Historical Legacy and Localized Increasing Returns

City-level competitive advantage displays a strong tendency to persist over long periods. Therefore, competitive cities and regions remain so over time, and it is difficult for less competitive ones to catch up. In Brazil, the most competitive cities remain in the southeast. São Paulo's GDP per capita, while declining relative to its national share over the preceding few decades, was still 67 percent above the national average in 2005. Yet cities' persistent economic success often outlasts the original reasons for existence. Although São Paulo initially developed because of the coffee trade, its current economic strength is of an entirely different nature. So although *comparative advantage* often explains the origins of many of today's most successful cities, continuing success rests on *competitive advantage*, or the ability for cities to renew, upgrade, and reinvent themselves.

Behind cities' persistent economic success are the processes of agglomeration by which competitive advantage is generated: positive feedback mechanisms from localized increasing returns, which bring self-reinforcing circles of success. In particular, urbanization economies are associated with the productivity benefits that a city enjoys because of its market size, which facilitates diversity in production and consumption and which simultaneously acts as a positive spur to competition and innovation. Localization economies are the productivity benefits that an individual industry (or cluster) in a city can gain as a result of its concentration. These benefits are the result of the combination of a skilled labor pool for that cluster, local businesses that are specialized in the supply of intermediate goods and services, and knowledge flows among firms. Urbanization economies help explain the persistent competitive success of cities, while localization economies partly explain the long-standing success of many clusters.

Innovative Environment

Innovation has been characterized as the lifeblood of competitiveness, and cities derive their competitive advantage from the geographic concentration of industries and *knowledge spillover effects*, or the unintended positive side effects (externalities) on productivity from the activities of individual local firms. These knowledge spillover effects occur in three ways:

- *Learning by observation* is seen when, through proximity, one local firm learns, by observation, new ways of doing business from another local firm.
- *Learning through meeting* takes place through direct face-to-face human interaction, including formal and informal discussions with peers, suppliers, and customers. Face-to-face interaction is important because of the tacit nature of much knowledge, and because it allows a higher frequency of exchanging ideas than alternatives such as emails.
- *Learning through leaving* happens when an employee leaves one firm to work for another firm, or to start his or her own business, thereby transferring knowledge outside the firm.

The knowledge spillover effects lead to complementary competitiveness among local firms and formation of an innovative environment. When the synergies between local firms are strong enough, the local economy will be able to achieve self-sustaining growth through exploiting an imitation–innovation nexus. But left on their own, local firms tend to overlook the positive spillover effects of knowledge generation and innovation, since the full benefits of these activities are not captured by individual firms. The result is a coordination failure that leaves local synergies underexploited. Local governments and other players can, therefore, play a facilitating role to help address this coordination failure to promote higher levels of innovation. It is also important to correct the misconception that innovation is equal to "high tech." According to Michael Porter: "There is no such thing as a low-tech industry. There are only low-tech companies—that is, companies that fail to use world-class technology and practices to enhance productivity and innovation" (Porter 1998, p. 89).

Human Capital

Human capital is an important input to innovative, knowledge-based activities, as a higher level of such capital permits the more efficient transformation of preexisting knowledge into new forms of knowledge. The level of local human capital is important also because direct face-to-face interaction for the transmission of tacit knowledge requires a high level of communication skills. Human capital also assists in attracting a favorable industry mix, and contributes to the ability of a city to reinvent itself. The existence of a talent pool—a skilled and specialized pool of labor—can be crucial in attracting the foreign direct investment (FDI) that helps a city gain a foothold in industries that are higher up the value chain. A case study of Boston, Massachusetts, by Edward Glaeser (2003) shows that the decisive factor separating Boston from Detroit, Michigan, and from Syracuse, New York (even though all three experienced poor performance from 1950 to 1980 as manufacturing cities), has been the highly educated nature of its workforce, which has been assisted by the city's historical strength as a center of learning and education, and its reputation as a livable city for the highly skilled.

Local Competition

Empirical research has found overwhelming evidence of the positive effects of local competition for local growth, because in a highly competitive environment a firm has to continue to engage in product, process, and marketing innovation to give it a competitive edge in the local marketplace. Firms accustomed to a competitive local environment are more likely to succeed in competition at the global level. Evidence also shows that as economic clusters mature, the presence of a local competitive environment generally becomes more important. Figure 1.4 (chapter 1) for example, from a study conducted by Claas van der Linde (2003), shows that while developing-country clusters relied more on comparative advantage, those in developed countries relied more on competitive advantage. The type of local competition affects overall local competitiveness.

The link is stronger if local competition is through innovation and adaptation, rather than through cut-throat local price competition.

Infrastructure

The contribution of infrastructure to economic growth has been well documented. One important dimension of infrastructure's contribution, as highlighted by the *World Development Report 2009: Reshaping Economic Geography* (World Bank 2008), is its instrumental role in allowing agglomeration economies to take place. From a competitiveness viewpoint, different types of infrastructure investment are important for different types of cities and at different stages of a city's development. Investment in basic public utilities and local public goods is important to provide the foundations for building density in small cities; spatially connective transport infrastructure is a further requirement for fast-growing, medium-size cities; and large cities additionally require spatially targeted investments in, for example, affordable housing to overcome divisions associated with the presence of slums. One other important result of infrastructure improvements is the enhancement of urban amenities—making a city more livable—which has become increasingly important for attracting and retaining high-level human resources.

Quality of Local Governance

The quality of local governance is important to city competitiveness because so much of the microeconomic environment of private businesses is affected or determined by the local public sector. For example, *local regulations* that enhance or constrain business activities, in areas such as starting a business, dealing with licenses, registering property, and employing workers, can have a significant impact on economic growth and competitiveness. Studies have found that the lower the entry barriers and state control, the faster the process of catch-up to best-practice technologies in manufacturing industries occurs. In fact, with a primary function of *providing local public goods*, local governments can play a leading role in the quality of infrastructure and human capital (through its role in providing education)—both important determinants for competitiveness, as discussed above. The ability of large cities to continue to grow and reinvent themselves can be facilitated or limited by the coverage and efficiency of infrastructure (especially transportation), which defines the effective labor market size (Prud'homme and Lee 1999). In other words, how much a city can grow also heavily depends on the effectiveness of its governance.

An efficient, professional, and participatory governance structure that can lead to high-quality public choices is especially important for high-density urban areas, where not only are a large part of public goods provided by the local government (including public security and recreation activities), but public choice also fundamentally shapes the future of the city through land-use planning and regulations, the formation of a shared city identity and vision, and activities that facilitate their realization.

Chapter 2. What Can Cities Do to Enhance Competitiveness?

The crucial contribution of knowledge and innovation to growth, as illustrated by these theoretical advances and successful examples worldwide, suggests opportunities for a broader scope of local interventions aiming at enhancing positive spillover effects among private firms and other players in the local economy. A more proactive role for local government may be warranted for cities to become and stay competitive in a global environment characterized by ever-increasing competitive pressures.

The Starting Point: Understanding the Local Economy and the Market

Local government intervention to boost competitiveness should start with a clear understanding of the market and the main drivers of city economic growth. Since it is the local private firms that determine competitiveness in most cases, local government intervention should complement the market and take effect in situations where market failure is present. Such scenarios include government provision of public goods, mitigation of negative externalities such as environmental pollution and traffic congestion, promotion of positive externalities such as knowledge sharing, and addressing coordination failures (promoting synergies and joint actions whose benefits go beyond individual local firms). It is important, however, to recognize the risks associated with these types of interventions. If they are of the wrong type or scale, or implemented poorly, the possibility of failure is significant.

How do local governments acquire a good understanding of the driving forces of the local economy and the market? Both quantitative and qualitative methods may be used. Quantitatively, local governments may collect and analyze information on local economic conditions to be used in decision making (Cities Alliance 2007). In Brazil, a significant amount of data is available at the municipal level, which provides a good base for analysis. The use of sector-specific data is particularly important for understanding the local economy. The case studies for the Cariri region and São Luís (chapters 4 and 5) present methodologies using employment data from the Relação Anual de Informações Sociais (Annual Records of Social Information, or RAIS) to analyze the local economic structure and identify the main driving sectors and critical clusters.

Qualitative methods can also be used to supplement quantitative analysis and to provide insight into the local economy not captured by existing data collection systems. Qualitative methods essentially entail structured involvement with the private sector (both locally and firms outside the region with local business links) through measures such as consultations, focus group meetings, surveys, and interviews. With key clusters identified, industry-level comparative analysis that benchmarks a city's specific cluster against the best performers nationally and globally can yield powerful results leading to policy actions (Palmade 2005).

In practical terms, the "cluster approach" (spearheaded by Porter) offers a pragmatic course of action as a framework for local government action plans on competitiveness to help organize public and private actions centered on competitive market forces. The essence of the cluster approach is not "cluster building," or to create competitive clusters that are currently nonexistent in a city, but to foster innovation and upgrading among the members of the existing or emerging clusters in the local economy.

Neither the cluster approach nor any one measure is a panacea for a city's economic competitiveness. There is no guarantee of success, and the risk involved in government interventions in economic development is often higher than that of other types of government activities. Forces outside local government control are often more important than policy interventions. It is therefore important to understand the key drivers of local growth, both internal and external, and to maintain a cautious approach toward government interventions.

Facilitating Private Sector Collaborations for Collective Efficiency

A critical premise of the cluster approach is that businesses compete not as isolated units but rather within complex webs of interdependence. The cluster concept involves the following elements: (a) leading firms that export products and services outside the region; (b) a supply network that provides inputs to these leading firms; and (c) the business environment and economic foundations, including such elements as human resources, technology, financial capital, and infrastructure. Figure 2 shows the footwear cluster in Cariri, Ceará, and its main members. The strength, or competitiveness, of the location is determined by

Figure 2. Cariri Footwear Cluster

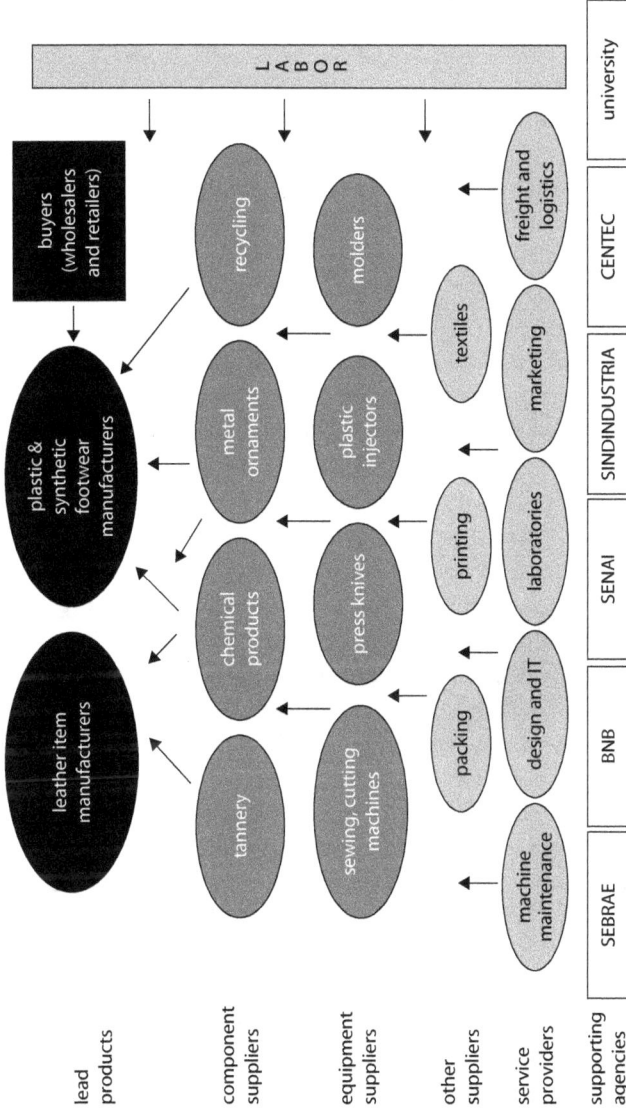

Source: Chapter 4 of this volume.

Note: IT = Information Technology, BNB = Banco do Nordeste do Brasil (Northeast Development Bank), SEBRAE = Serviço Brasileiro de Apoio às Micro e Pequenas Empresas (Brazil Micro and Small Business Services), CENTEC = Instituto Centro de Tecnologia do Ceará (Technology Center Institute of Cariri), SENAI = Serviço Nacional de Aprendizagem Industrial (National Industrial Training Service) the presence of this sophisticated, closely integrated network of private, public, and semipublic entities. Moreover, a competitive cluster is a network of such magnitude that its members continuously learn, innovate, and improve, resulting in the continual upgrading of quality and efficiency. The sophistication of such a web and its ability for continued renewal and innovation are, in the end, the source of sustained competitiveness.

Local governments can help facilitate collaborative actions among private sector players that would lead to *collective efficiency*, or the competitive advantage derived from external economies and the conscious pursuit of joint actions. By strengthening networking and associative behavior of the local private enterprises, government can support building the relational assets, or "social capital," of a cluster and provide local collective goods.

The institutional forms of such relational assets, or "institutions for collaboration," include trade associations, entrepreneur networks, standard-setting agencies, quality centers, and technology networks. The process of cluster organization is of great importance. The essence of a cluster initiative is to stimulate firms to cooperate, share information, and organize themselves for the common good. Building collaborative organizations requires building trust, often among competitors, and therefore it may take a long time; it also needs considerable support. Cluster organization is therefore frequently characterized by an initial phase that requires intensive support, and should be a concurrent process of diagnosis, group discussions, and leadership actions, all of which constitute a system of continual feedback among the elements. This indicates an action-oriented process, where the cluster members desire and expect quick results and actionable items, as opposed to waiting for prolonged diagnosis and planning without intermediate results. Figure 3 shows the overall cluster working group process that the authors of chapter 5 recommended for São Luís.

Examples of Specific Actions to Enhance Competitiveness

In pursuing competitiveness, each city must formulate a unique set of strategies and actions that are suitable for its own situation and differentiated from other cities. Self-evidently, no single approach is applicable to all cities. In fact, the most important challenge is to propose a unique value proposition and formulate a strategy that differentiates the city from the rest. Nevertheless, certain actions have been used by many cities, and the following examples are likely to be more relevant to Brazil.

Figure 3.   The Cluster Working Group Process

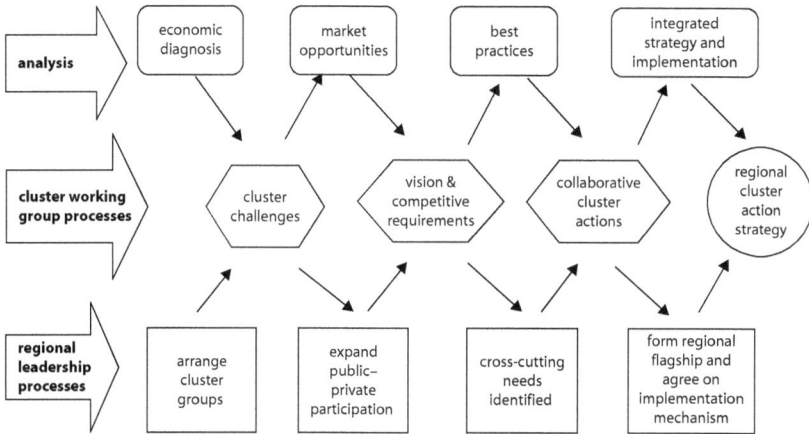

Source: Chapter 5 of this volume.

Joint marketing and investment, and export promotion. Through these supporting activities, the local government can help expand the demand for local products and services and attract external investment (foreign or domestic). Collective marketing is certainly more effective than uncoordinated efforts by individual firms. The key is to link joint marketing and promotion efforts closely with the local private sectors and the collaborative cluster enhancement process. One good example is the Ceará Footwear Technology Trade Fair, held annually in Juazeiro do Norte, which has become particularly important for the footwear cluster in Cariri.

Value chain integration. An important feature of today's global economy is the presence of global value chains, where the research and development (R&D), design, manufacturing of different components, and marketing are undertaken in a highly integrated fashion but from different locations (cities in different countries) and by different firms. One way to quickly catch up in productivity is to join such a value chain, often starting with a less lucrative segment and then moving on to higher value-added segments. Value chain analysis helps the policy maker both identify the bottlenecks in the productive chain and determine three things: which bottlenecks deserve the priority attention of government, which can be expected to be resolved by the private sector, and which require public–private partnerships.

Entrepreneurship development and support to small and microenterprises. Significant scope exists for public policies and actions to address market failures that limit supply of finance, business development services and training, industrial real estate, information problems faced by start-up enterprises, and noncompetitive market structures dominated by one firm or a small number of firms.

Support to R&D. Local government can support well-focused R&D expansion by motivating university-industry linkage for applied innovative research with business potential, supporting targeted business incubators, and by seeking and attracting talent to the city. A good example is the Center for Information and Technology for Footwear that is being established in Cariri, and already operational in other cities in Brazil and in other countries.

Skills upgrading. Two of the highest priorities of almost any cluster's plan should be the availability of experienced and skilled labor and the customized and specialized education and training that produce and upgrade skills and knowledge. Specific local government actions include analyzing and anticipating the skills needed, promoting employer provision and participation, and creating close partnerships with SENAI.

Economic zones. These offer a combination of benefits by facilitating the land-assembly process for industrial development; providing specialized infrastructure needed by a group of firms; facilitating interfirm learning, exchange, and collaboration through physical colocating of firms; and creating a cluster identity that facilitates marketing and investment promotion. But attention to market, demand, R&D capacity, and professional management is especially important for economic zones, as the all too frequent emphasis on fiscal incentives and physical infrastructure alone has often led to failure.

Specialized infrastructure or services. High-quality infrastructure, such as transport, power, water, and telecommunications, is always important for the local economy. In addition, depending on the unique local competitive advantage, it may be important to enhance certain types of specialized infrastructure, such as tourism facilities or logistics infrastructure, which may play an instrumental role for the particular clusters or strategies that a city pursues.

Community economic development. In promoting competitiveness, local officials also need to look for solutions to address the livelihood and job needs of their low-income communities. In Brazil, many of these communities are also informal settlements. While national, state, and municipal governments have been upgrading slums to improve services, support efforts for economic development have thus far been limited. Some of the models used for community economic development in distressed areas in the United States and Europe, often based on nurturing and leveraging local entrepreneurship within these communities, can be of useful reference. Measures to support entrepreneurship and small and microenterprises, highlighted above, are especially relevant for these communities.

Pulling It Together: Strategic Plan for Competitiveness

A clear, visionary, and credible strategic plan (not to be confused with the traditional master plan, or *plano diretor*) articulated by policy makers can send signals on government policy priorities and desired outcomes to the private sector. Local strategies should be more than just an aggregation of considerations and policy principles compiled in a plan or document. The challenge is to identify the critical relationships among the many agents that are likely to shape the future economic, social, political, and environmental quality of the territory, through answers to such questions as: "How will the city be distinctive?" "What is the city's economic role in its region or neighborhood?" "In which clusters can the city build an advantage?" "What aspects of the business environment are crucial to success when compared to other locations?" To attract investment, the city needs to offer a unique mix of strengths in terms of business environment conditions and cluster positions; the mere absence of weaknesses is not enough.

The process of strategic planning is therefore threefold: to identify the unique, hidden (intangible) capacities of a location, to achieve a broad-based agreement on the unique value proposition and direction for a city, and to develop an actionable road map to achieve a common vision.

Developing a strategic plan is not easy, especially in the context of a globalized market economy where technology and innovation advance rapidly. Local and national political systems often complicate the situation by making it hard to build consensus among different parties or achieve a shared long-term perspective. Some of the key elements of a successful strategic plan include:

- A balanced combination of broad public participation and top expert inputs with in-depth diagnoses, innovations, and global best practices
- Integration of physical investments with economic and social transformation

- Effective communication of results in a form easily understood by the public (such as graphics)
- Careful consideration of implementation through public–private partnerships during the strategy formulation phase.

Building Institutions and Capacity for Local Competitiveness

The task of promoting city competitiveness poses severe institutional challenges to local governments in several areas, especially the need to:

- Coordinate efforts within a municipal authority, because government services are often dispersed across different departments, making it difficult for businesses to access them
- Involve and ensure the strong commitment of a large number of stakeholders—particularly in the private sector—to develop and implement a common strategy
- Introduce business know-how and sometimes even take informed business risks, which would require a different set of competencies and skills from the usual bureaucratic ones
- Coordinate—often—the efforts in a metropolitan region, including several municipalities, and involve the state and national governments.

Different models for building institutions and capacity have been used across countries, from public to private domains. The exact form that each authority takes will depend on the local situation and should be adapted accordingly. Whatever the institutional form, local governments should proceed with caution in recruiting staff in their economic development efforts, and seek people with business experience and expertise in dealing with the private sector. Partnership with the private sector becomes important in terms of bringing expertise, discipline, and a sense of ownership.

Moreover, the type and level of engagement by the local governments in competitiveness enhancement measures need to be matched by local capacity. Some types of interventions entail greater risks, including business and market risks, than others. It is therefore important to ensure sufficient capacity to analyze, assess, and prepare for the risks involved in the interventions.

Chapters 3, 4, and 5. Competitiveness of Brazilian Cities: Initial Benchmarking and Case Studies

Initial Competitiveness Benchmarking

Competitiveness indexes, such as the national competitiveness ranking conducted annually by the World Economic Forum, have been widely used to identify and benchmark the productive potential of nations and regions. In general, these indexes show the "drivers" of competitiveness in multiple dimensions. Chapter 3 presents an initial benchmarking of the competitiveness of Brazilian cities. The results are limited due to resource constraints, with analysis mostly based on available data, with no first-hand survey or poll data. This initial benchmarking uses Brazilian population census data for the year 2000. The cities were benchmarked along four dimensions: urban, sociodemographic, institutional/fiscal, and economic. Each dimension incorporates a series of variables from the census data. The principal component analysis method was used to construct the indexes. Unsurprisingly, the top-ranked cities are from the southeast region, and the least competitive cities are overwhelmingly from the northeast region. Further improvements can be made to these initial benchmarking results with more systematic data collection efforts, in combination with survey work. But these results can already serve as a powerful instrument for municipal officials, citizens, and businesses to assess where each city stands relative to others, its strengths and weaknesses, and the areas for improvement.

Case Studies on Cariri, Ceará, and São Luís, Maranhão

Chapters 4 and 5 each present a case study on strategies to enhance city and regional economic competitiveness. Both urban areas are in the northeast region. In analyzing citywide economic structures, both case studies use employment data from RAIS as a base for identifying the important clusters in a city.

The case study on Cariri focuses on one cluster (footwear), and analyzes in detail the dynamics of the cluster—its history, leading firms and followers, inputs and suppliers, demand and buyers, support agencies, organization of social capital, and sources (or lack) of innovation. The analysis shows that the cluster is functioning vibrantly with the emergence of key agents for collaborations, a gradual process of value chain integration, movement toward innovation, and product upgrading. The analysis also identifies weaknesses: the need for technology upgrading and skills improvements, closer collaborative efforts, and continued innovation. A vision and strategy for the footwear cluster is presented in chapter 4.

The case study on São Luís, the capital city of the state of Maranhão, presents a situation where the cluster organization process is in its early stages. The case study was written as a result of the initial cluster mobilization process led by the municipal government (with support from the authors). While the chapter's economic structural analysis helps identify the key strengths, weaknesses, and the main economic clusters in the city, the chapter focuses specifically on two clusters—the port-industrial and tourism clusters. Workshops, with the participation of the key cluster stakeholders and facilitated by external experts, were the main method used to conduct a quick analysis and develop short-term actions and road map for a cluster-based strategy for local economic development in the city. The results demonstrate how a cluster-based, local economic development strategy may be started in a city.

Main Conclusions

Local Policy Framework for City Competitiveness

To become and stay competitive, cities need to strive to reduce the cost of doing business by improving services and infrastructure and reducing bureaucracies. But for a middle-income country like Brazil, which needs to be economically competitive in a globalized environment, this is not sufficient. Cities also need to strive to add value to local businesses. A crucial part of the strategy should be to create and sustain an environment that stimulates local firms to innovate and learn from each other, to nurture and facilitate the creation of synergies generated by the presence of interconnected economic clusters in the city, and to provide incentives for all local players to continuously upgrade the level of competitiveness—to become better and the best.

With regard to the areas of policy interventions by municipal and state governments for enhancing local economic competitiveness, this report has focused on the cluster approach to competitiveness. As an expanded version of the widely used approach of *arranjos produtivos locais*, the cluster approach in essence is to facilitate private sector collaborations for collective efficiency: organizing and facilitating private and public institutions to arrive at a common cluster vision; identifying opportunities for growth and collaboration; promoting joint actions such as co-information, co-learning, co-marketing, and co-purchasing; and jointly building economic foundations such as R&D capacities, infrastructure, skills upgrading, and public–private sector support institutions.

While this report has provided many examples of actions that may be undertaken, it emphasizes the critical importance of cities pursuing their own unique strategy based on their comparative and competitive advantages, rather than blindly applying different actions. Finally, the more active approaches discussed in the report will require the presence of stronger governance and management capacity at the local government level. Local governments should be fully aware of the market and governance risks involved in their actions, and should match the level of policy actions with the competence of local institutions and staff capacities.

Toward a National Policy Framework for City Competitiveness

The wide range of possibly powerful actions by local governments for city competitiveness and growth raises the question: "What is the proper role of the federal government in Brazil?" There is a case to move toward a national policy framework for city competitiveness, as has been done or proposed in China, the United Kingdom, United States, and other countries. Some of the elements of a potential framework are:

- Guidance to municipal and state governments on how to compete and disseminate best-practice examples
- Performance measurements and benchmarking to enable cities to compare their performance in competitiveness in different dimensions
- Provision of the right incentives for competition, for example, discouraging fiscal wars and encouraging human capital enhancements and innovation efforts
- Provision of incentives on cross-jurisdictional efforts, especially for economic collaboration and integration of metropolitan regions, by establishing a metropolitan governance framework and channeling federal funding through cross-jurisdictional metropolitan entities

Note

1. This term refers to a situation where state and municipal governments competitively offer appealing fiscal incentives (tax breaks or other subsidies) to attract investments, often resulting in high fiscal cost and relatively low benefits to the local economy.

CHAPTER 1

What Makes Cities Competitive? A Selective Review of Theories and International Experiences

Mark Roberts and Ming Zhang

Introduction

A key question confronting policy makers the world over is how best to ensure competitive economic success in a rapidly evolving global environment. This question confronts both municipal and local policy makers (city mayors and other local officials) as well as national policy makers. Indeed, policy maker interest in city competitiveness—how it can be built and sustained—has increased dramatically in recent decades, and new approaches have emerged. In particular, there has been a shift in emphasis from spatially targeted fiscal incentives, based on employment creation and the attraction of business, to an increased awareness of such concepts as agglomeration economies, clustering, and knowledge spillovers. This shift, in turn, has led to the adoption of more sophisticated and holistic approaches to local development that involve a greater array of local stakeholders than in the past.

In high-income countries, evidence of this shift can be found in the policies adopted over the last decade or so by such G-8 countries as Canada, Italy, and the United Kingdom; by individual states in the United States such as Arizona and Massachusetts; and by the series of Territorial

Reviews from the Organisation for Economic Co-operation and Development (OECD)—most notably, the publication *Competitive Cities in the Global Economy* (2006a). For middle-income and developing countries, the cluster concept has gained growing popularity: at least 10 countries in the Latin America and Caribbean Region of the World Bank have pursued cluster policy initiatives, as have Malaysia, Morocco, Senegal, and South Africa (Enright 2000).

The emergence of new policy approaches to city competitiveness is mirrored by developments in several academic fields, most notably economics, management science, regional science, and human geography. In economics, for example, endogenous growth theory (Lucas 1998; Romer 1986, 1990) and the new economic geography (Krugman 1991a, 1991b; Fujita, Krugman, and Venables 1999) have emerged to emphasize the key roles of, respectively, knowledge and agglomeration economies in driving local development outcomes. Each of these "subfields" is concerned both with the positive and negative externalities of decisions by local players (notably, businesses, workers, and consumers) on other local players, and with the implications of these effects for local and regional development. The literature also emphasizes the importance of knowledge spillovers and the spatial impacts of declining transportation and telecommunications costs. This emphasis is consistent with policy maker concern about how cities should compete in a globalizing world that is characterized by new, knowledge-intensive industries.

Research on the empirical determinants of local competitiveness has also shown rapid growth, and, although much of this research has been confined to the traditional industrial countries, it has greatly improved academic understanding of these determinants. Elsewhere, in the field of management science, the Harvard Business School academic Michael Porter has pioneered the cluster approach to local development, inspiring a vast body of case study evidence on the sources of cluster success and failure.[1] Generally, it is possible to talk of a new field of spatial economics under whose umbrella all these developments fall, and of which the various literatures on city competitiveness are but one part.

This chapter draws on the above developments to provide a broad answer to the question: "What makes cities competitive?" The chapter is intended to be accessible to local policy makers and practitioners in the field of local economic development, and is based on a selective review of the relevant academic and policy literature.[2] Rather than providing an exhaustive account of all possible determinants of city competitiveness, it emphasizes a (relatively) small list of six key drivers, and, within this list, gives special attention to factors that have become more important in light of globalization and global technology trends.[3] The chapter also emphasizes state-of-the-art approaches that maximize the chances of modern-day success, rather than dwelling on the policy experiences, and mistakes, of the past.

Key Messages

The key messages of the chapter are as follows:

- In a global environment characterized by rapidly expanding trade and foreign direct investment (FDI) flows, as well as the breaking up and globalization of many production value chains, the key to success for any city lies in building competitive advantage.

- Competitive advantage is distinct from comparative advantage—it is a dynamic concept associated with both the continual economic and social upgrading of a city, and a city's ongoing reinvention to deal with the decline of old industries. In turn, a city's competitive advantage is driven by its level of productivity.

- The tendency for spatial disparities in productivity and well-being to persist over long periods of time underscores the importance of agglomeration economies to competitive advantage. Agglomeration economies consist of urbanization economies (the productivity advantages of a city's market size and density) and localization economies (productivity benefits from the concentration of an individual city-industry). Urbanization economies are important to the competitiveness of large cities, and localization economies to small and medium cities, as well as to individual industry clusters.

- Historical examples of once great cities that have lost competitive advantage demonstrate that competitive advantage also requires a city to have the ability to reinvent itself through positive structural change and the cultivation of a citywide learning environment.

- Without innovation, a city's competitiveness is doomed to stagnation. In the world's most competitive cities, innovation is associated with clusters of firms in strong value-added activities. The knowledge spillover effects that characterize such industries are, however, also present in apparently more mundane industries, but are often less exploited because of coordination failures. In the strongest clusters, other players—universities, local and regional economic development agencies, and competitiveness councils—step in to resolve these failures. By helping leverage competitive advantage through strategic planning based on the identification of a locality's unique, perhaps hidden, capacities, a cluster-based approach to policy may help stimulate innovation.

- Human capital (skills, training, and education) promotes a city's competitive advantage through a diverse array of mechanisms, most notably by contributing to a city's capacity to reinvent itself, acting as a key input into innovative activities, facilitating knowledge spillovers, and helping to attract FDI and a favorable industry mix. Policy measures to improve skills, training, and education must, however, be accompanied by measures that boost the demand for human capital if a local "brain drain" is to be avoided.

- Empirical evidence overwhelmingly points to a positive impact of local competition on productivity growth and, therefore, on competitive advantage. Competition, however, works best when it coexists with cooperation among local firms to overcome coordination failures and to help create a common brand. Competition also works best when it is based on quality rather than price.

- While important, private investment is, by itself, insufficient to produce ongoing improvements in competitive advantage; past policy approaches based on spatially targeted fiscal incentives to stimulate private investment have largely failed.

- From a competitiveness viewpoint, different types of infrastructure investment are important for different types of cities and at different stages of a city's development. Investment in basic public utilities and local public goods is important to provide the foundations for building density in small cities; spatially connective transport infrastructure is a further requirement for fast-growing medium-size cities; and large cities additionally require spatially targeted investments in, for example, affordable housing to overcome divisions associated with the presence of slums.

- The quality of local governance has an important influence on the other key drivers of city competitiveness; burdensome regulations stifle competition, low public sector capacity hampers quality public services, and lack of government credibility prevents the formation of a shared, strategic vision. High-quality local governance is also important for attracting FDI in higher-value-added activities. Such FDI can encourage knowledge spillovers to the local economy.

The Rapidly Changing Global Environment and the Need for Competitiveness

In recent decades, advances in transportation and telecommunications technologies have coincided with policies of increased international openness to create a highly dynamic global environment in which cities must compete. It is against this backdrop that the issue of city competitiveness has come to the top of the policy agenda. Since the mid-1970s, freight costs have approximately halved (Krueger 2006, cited in World Bank 2008) as maritime transport has gone through the containerization revolution and open registry shipping has grown. Airfreight, helped by the invention of the jet engine in the 1950s, has become an increasingly viable option for activities with high value-to-weight ratios and has simultaneously allowed for the transport of perishable goods over long distances, such as cut flowers from Kenya,. The average cost of a three-minute telephone call to the United States has likewise plummeted over the last decade. Whereas in 1997 the average cost from the Latin American region was US$4, by 2003 it had fallen to approximately US$1.[4] With respect to increased international openness, China and the former Communist countries of Eastern Europe and Central Asia have opened up to international trade, as has India, while the World Trade Organization, and before it the General Agreement on Tariffs and Trade, has overseen a broad process of multilateral trade liberalization.

Several facts bear testimony to nature of the changes that have occurred in the global environment and that are a consequence of the above developments (Venables 2006, pp. 15, 32):

- *The global workforce has doubled, increasing by 1.46 billion workers.* This is a result of the collapse of the Soviet bloc, and unilateral trade liberalization in China and India, beginning in the early 1990s.

- *World trade has grown at twice the rate of world income.* This is a consequence of falling export costs driven by trade liberalization and technological progress in transport.

- *Trade in intermediate goods (parts and components) has grown and now represents approximately 30 percent of world trade.* This reflects the fact that many goods and services that were once nontradable have become tradable. It is one important consequence of the global division of the production value chain in many industries, whereby component parts and semifinished goods are able to cross national borders several times. This has led to the emergence of vertical specialization processes whereby countries, and cities, are now more able to achieve competitiveness through specialization in a single fragment of the production chain of a particular commodity.

- *FDI has grown at twice the rate of world trade.* This also comes partly as a consequence of the global fragmentation of production processes and the attendant rapid growth of multinational corporations.

Reductions in telecommunications costs and the broader information and communication technology (ICT) revolution have also helped usher in a new information age in which new types of knowledge-intensive industries have emerged and the marginal cost of digitally transmitting information has fallen to close to zero. As a result, the world appears to have crossed a threshold of information connectivity.

Against this backdrop, competitive advantage represents, regardless of location, the key to success for any city that is seeking to improve the standards of living of its inhabitants. It provides the means by which a city can take full advantage of globalization's benefits, while simultaneously minimizing the associated risks. Competitive advantage is logically distinct from comparative advantage (Porter 1998, p. 78). While the latter is a static concept linked to the existence (or lack) of natural endowments, the former is a dynamic concept associated with both the continual economic and social upgrading of a city and its ongoing reinvention to deal with adverse economic shocks and the associated decline of old industries. The building of competitive advantage therefore provides a means of helping major cities in Latin America to cope with the premature onset of deindustrialization, partly as a result of the rapid growth and industrialization in Asia. This includes such major cities in Latin America as Mexico City, where three-quarters of the workforce is now engaged in service sector activity (OECD 2006a, p. 132).[5]

How is competitive advantage to be measured? This is a controversial question on which full consensus is lacking.[6] From a practical and policy viewpoint, however, the simplest, albeit highly imperfect, measure is GDP per capita.[7] Evidence both for OECD cities (OECD 2006a, p. 56) and for U.K. regions (HM Treasury 2001, p. 5) in turn suggests that the main determinant of GDP per capita is labor productivity,[8] so that it is the evolution of productivity that is the primary driving force behind a city's competitive advantage. This view is supported by basic economic theory. Notably, while other proximate determinants[9] of GDP per capita can influence a city's level of competitiveness, productivity is unique in being able to increase without bound and, therefore, in being able to influence the long-term growth rate of competitiveness. It follows that only through making long-term gains in productivity can a city build competitive advantage and achieve a high level of prosperity.

Key Drivers of City Competitiveness

The potential determinants of a city's competitive advantage are many and varied. Rather than providing an exhaustive discussion of all such factors, this chapter emphasizes a relatively small subset of six

Figure 1.1   Key Drivers of City Competitiveness and Their Interlinkages

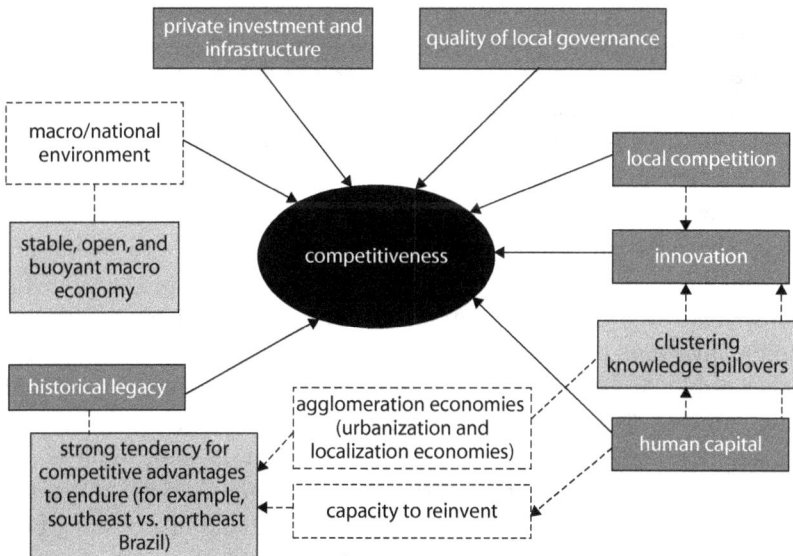

Source: Authors, based on various sources.

key drivers based on a reading of academic, empirical, and policy literature (figure 1.1):

- Historical legacy
- Innovation
- Human capital (skills, training, and education)
- Local competition
- Private investment and infrastructure
- Quality of local governance.

Innovation, human capital, and local competition all command strong empirical support, and, particularly human capital, support competitive advantage through an array of mechanisms. There are good reasons too for believing that these key drivers have become relatively more important in recent decades as a result of the increased dynamism and openness of the global economy.[10] The same is true for the quality of local governance as a driver of competitive advantage. A city's historical legacy, meanwhile, is emphasized because it highlights the key role of agglomeration economies (economic advantages arising from the density of economic activity) in driving spatial economic outcomes, and, therefore, competitive advantage. Agglomeration economies may arise from either the clustering together of firms and businesses in the same industry (localization economies) or of firms and businesses in different industries (urbanization economies). Within any country there exists a hierarchy of cities and, as we move up this hierarchy, a city's competitive advantage comes to depend less on localization economies and more on urbanization economies. As a consequence, the determinants of a city's competitive advantage depend to some extent on the city's size and position in the country's urban hierarchy or portfolio of places.

Finally, infrastructure comes in several forms, which are all important. Transport infrastructure promotes spatial connectivity both within and around a city, and acts as an antidote to congestion that might otherwise threaten to strangle agglomeration economies. When directed at households, investment in housing and basic utilities (water, electricity, and other public services) can help in the integration of informal communities, reducing divisions within a city and promoting greater cohesiveness. In addition, when directed at firms, investment in basic utilities can reduce the costs of doing business and promote productivity. Investment in cultural and other amenities, meanwhile, can help in attracting both tourists and skilled workers, which is important given the status of human capital as a key driver.

Although the six key drivers of competitive advantage are discussed here as discrete entities (shown in figure 1.1 as boxes with solid borders), it is essential not to neglect the synergies that exist between them, some of which are illustrated as boxes with dashed borders. These synergies imply that competitive advantage is best achieved by a holistic approach to policy that simultaneously targets local constraints operating on all drivers. Importantly, the exact nature of these constraints will, even within the same country, differ markedly from city to city. This strongly suggests that policy needs to involve a wide array of local players. And, because local policy makers may overlook both positive and negative synergies between their own and other cities, it is also important that some role exists for national government. The national government is also important in establishing general macroeconomic stability, the absence of which is likely to severely undermine the competitive advantage of all of a country's cities, irrespective of the effectiveness of their individual local policies.

Historical Legacy and the Associated Importance of Agglomeration Economies

Cities are not hostages to their histories. As discussed in more detail in chapter 3, a city that lacks competitive advantage does have options for building it. Likewise, once acquired, competitive advantage can be lost through a combination of bad policies, lack of resilience to long-term structural transformations in the wider economy, and even bad luck, as will be discussed below.

Notwithstanding the above, there is a strong tendency for city-level disparities in competitive advantage to endure over long periods of time. In France, no city that was relatively big (that is, had a population of greater than 50,000) in 1911 "died" in the ensuing 97 years, and virtually no new cities have been born. The same is true for Japan; the top 30 cities in 1985 were the same as in 1925, and there has been remarkable constancy in the relative populations of cities (Eaton and Eckstein 1997). This evidence of persistence in relative performance mirrors, and is an important cause of, performance that exists at the level of more aggregated subnational areas.

The so-called convergence literature shows that over 120 years, the tendency of the poorest U.S. states to grow faster economically and catch up with the richest has been extremely weak. Between 1880 and 2000, the productivity gap between any two states showed a tendency to close at a rate of only approximately 1.5 percent a year. This implies that, in the absence of shocks, it takes almost half a century for one-half of a productivity gap between a rich and a poor state to be closed (Barro and Sala-i-Martin 2004, p. 409, table 11.1). Similarly for European regions, despite ever-deepening economic and political integration, there has been little evidence of a catch-up tendency over the last quarter of a century (Roberts and Setterfield 2007, p. 22). This lack of catch-up is aptly summarized in the title of an academic article by the economists Fabio Canova and Albert Marcet (1995), "The Poor Stay Poor: Non-Convergence across Countries and Regions."

In middle-income and developing countries such as Brazil, city-level disparities in competitiveness have also been left relatively untouched by the passage of time. Despite a history of regional development initiatives dating back to the 1950s, the most competitive and dynamic cities in Brazil remain very much in the Southeast. While declining relatively over the preceding few decades, São Paolo's GDP per capita was still 67 percent above the national average in 2005, according to data from Instituto Brasileiro de Geografia e Estatistica (Brazilian Institute of Geography and Statistics, or IBGE). Likewise, per capita income in the Southeast was 2.9 times that in the Northeast in 1939, and still 2.8 times in 1992 (World Bank 2008, chapter 8).

Competitive advantage also persists, although not as strongly, at the level of many individual city-industries, as is demonstrated by the long-standing success of many of the world's most visible and well-known clusters. For more than 50 years, Silicon Valley in San Jose, California (United States), has maintained a competitive advantage in cutting-edge ICT industries. This pales in comparison, however, with the 300 years over which the financial industry cluster in London (United Kingdom) has sustained competitive success. In turn, this is less than half the period over which Solingen (Germany) has been home to a world-class cluster in the cutlery industry.[11]

Although the existence of a city or a city-industry frequently has its origins in some natural, "first nature" advantage, such as a favorable coastal location or a location that was once strategically advantageous from a military/defense viewpoint, this factor has often long disappeared in importance (Krugman 1991b). A number of U.K. cities had their origins as "burhs," or fortress towns, in the national defense system designed by King Alfred the Great in the Middle Ages to ward off raiding Vikings. Although it was eventually to wane, the cities of the traditional U.S. manufacturing belt were able to maintain a competitive advantage long after the reasons for the early dominance of the belt—an initial advantage in access to such natural resources as coal and oil—had disappeared (Krugman 1991b, pp. 13–14). Likewise in Brazil, the favorable competitive position of the

Southeast in relation to the Northeast can be traced back to the more favorable conditions for industrialization created in the second half of the 19th century (World Bank 2005, p. 11).

The tendency for success to outlast the factors that sparked it highlights the fact that, although comparative advantage may explain the origins of many of today's most successful cities, continuing success rests on competitive advantage. It also sheds light on the mechanisms that help both generate and sustain competitiveness. In particular, this tendency reveals that the process by which competitive advantage is generated is characterized by positive feedback mechanisms, or "second nature" advantages, which bring with them self-reinforcing circles of success (Kaldor 1970; Krugman 1991a, 1991b; Venables 2006, p. 27). These feedback mechanisms emanate from agglomeration economies, which can arise at either the urban level (urbanization economies) or the individual city-industry level (localization economies).

Urbanization economies are associated with the productivity benefits that a city is able to enjoy primarily on account of its market size and density, which facilitate diversity in production and consumption, as well as simultaneously acting as a positive spur to competition and innovation. These productivity benefits can be both static and dynamic in nature, so that they can benefit both a city's level and growth rate of competitiveness. Evidence on the static productivity benefits of urbanization economies is strong for developed countries—consensus indicates that a doubling of city size, over a wide range of city sizes, is associated with a productivity gain of 3–8 percent (Rosenthal and Strange 2004). For Mexico, empirical work shows that wages decline with distance from Mexico City, which indicates that productivity must be highest where agglomeration is strongest, for it is only through high productivity that businesses can afford to pay high wages (Hanson 1997). Evidence of dynamic urbanization economies is both more difficult to come by and subject to controversy. However, consistent with the existence of such economies, a number of studies for the United States (Glaeser et al. 1992) and Europe (Van Stel and Nieuwenhuijsen 2004) report a positive relationship between the diversity of a city's industrial base and its growth.

Localization economies are the productivity benefits that an individual city-industry enjoys as a result of its concentration. These benefits derive from three distinct sources: (a) the presence of a skilled pool of labor; (b) the presence of local businesses specialized in the supply of intermediate goods and services; and (c) knowledge flows between firms.

In cases (a) and (b) above, the competitiveness benefits are static (level effects); in case (c) they are dynamic (growth effects).[12] Whereas urbanization economies help account for the persistent competitive success of larger cities, localization economies are essential ingredients in the competitive advantage of small and medium cities, and form part of the explanation for the long-standing success of many industry clusters. Respectively, they help "lock in" competitive advantage at the city and city-industry levels (Arthur 1994). Such lock-in helps simultaneously "lock out" other potential competitor cities and locations for a city-industry. In the case of urbanization economies, the literature on the new economic geography has theorized that this helps create an "urban shadow," whereby the competitive advantage of a city is such that it is extremely difficult for other cities to even become established within a certain geographic radius (Fujita, Krugman, and Venables 1999). The implication is that it is very difficult for a single country, no matter how well developed, to have more than a small number of truly world-class cities.

As stated earlier, however, it would be an overstatement to say that the tendency for competitive advantage to persist is all pervasive. The post–Second World War experience of the traditional industrial countries provides plenty of examples of cities that have lost competitiveness, and, with it, population, as a result of a combination of bad policies, an inability to respond to long-term structural changes in the wider economy, and bad fortune. Consider, for instance, the U.S. "Rust Belt" cities of Detroit, Michigan, and Syracuse, New York. In the words of the prominent urban economist Edward Glaeser (2003, p. 143), these have experienced a "sad path to urban irrelevance." Consider also the once great shipbuilding and manufacturing cities of northern England and of Scotland. Once the most important port in the British Empire, Liverpool has been in virtually continuous decline since the 1930s, hemorrhaging population as a consequence. Between the census years of 1931 and 2001, its population fell by almost half from 846,000 to 435,000.

The above examples provide an important lesson. Part of the reason why cities such as Detroit and Liverpool have lost competitive advantage, and slid down from their respective national hierarchies of cities, is that, for a variety of reasons, they have been unable to reinvent themselves in the face of long-term adverse economic shocks. In contrast, other similarly placed cities have managed to effectively reinvent themselves. In the United Kingdom, both Manchester and Glasgow, not to mention Newcastle and Leeds, have proved more capable of reinventing themselves than has Liverpool. Likewise in the U.S. Rust Belt, Boston has been able to reinvent itself despite the fact that "an urban observer looking at Boston in 1980 would have every reason to believe that it would go the way of Detroit and Syracuse" (Glaeser 2003, p. 143). Clearly then, the message coming from international experience is that competitive advantage rests on more than agglomeration economies—it also requires the ability to reinvent through positive structural change and the cultivation of a city-wide learning environment.[13] The remaining key drivers of competitive advantage play an important part in helping determine a city's ability to effect positive structural change and to create such an environment.

Interestingly, the very localization economies that are important in helping build the competitive advantage of small and medium cities can also become problematic once the industry specialized in enters a decline. This is because they can help lock such cities into an industrial structure that becomes unfavorable once the industries in question experience long-term adverse economic shocks. Diversification of industrial structure, therefore, represents an important factor in a city's ability to reinvent itself. It follows that reinvention may also come more easily, if other conditions are right, for large metropolises than for smaller cities. Diversity helped Boston in its reinvention (Glaeser 2003); and for mature U.S. cities during 1956–1987 (a time of unfavorable economic shocks for such cities), diversity of industrial structure was beneficial for both employment and wage growth (Glaeser et al. 1992).

Innovation

Innovation lies at the heart of a city's competitive advantage. According to economists' standard model of economic growth, the Solow-Swan model (Solow 1956; Swan 1956), an economy's competitive position is ultimately doomed to stagnation in the absence of innovation.[14] Realizing this, both the European Union (EU) and the OECD have put emphasis on innovation in their local economic development policy thinking. The promotion of innovation, therefore, represents a key component of the EU's Lisbon Agenda for regional development; it is one of the U.K. government's five key drivers of productivity growth at national, regional, and local levels (HM Treasury 2001, pp. 23–25); and it has been trumpeted by the OECD.[15] In many of the most globally competitive cities, innovation is associated with clusters of firms in strong, value-added, and R&D-intensive activities, including high-tech manufacturing, telecommunications, biopharmaceuticals, and financial services. In this context, the OECD has defined clusters as "geographical

concentrations of groups of industries within which firms and other ...
[players] ... in the spatial economic systems are formally or informally
linked through their activities" (OECD 2006a, p. 104).

Such industries are distinguished by particularly powerful localization
economies of the sort discussed in the previous section. Most importantly,
they are characterized by extremely strong knowledge spillover effects,
which have become increasingly important as the global economy has
become more dynamic and interrelated. In this context, "spillovers" are
the positive knock-on effects, or externalities, on productivity that arise
from the activities of one local player, but benefit other local players.
These externalities emanate from the frequently unintentional passing on
of knowledge, which explains the reference to players being "informally
linked" in the OECD definition of clusters. Three primary mechanisms
transmit knowledge spillover effects (table 1.1).

The knowledge transmission mechanisms described in table 1.1 imply
that the productivity, and therefore the competitiveness, of firms within
a cluster are complementary. This indicates the existence of positive
local synergies between clustered firms.[16] According to economists' theories of endogenous growth, which attempt to explain technological
progress, if these synergies are sufficiently strong within a cluster, the
cluster will achieve self-sustaining growth through the exploitation of an
imitation-innovation nexus. In this nexus, firms will be engaged in continual co-learning in a dynamic process of circular and cumulative cau-
sation (Romer 1986, 1990; Lucas 1988). Furthermore, the cluster will
naturally tend to be a "traded cluster" (Porter 2002). This implies that
the growth exhibited will be export-led, of a kind that economists have
long associated with the promotion of local prosperity (North 1955;
Kaldor 1970; Dixon and Thirlwall 1975; Rowthorn 2000, 2005). This is
precisely the situation achieved in the strong value-added clusters that
characterize the world's leading competitive cities.

However, as the OECD definition indicates, clusters also involve
other players than firms. These other players—which might include
universities, specially established local and regional economic development agencies, and competitiveness councils (chapter 2)—are
important because endogenous growth theory also implies that, if left
to their own devices, local businesses will tend to overlook the positive externalities of their business decisions. This is especially true of
small and microenterprises (SMEs), not only because the externalities
are largely unintended, but because the indirect feedback effects for
such businesses are likely to be negligible. Although a decision by an

Table 1.1   Mechanisms for the Transmission of Knowledge Spillovers

Mechanism	Description
Learning by observation	This happens when, by virtue of proximity (spatial and/or industrial), one local firm learns, through observation, from another local firm about, for example, a new best-practice technology, or a new way of better adapting an existing technology. This mechanism might also involve learning about a new way of doing business in terms of the appropriate design of management systems, new methods of marketing, and others.[1]
Learning through meeting	This takes place through direct face-to-face interaction or associative behavior. It may occur, for example, through both formal and informal discussions not only with peers, but also with suppliers and customers.[2] Face-to-face interaction is required because of the tacit nature of much knowledge, particularly highly contextual and uncertain knowledge. In this sense, knowledge is distinct from information—while the latter can be codified, the former cannot.[3] Face-to-face interaction also allows for a higher frequency exchange of ideas than in alternative means of communication, such as e-mail, and allows for parallel means of communication, such as body language. These parallel means help ensure the correct transmission of meaning. Finally, face-to-face contact builds trust, facilitating the flow of knowledge and reducing the costs of doing business.[4]
Learning through leaving	This occurs when (a) an employee leaves one firm in a cluster for another, or (b) through acts of entrepreneurship[5] whereby an employee leaves to start his or her own business.[a] It can also involve the movement of individuals from research-based institutions, including universities, into the private sector.

Sources: (1) National Governors Association (2002, p. 13); (2) Lucas (1988); National Governors Association (2002, p. 10); (3) Feldman and Audretsch (1999, p. 411); (4) Venables (2006, p. 23); (5) National Governors Association (2002, p. 25).
a. In this context, a flexible local labor market in which workers can easily move from one firm to another might be thought to be good for city competitiveness. However, this has to be balanced against the fact that such a market generates an incentive for one firm to free ride on the costs of training provided by other firms. Just as with knowledge spillovers per se, this creates a coordination failure in the form of collective cluster underinvestment in education and training. This provides logic for some form of collective action to overcome the coordination failure.

SME might increase the productivity of other firms in the same cluster through a spillover effect, which then indirectly spills back to the SME itself, the impact is likely to be so small that it goes unnoticed by the owner or manager of the SME. The feedback will be more noticeable for larger enterprises, and so is more likely to be factored into business decisions. Even in this case, however, the tendency will be for firms to underinvest in activities that are of mutual competitive benefit. The result is a coordination failure that leaves local synergies underexploited.

In the strongest clusters, it is precisely the existence of the other players referred to in the OECD definition that helps resolve coordination failures. Part of this can simply involve the existence of cluster institutions that make local firms aware of the positive synergies between them, thereby encouraging them to "internalize" the synergies into their business thinking. Such a mutual awareness of beneficial synergies is seen, for example, within North Carolina's hosiery cluster. Members of this cluster "proudly note there are no secrets between them. They are competing far less with one another than collectively with Turkey, [the Republic of] Korea, and Mexico" (National Governors Association 2002, p. 14). The other players might themselves facilitate the mechanisms through which knowledge spillovers occur, while also acting as sources of spillovers themselves—consider the fee-paying Industrial Liaison Program operated by the Massachusetts Institute of Technology (MIT), which helps support the competitiveness of the Massachusetts biotech cluster (OECD 2006a, p. 120, box 2.6).,The collection of firms and other players that defines a successful cluster represents a "regional innovation system" or a "regional innovation network," which helps a city both build and sustain its competitive advantage (Hotz-Hart 2000).

From the viewpoint of many if not most cities in the developed or developing world, a problem exists: attempting to specialize in the very knowledge-intensive and high-tech industries that characterize the most globally competitive cities is an extremely risky strategy, with a very high probability of failure. Such a conclusion follows from the logic of agglomeration economies—in particular, from the earlier-stated fact that such economies promote the lock-in of competitive advantage in the cities where it is already enjoyed and, therefore, the lock-out of cities that do not already have a competitive foothold. The consequence is that at the very highest end of the value chain, a single city can often achieve global domination of an industry or subindustry. Take, for instance, the ion implanting equipment cluster located close to Boston, Massachusetts. This cluster produces a type of semiconductor manufacturing machinery and has a world market share of almost 90 percent (van der Linde 2003, p. 136). Likewise, the same agglomeration economies imply that a single city will frequently dominate formal R&D within a country. This is the case in Canada, Finland, Greece, Ireland, Japan, Korea, and the Netherlands, where a single metropolitan region is responsible for almost half of the national innovative activity, as measured by patenting activity (OECD 2006a, p. 59).

Fortunately however, innovation and the forces of knowledge spillovers should not just be associated with Silicon Valley–style clusters. Indeed, they are a much more generalized phenomenon, just as characteristic of many apparently mundane industries as they are of high-tech industries. The concept of a knowledge spillover predates modern ICT industries by almost a century (Glaeser 2003, p. 143). Indeed, Porter (1998, p. 89) has argued that:

> There is no such thing as a low-tech industry. There are only low-tech companies—that is, companies that fail to use world-class technology and practices to enhance productivity and innovation. A vibrant cluster can help any company in any industry compete in the most sophisticated ways, using the most advanced, relevant skills and technologies.

Consider the flower cluster in the Netherlands, which, despite the apparently low-tech nature of its business, represents one of the largest documented clusters in the world (van der Linde 2003, p. 136), and relies for its competitive advantage partly on the collective provision of highly specialized, even sophisticated, auction and handling facilities (Porter 1998, p. 89). Consider also the successful replication of this cluster in Brazil by the Dutch community that migrated to the São Paulo countryside. The three municipalities that the community used to live in have recently merged into one municipality under the name of Holambra, and this is responsible for 70–90 percent of Brazilian flower exports. The immigrant Dutch community heeded the lock-in lesson. Before switching to flowers, they attempted to compete in coffee, but found themselves too late in the game to be successful.[17] This example demonstrates, first, the importance of the cluster concept to Latin American cities, as well as the need for intervention to tackle coordination failures. What is more open to question is the appropriate form of intervention. Certainly, as the above examples demonstrate, it need not take the traditional form of direct government intervention. Second, the example provides local policy makers with an important motto: "Know your economy." Leveraging competitive advantage requires strategic planning based on the identification of a locality's unique, perhaps hidden, capacities. This is consistent with theory from the new economic geography, that second nature advantages have a greater probability of taking hold if they build on preexisting first nature advantages.[18]

Despite the above emphasis on proximity in knowledge transfer, local synergies are not the only type of synergy that helps create competitive advantage. Also important are synergies—nonlocal synergies—that might be thought of as being external to a city. For example, one type of synergy that might be less local in scope, but that is nevertheless important to competitive advantage, is the home market effect.[19] This is a type of positive synergy that results from the interaction of the costs of starting a business with transport costs and labor mobility, and its spatial range might extend across several regions of a country (Venables 2006, pp. 23–24). The cluster concept does not, therefore, provide a panacea for competitiveness. Policy makers must also be cognizant of other types of synergies, which are unrelated to clustering and which yet might be equally important to competitive advantage (Feser 2002).

Human Capital

It has been argued that "if innovation and knowledge represent the lifeblood of city competitiveness, human capital [skills, training, and education] acts as the gene pool" (National Governors Association 2002, p. 15). This reflects the fact that human capital both acts as an input into innovative, knowledge-based activities and forms a pivotal component of the transmission mechanism for certain types of knowledge spillover (figure 1.2). The former role has again been emphasized by economists in their models of endogenous growth. In many such models, a city's or cluster's rate of innovation, and therefore growth, is positively related to its level of human capital (Romer 1990). This is because a higher level of human capital permits the more efficient transformation of preexisting knowledge into new forms of knowledge. Meanwhile, the latter role of human capital emanates from the need for associative behavior—direct face-to-face interaction and networking—for the transmission of tacit knowledge. Given the typical subtleties involved with such knowledge, communication skills are vital for successful transmission, and these skills are typically associated with a more educated local workforce. For instance, empirical work for the United States shows that a worker's individual wage is positively related to the average level of schooling in the city in which he or she currently resides and works. This implies a substantial knowledge spillover effect working through human capital—an additional year of average city-level

Figure 1.2   Channels of Human Capital Contribution to a City's Competitive Advantage

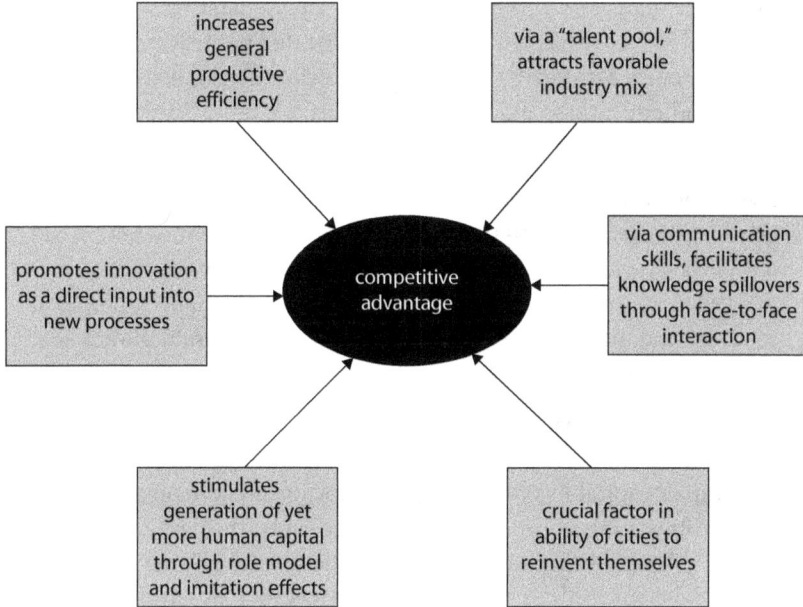

Source: Authors.

education is associated with a local productivity increase of 2.8 percent (Rauch 1993). An increase in educational attainment, therefore, not only benefits the direct recipients of the additional education, but also workers in general.

The importance of human capital as a key driver of a city's competitive advantage is by no means limited to the above roles. Its part in attracting a favorable industry mix and in contributing to a city's ability to reinvent itself is arguably just as important. The existence of a talent pool—a skilled and specialized pool of labor—can be crucial in attracting the FDI that helps a city gain a foothold in industries that are higher up the value chain. This is one dimension in which human capital has become a more prominent driver of city competitiveness given the above-mentioned fact that FDI flows have grown at twice the rate of world trade (and, therefore, at four times the rate of world income).

With respect to human capital as a determinant of a city's capacity to reinvent itself, recall the earlier discussion of Boston's ability to reinvent itself following a 60-year downturn in fortunes between 1920 and 1980.

Also remember the contrast with other U.S. cities such as Detroit and Syracuse, which failed to reinvent themselves, despite being in a similar situation around 1980. The decisive factor separating Boston from Detroit and Syracuse has been the highly educated nature of its workforce, which has been assisted by the city's historical strength as a center of learning and education, and its reputation as a livable city for the highly skilled (Glaeser 2003):

> Like Syracuse and Detroit, Boston was a cold, manufacturing city that had done poorly over the 1950–1980 period. But unlike those cities, Boston had universities, a well-educated workforce and a residual finance industry. In the 1980s, the return to schooling skyrocketed. The computer revolution sped up and demand for education soared. As a result, Boston did extremely well.

Hence, against the backdrop of the rapid global evolution of technology—which, as the quote states, has increased the returns to such capital in any case—human capital has been central to Boston's reinvigoration and, as a result, to its strong competitive advantage over the last two to three decades.[20] Moreover, human capital has been pivotal not only to Boston's ability to reinvent itself in the late 20th century, but also at previous periodic intervals since its origins as a city in the first half of the 17th century. At critical junctures in Boston's history, therefore, human capital has allowed the city to overcome long-term adverse economic shocks and assisted it in retaining competitive advantage. It has done this through facilitating positive structural change and allowing for the cultivation of a citywide learning environment.[21]

The problem that middle-income and developing-country cities face is that they are often severely disadvantaged with respect to the local availability of human capital. Part of the reason is the existence of large informal labor markets, which deny workers access to on-the-job training and other mechanisms for accumulating human capital. Consider Mexico City, where informal activities account for around one-third of all employment, or Istanbul, where they account for approximately half the local economy (OECD 2006a, p. 132–33). The situation is even worse in the cities of developing countries that lag far behind Mexico and Turkey. This indicates the importance of bringing such workers into the formal sector and providing them with access to education.

While promoting human capital accumulation is necessary to achieve a high level of competitive advantage, it is not enough. Without accompanying policy measures that succeed in boosting the demand for high-skilled workers, there is a very real risk of local "brain drain" as workers selectively migrate to other more competitive cities. In effect, this means that initiatives that boost the level of human capital accumulation in less competitive cities can subsidize accumulation in more competitive cities. Indeed, it is even possible to imagine a negative net impact on local competitiveness if such initiatives are locally financed.

Local Competition

Economic theory points to an ambiguous relationship between the level and intensity of local competition (whether at the city or individual cluster level) and competitive advantage (figure 1.3). On the one hand, fiercer local competition is theorized as having a negative impact on competitiveness because by undermining the monopoly privileges from innovation, it reduces the expected return to undertaking such activity in the first place.[22] On the other hand, it is theorized as having a positive impact on competitiveness because, in a highly competitive environment, a firm cannot afford to rest on its past achievements—if it fails to innovate, it will soon find its market usurped by a rival that is only too willing to steal its customers through engaging in product, process, and marketing innovations, which serve to give it a competitive edge in the local marketplace.[23]

Figure 1.3   Theoretical Relationships between Local Competition and Competitive Advantage

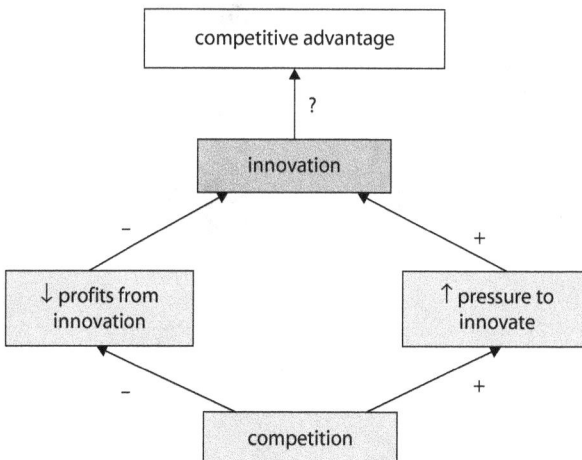

Source: Authors, based on Glaeser et al. (1992).

Despite the theoretical ambiguity, however, the message from the empirical literature is loud and clear—stronger competition between local firms is unquestionably good for city competitiveness. Glaeser underlines this: "Every piece of research in this area that I am aware of finds a positive effect of competition on later growth" (Glaeser 2000, p. 93). This empirical consensus corresponds with intuition—it seems only right to argue that, if a city is to successfully compete in today's rapidly evolving global environment, its firms must first of all be able to compete locally. In this respect, local competition has increased in relative importance as a key driver. Consistent with this, the existence of local competition as a dominant determinant of competitiveness is one of the primary factors that differentiates developed country clusters from developing country ones (figure 1.4). The key to success for a middle-income or developing-country city therefore lies in securing a movement away from competitiveness of its clusters based on comparative

Figure 1.4   Primary Determinants of Cluster Competitiveness in Developing and Developed Countries

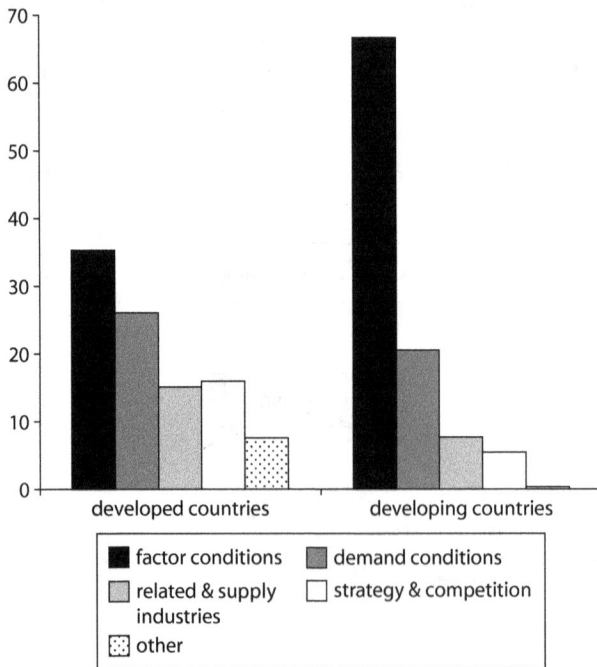

Source: Adapted from van der Linde (2003, p. 146, figure 7.11), based on a meta study of literature covering 833 clusters in 49 countries, 24 of which are developing.

advantage to competitiveness based on competitive advantage. It is this movement that represents the secret to achieving sustainable increases in prosperity. There is a clear interaction with human capital here—the higher is the level of human capital, the more effectively will any given increase in local competition translate into innovative activity. Again therefore, positive synergies exist among the key drivers of city competitiveness.

Notwithstanding the above, the positive link between local competition and competitive advantage is contingent upon the competition taking place along the correct vector. The links that have been made between competition and competitiveness above operate through innovation. It is not cut-throat local price competition that is required, rather nonprice competition in branding, innovation, and adaptation. It is on the basis of such competition that developed countries compete and it is the type of competition that is characteristic of a positive competitive dynamic in which the trajectory of local growth moves toward industries and activities of greater value added.[24]

The need for such competition does not stand in contradiction to the need for cooperation between firms to exploit local synergies and overcome coordination failure. This is because the two elements—competition and cooperation—can operate on different planes. In particular, cooperation should occur where there would otherwise be areas of coordination failure, as with uninternalized knowledge spillovers or failures of the market to provide jointly beneficial physical and marketing infrastructure. For example, local businesspeople may cooperate to create a common brand or identity (for instance, Napa Valley wine) from a nonlocal viewpoint.[25] However, behind this exterior image there needs to be strong competition based on quality.

Private Investment and Infrastructure

Private investment by firms in plants and equipment, though undoubtedly important, is a factor that, by itself, is insufficient to launch a city on a positive path of co-learning and continual improvement. According to economists' standard model of growth (Solow-Swan), any increase in private investment will, unless accompanied by simultaneous innovation, only provide a temporary boost to local economic growth. The evidence agrees that the belief that private investment is, by itself, able to bring about sustained improvements in competitive advantage is more in line with old-style approaches to the problem of local development. These approaches, based on spatially targeted fiscal incentives, have largely failed to live up to expectations and are now widely considered inadequate for the task at hand—building city competitiveness in an open and highly dynamic global environment. In Canada, Italy, and the United Kingdom, decades of policies based primarily on the subsidization of private investment failed in their objective of narrowing regional disparities (Armstrong and Taylor 2000). Likewise in Brazil, while some footloose manufacturing firms have been attracted to the lagging northern and northeast regions of the country, the "constitutional funds"—on which annual expenditure has reached US$3–4 billion—have failed to attract vertically integrated industries (Carvalho, Lall, and Timmins 2008; cited in World Bank 2008).

Infrastructure investment may take several forms. Although the macroempirical evidence on the causal relationship between these various forms of investment, on the one hand, and development, on the other, is plagued by contradictory results,[26] it has been forcefully argued that the types of infrastructure investment that are important for a city at any given moment are dependent on the city's size and level of development (World Bank 2008). For a small city or one that is just in the process of getting established, investment in basic public utilities and local public goods is important. This includes investment in energy and water supply infrastructure, as well as in basic health and sanitation facilities. These types of infrastructure investments provide the foundation on which the city may be able to build density, thereby reaping the benefits of agglomeration economies and building competitive advantage.

In contrast, a medium-size or rapidly growing city requires, in addition to basic public utilities and local public goods, investment in spatially connective infrastructure. This consists predominantly of transport infrastructure—roads, rail, and various other forms of public transportation—and assists in tackling problems of congestion that might otherwise threaten to choke off agglomeration economies, strangling competitive advantage in the process.

An important distinction here is between intra- and interurban transportation infrastructure. The former improves spatial connectivity within a city, which, as well as improving intraurban movements of goods and services and reducing travel-to-work times, may facilitate associative behavior between individuals and businesses located in different neighborhoods. The latter improves spatial connectivity between a city and (a) the wider subnational region of which it is a part, and (b) other cities in a country's urban hierarchy or portfolio of places. For a medium-size city, (b) may be particularly important in helping it capture maturing industrial activities that are looking to relocate from cities higher up the urban hierarchy, where the price of land and commercial property, not to mention labor, is more expensive. In Korea, for example, the early decentralization of manufacturing activity from Seoul was made to locations that were within an hour's drive of the capital; in Brazil, industries that relocated from São Paulo followed transport corridors into the neighboring state of Minas Gerais (World Bank 2008, chapter 2).

Importantly, investments in spatial connectivity with other cities are likely to fail unless they are sequenced correctly and accompanied by attempts to simultaneously address constraints to the other key drivers of city competitiveness. This is because, as the literature on the new economic geography shows, major intercity transportation projects increase not only the access of the city that is the intended beneficiary of the projects to the markets of other cities, but also vice versa. If the other key drivers are not in place, this could well result in a loss of industry share, not to mention human capital.

For a large city in a middle-income or developing country, general investments in basic public utilities, local public goods, and spatially connective infrastructure need to be supplemented with spatially targeted infrastructure investments, including investments in the supply of affordable housing. This is to overcome intracity divisions, such as informal settlements or slum communities, which have arisen, in part, because of a city's very success in growing and attracting both rural and other migrants. Consider Goiânia, the state capital of Goiás in Brazil. Since 1950, Goiânia has been transformed from a medium-size city of 40,000 inhabitants to one with a population of more than 1 million. Much of this population growth, however, has been accommodated in slums—the number of slum clusters has increased from 200 to 1,160. Without investments in affordable housing and other infrastructure aimed at better integrating their inhabitants with the rest of the city, these settlements will act as a potential drag on Goiânia's competitive advantage (World Bank 2008, chapter 1).

One further type of infrastructure investment that may be important for competitive advantage is investment in urban amenities or cultural facilities (museums, art galleries, sporting and entertainment venues, and more). These amenities can help a city establish itself as a place of tourism—consider the Guggenheim Museum in Bilbao, Spain, which has helped transform a depressed industrial city into a tourist center by attracting over 9 million visitors since its opening in 1997.[27] They can also be important in attracting and retaining human capital. The centrality of human capital to Boston's ability to periodically reinvent itself has already been emphasized. What has not been mentioned, however, is that Boston's high level of urban amenities and historical status as a consumer city have been vital to its reputation as a livable city, which, in turn, has played a crucial role in its ability to retain human capital in periods of economic downturn (Glaeser 2003).

Table 1.2 summarizes these five main forms of investment and their relationship to a city's competitiveness.

Quality of Local Governance

The quality of local governance is an influential factor in determining the cost of doing business within a city and, through this, crucially affects the favorability of the local investment climate (Dollar et al. 2003, p. 6). In turn, the favorability of the local investment climate affects the attractiveness of a city to inward investment, including, most importantly, FDI. In this sense, the quality of local governance cannot, correctly speaking, be considered an independent driver of its competitiveness. Nevertheless, an efficient and market-oriented institutional environment is needed not only to attract FDI, but also to create the incentives through which longer-term local economic growth can be sustained (Jacobs 2003). Regulations that enhance or constrain business activities, in areas such as starting a business, dealing with licenses, employing workers, registering property, getting credit, protecting investors, paying taxes, enforcing contracts, and closing a business, can have a significant impact on economic growth and competitiveness (World Bank 2007), and governments at the local level have more leverage over these factors than perhaps most others. It has been found, for example, that countries that regulate market entry more heavily have more corruption and larger unofficial economies, without the compensation of a better quality of public or private goods (Djankov et al. 2002). Work by the OECD suggests that easing product market regulations and administrative burdens is associated with accelerating multifactor productivity growth across the economy (Bassanini, Scarpetta, and Hemmings 2001).

In fact, the quality of local governance has strong implications on most of the competitiveness drivers highlighted in this chapter. Infrastructure provision is a primary function of local governments, given their role as providers of local public goods. Human capital is to a large extent dependent on the quality of education, which is often provided by local governments. The ability of large cities to continue

Table 1.2   Different Forms of Investment and Their Relationship to City Competitiveness

Type of investment	Relationship to city competitiveness	Type of city for which most important
Private investment by firms in plants, machinery, and equipment	• Helps in upgrading capital stock of firms and facilitating introduction of up-to-date technologies. Importance underscored by existence of a positive relationship between private investment and productivity for 23 Chinese cities, 2002–03.[1] • Reflects importance of efficient allocation of finance to local firms, which is free from informal payments to bank and other officials. Such finance "significantly reduces the transaction costs ... compared to the scenario in which the firm has to secure development funds for themselves (via informal loans, personal wealth, or direct soliciting of private investors)."[2] • Access to formal sources of finance (venture capital and angel finance) is a particular problem for SMEs in most cities, even in developed countries.[3]	All cities
Investment in public utilities and local public goods	• Energy and water supply infrastructure; basic environmental, sanitation, and health facilities.	Small cities laying the foundations for agglomeration economies and competitive advantage; important in spatially targeting problems of slum communities in large cities
Spatially connective infrastructure investment	• Takes several forms, such as improving transport links: (a) within a city; (b) between a city and the wider metro region of which it is a part; and (c) between a city and other cities. • Benefits of (a) and (b) are emphasized by stakeholders in local development in the United Kingdom;[4] the World Bank's (2008) *World Development Report 2009: Reshaping Economic Geography*, emphasizes the importance of (a)–(c).	Rapidly growing medium-size cities suffering from emerging congestion problems; large cities with long-standing congestion problems

(continued)

Table 1.2   Different Forms of Investment and Their Relationship to City Competitiveness *(Continued)*

Type of investment	Relationship to city competitiveness	Type of city for which most important
	• Also includes investment in ICT infrastructure (landline and mobile telephone networks and broadband Internet capacity), which is important in facilitating connectivity to markets and market information, thereby reducing the costs of doing business. Has the potential to stimulate innovation through facilitating certain types of knowledge spillovers, with some evidence of positive knock-on effects for Europe.[5]	
Housing investment	• Investment in affordable housing helps reduce intraurban disparities in living standards between neighborhoods (for example, the existence of slums) that might otherwise be a source of division and tension, undermine the health and productivity of the affected population.	Large cities
Investment in urban amenities	• Significant contribution in making a city livable, and hence in the attraction and retention of human capital. Might also contribute to the building of a tourism cluster.	Declining industrial cities

Sources: (1) Dollar et al. (2003, p. 47) ; (2) Dollar et al. (2003, pp. 41–42); (3) Armstrong and Taylor (2000); (4) Office of the Deputy Prime Minister (2003); (5) Martin (1998; cited in World Bank 2005, p. 7).

growing and reinventing themselves can be facilitated or limited by the coverage and efficiency of infrastructure (especially intraurban transportation), which defines the effective labor market size (Prud'homme and Lee 1999). Finally, business regulation can have a significant impact on the presence and level of local competition. For OECD countries, it has been found that the lower the entry barriers and the less state control, the faster the catch-up to best-practice technologies in manufacturing industries (Nicoletti and Scarpetta 2003).

As mentioned, local governance also affects competitive advantage through its influence in attracting FDI, a type of investment that has become relatively more important with the advent of globalization (see the previous section, "The Rapidly Changing Global Environment and the Need for Competitiveness"). Even if private investment is, by itself, unable to set a city on a path of continual competitive improvement, the fact that FDI has become relatively more important indicates that the quality of local governance will be an important factor in deciding whether cities in the Latin America and Caribbean region and elsewhere end up as winners or losers from globalization. Furthermore, out of all the types of private investment, FDI is the one most likely to energize beneficial synergies in relation to innovation and human capital accumulation.

In the above context, it has been argued that, as globalization occurs, a city where the quality of local governance is good becomes more likely to attract FDI that places a high premium on this factor (Venables 2006, p. 31). Such investment will tend to be in higher-value-added activities, which can provide a medium for the introduction of new technologies to a locality. This in itself can encourage knowledge spillovers to the local economy, particularly through the entrepreneurial mechanism of local workers leaving a foreign-sponsored plant to set up business themselves and, in so doing, taking the acquired knowledge with them. A vivid example of this is the garment industry in Bangladesh. This industry started in April 1980, when a shirt factory was opened with a joint venture between Desh Garment Ltd., owned by the Bangladeshi entrepreneur Noorul Quader, and the Daewoo Corporation of Korea. Subsequently, "Of the 130 Desh workers trained by Daewoo, 115 of them left Desh during the 1980s to set up their own garment export firms. They diversified into gloves, coats, and trousers. This explosion of garment companies started by ex-Desh workers brought Bangladesh its $2 billion in garment sales today" (Easterly 2002, p. 147–48).

It is therefore important for cities to improve their areas of substandard performance in local governance. They need to ensure that both local government and the local judicial system operate in an open and transparent manner. This is because increasing accountability and transparency provides protective insulation against distorting corruption and acts as a deterrent against rent seeking by local economic players and as a stimulus to engaging in productive behavior.

A responsible and transparent fiscal framework—particularly for local government operations—can help prevent a city from becoming saddled with an unmanageable burden of debt. It can also assist in tax-raising efforts by local government to finance its spending plans. This is because such a framework helps civil society see the relationship between the taxes that are levied and the spending that results, providing reassurance that the revenue is not being mishandled or wasted. In this way, in the words of the economist David Dollar et al. (2003, p. 36), the local populace sees local government as playing the role of "helping hand" rather than "grabbing hand." In addition, in terms of local regulations on legitimate public interests such as the environment, health, and safety, transparency is important in creating a level local playing field. On such a playing field, "an economy … [can be] … expected to work much better" (Dollar et al. 2003, p. 36).[28]

An efficient, professional, and participatory governance structure that can lead to high-quality public choices is especially important for high-density urban areas, where not only are a large part of public goods provided by the local government (including public security and recreation activities such as parks, museums, and sports), but public choice also fundamentally shapes the future of the cities through land use planning and regulations, the formation of a shared city identity and vision, and activities that facilitate their realization.

Summary and Conclusions

The aim of this chapter has been to address the question: "What makes cities competitive?" To try to answer this question, the chapter has drawn on academic research from the fields of economics and management science, among others, and on international policy experience. It has presented a list of six key drivers of a city's competitiveness or competitive advantage—historical legacy; innovation; human capital; local competition; private investment and infrastructure; and the quality of local governance. The exact relative importance of these determinants will vary from city to city according to their size, stage of development, and position in the national hierarchy of cities. In general, however, the building of competitive advantage requires the simultaneous tackling of key constraints affecting all these drivers.

Chapter 2 will take forward the argument that a cluster approach is well suited to local economic development. This approach also helps deal with one of the main policy lessons to emerge from this chapter: namely that, because of the logic of agglomeration economies and the associated tendency for industries to become locked in to certain locations and locked out of other locations, local policy makers will have the best chance of achieving competitive success if they seek to build on a city's preexisting strengths. As stated earlier, this leads to the motto: "Know your economy." Again, by providing the diagnostic tools to help identify a city's strengths and weaknesses, as well as its opportunities and threats, a cluster approach provides a potential way forward to those local stakeholders who have a positive policy agenda.

Notes

1. Other developments of relevance from economics and other fields include territorial innovation systems models, evolutionary and path-dependence models, social capital approaches, and creative cities approaches.

2. With reference to the academic literature, the primary focus will be on insights arising from economics.

3. One further factor—a city's historical legacy—is also given special attention, because of the insights into the mechanisms generating competitive advantage that historical factor provides.

4. For greater discussion of these developments see World Bank (2008, chapter 6).

5. This figure is for 2003.

6. Indeed, some economists, most notably Krugman (1996), have questioned the extent to which it is meaningful to even apply the term "competitiveness" to entities other than firms.

7. This is the measure used by the OECD (2006a, p. 56). One reason why it is imperfect as a measure of competitiveness is because the mobility of labor and capital creates a tendency toward the equalization of factor rewards at the margin. This implies that GDP per capita growth differences might not reveal the true extent of underlying differences in competitive advantage.

8. For brevity, "productivity" from this point forward will be used to mean "labor productivity."

9. There are two of them: labor market efficiency as measured by the employment rate; and the activity rate, which is affected both by the proportion of the working-age population participating in the local labor market (the participation rate) and the size of the working-age population relative to the aggregate population.

10. Caveats include, for example, Simon and Nardinelli (1996), who provide evidence on the central importance of human capital in explaining the growth of English and Welsh cities between the late 19th and 20th centuries. Likewise, Glaeser (2003) documents the importance of human capital, albeit of radically different forms, in helping Boston periodically reinvent itself over a period of more than three centuries.

11. This cluster can be traced back to 1348 (van der Linde 2003, p. 141).

12. Recognition of these benefits dates back to the late 19th century (Marshall 1920).

13. This requirement for cities to be able to reinvent themselves to ensure enduring competitive advantage is consistent with a more "path-dependent" view of the importance of history in determining long-run competitive outcomes. In truth, even for cities like Boston, reinvention has not been without hardship-Boston experienced a population decline relative to the United States for six decades from 1920 to 1980. The relevant policy question therefore becomes: How quickly can a city reinvent itself in the face of negative long-term economic shocks and are there factors, open to policy influence, which can facilitate the reinvention process?

14. Innovation in this chapter is taken to mean both the creation of new products, devices, methods and processes, and the adaptation/improvement of existing products, devices, methods, and processes. Crucially, therefore, innovation includes the successful adaptation of foreign (that is, nonlocal) ideas to the local context.

15. OECD (2006a, p. 59) associated innovation with a "more favorable" industrial mix.

16. These positive local synergies will, because of the need for proximity, tend to be very spatially concentrated. Indeed, work by Rice, Venables, and Pattachini (2006) suggests that, in the United Kingdom, these synergies die out beyond an 80-minute driving range. In middle-income and developing countries, where transport infrastructure is less developed, this range will be less. This underscores the importance of synergies between the six key drivers.

17. We are grateful to Giorgio Romano Schutte from the São Paulo office of the Cities Alliance for this example.

18. This assumes an enlarged definition of first nature advantages to include not just the physical geographic characteristics of a particular location, but also aspects of its cultural, institutional, and historical heritage.

19. The existence of such an effect was first theorized by Krugman (1980).

20. It should be noted, however, that Boston's competitive advantage has been threatened more recently by its tight regulations on new construction.

21. Besides the research already cited in this section, evidence on the importance of human capital to local competitiveness is provided for the United Kingdom by Roberts (2004), for the United States by Glaeser, Scheinkman, and Shleifer (1995), and for Brazil by da Mata et al. (2007).

22. This is the position taken in the Marshall-Arrow-Romer theory of city growth, as stylized by Glaeser et al. (1992).

23. This is consistent with the Jacobs and Porter theories of city growth, as again stylized by Glaeser et al. (1992).

24. In this context, there is a strand of economic theory that models the economic growth of a locality as depending positively on the income elasticity of demand for its tradable goods and inversely on the income elasticity of demand for the goods it imports (Thirlwall 1980; McCombie and Thirlwall 1994). Within this framework, successful nonprice competition can be interpreted as increasing the income elasticity of demand for tradable goods and reducing that for imports. The result of this is an increase in the sustainable rate of local growth.

25. Such joint actions may be characterized as precompetition cooperation.

26. See Straub (2008) for a survey.

27. "Bilbao, 10 years later," *The New York Times*, September 23, 2007.

28. Bombay First-McKinsey (2003) highlighted that poor governance is a key constraint to Mumbai becoming a world-class city.

CHAPTER 2

What Can Cities Do to Enhance Competitiveness? Local Policies and Actions for Innovation

Ming Zhang

This chapter summarizes the practical policies and actions that local governments in Brazil can adopt in their efforts to enhance local economic competitiveness. It stresses measures to enhance the innovative and learning aspects of local economies.

To address one of their most important challenges, economic growth, municipal leaders ask: "What can be done to enhance my city's economic competitiveness?" Policies on municipal actions to promote local competitiveness have typically focused on three areas:

- Providing infrastructure, such as transportation, telecommunications, water, and sanitation
- Improving public services, including education, health, public security, and housing
- Reducing the cost of doing business through simplifying regulations, making it easier to open businesses, pay taxes, hire workers, acquire land, and exit from businesses.

These three broad areas of action are critical, especially in the Brazilian context where infrastructure and bureaucracy have been identified as among the top constraints to economic competitiveness. The *Global Competitiveness Report 2007–2008* (Porter, Sala-i-Martin, and Schwab 2007), for example, out of 131 countries ranked Brazil 128 in "burden of government regulation"; 120 in "quality of the educational system"; 121 in "business cost of crime and violence"; and 97 in "quality of overall infrastructure." These are unquestionably crucial factors that have brought down the overall competitiveness of the Brazilian economy, which was ranked 72 overall. At the municipal level, the International Finance Corporation's Municipal Scorecard 2007 for Latin America places the majority of the 25 participating Brazilian municipalities toward the bottom of the regional ranking (IFC 2007). Their greatest weaknesses are in the performance index for the operating license and the construction permit. Efforts by local governments can therefore contribute significantly to addressing such major competitiveness constraints.

However, theoretical advances and successful examples suggest that these three broad areas of action alone are not sufficient. To be competitive globally, it is not enough to simply offer lower-cost, or even superb infrastructure. Knowledge and innovation, which can be significantly enhanced by positive spillover effects among private firms and other players in the local economy, provide opportunities for a broader scope of local interventions. A more proactive role for local government may be warranted for cities to become and stay competitive in a global environment characterized by ever-increasing competitive pressures. This chapter focuses on possible courses of actions in this area.

The review of recent literature in chapter 1 suggests that there are market failures of coordination: if left to themselves, local players are unlikely to coordinate and take joint actions that will benefit the local economy as a whole. Active government involvement in providing incentives or mechanisms to coordinate has the potential to fill this gap and benefit individual firms. Yet the risk of government involvement can be high, as such coordination is complex and the tendency of governments to overstep and replace, rather than supplement, the forces of the market has often resulted in can be significant.

This chapter tries to highlight a range of possible local government actions for Brazilian municipal, state, and federal policy makers in promoting local economic competitiveness. Going beyond the well-covered areas of infrastructure, services, and business cost, the chapter focuses on policies to promote knowledge and innovation in the local economy for competitiveness, drawing on a wide range of international and Brazilian experiences taken from different sources, as well as the two case studies conducted for the Cariri region, Ceará, and São Luís, Maranhão (chapters 4 and 5). In reviewing international experiences, we have tried to select examples that we feel are relevant for Brazil. The preliminary results were presented at a number of forums in Brazil with the participation of policy makers at different levels. Feedback from these exchanges helped improve this chapter.

The key message of this chapter is that for the local economy to be competitive in a globalized environment, simply reducing the cost of doing business—through providing high-quality infrastructure and public services and lowering business transactions costs—while critical, is not sufficient. Leading cities are also taking action to add value to local businesses by creating an environment that incentivizes local firms to innovate and learn from each other, and upgrade the level of competitiveness of the overall local economy.

The Starting Point: Understanding the Market and the Local Economy

Local governments' interventions to boost competitiveness should start with a clear understanding of the market and the main drivers of city economic growth. It is critical for local policy makers to bear in mind that, in most cases, it is the local private firms that determine competitiveness, and local government intervention should merely complement the market and take effect only where market failure is present. Such scenarios include government provision of public goods, mitigation of negative externalities such as environmental pollution and traffic congestion, promotion of positive externalities such as knowledge sharing, and addressing coordination failures. It is also important, however, for local policy makers to recognize the risks associated with an intention to correct market failures. As the planned interventions may be of the wrong type or scale, or implemented poorly with inadequate competence, the possibility of public interventions failing can be significant.

How do local governments acquire a good understanding of the driving forces of the local economy and the market? Both quantitative and qualitative methods may be used.[1] Quantitatively, local governments may collect and analyze information about local economic conditions to be used in decision making (Cities Alliance 2007). In Brazil, a significant amount of data is available at the municipal level. Figure 2.1, which plots sector importance against growth with employment data from the Relação Anual de Informações Sociais (Annual Records of Social Information, or RAIS),[2] can be used to detect the critical local economic clusters in a city. Sector importance is measured with a "location quotient," which ranges between 0 and 1. The figure will help a city identify important and emerging clusters. More detailed explanations are given in the case studies on Cariri and São Luís.

Qualitative methods can also be used to supplement the results of quantitative analyses and provide insight into the local economies not captured by the existing data collection system. These methods essentially entail structured involvement with the private sector (both locally and firms outside the region with local business linkages) through measures such as consultations, focus group meetings, surveys, and interviews.

In practical terms, the "cluster approach" (spearheaded by Porter [2000]) offers a pragmatic course of action for local government action plans for competitiveness. While there are debates about the concept and theory of the cluster approach (Martin and Sunley 2003), we believe that many of the policy recommendations from the cluster

Figure 2.1   Detecting Local Economic Clusters: Using Location Quotient and Employment Growth Rate

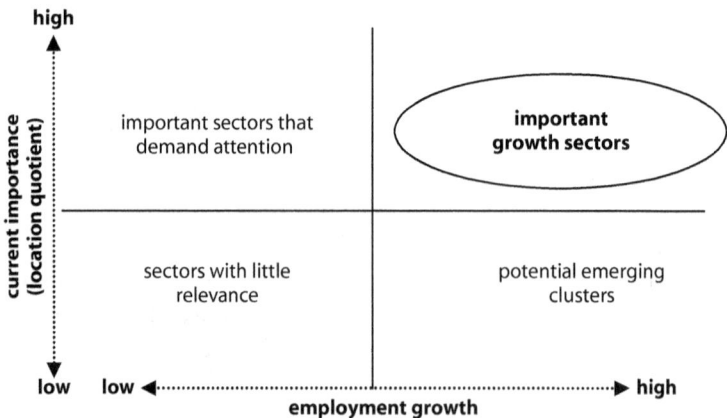

Source: Authors.

approach, such as the emphasis on private sector networking, regulatory environment, and constant learning, are consistent with recent theoretical and empirical advances. The cluster approach offers a practical framework for policy makers to organize public and private actions (social capital) centered on competitive market forces. The essence of the cluster approach is not "cluster building," or creating competitive clusters that are currently nonexistent in a city,[3] but fostering innovation and upgrading among the members of the existing or emerging clusters in the local economy.[4]

Neither the cluster approach, nor any one measure, is a panacea for city economic competitiveness. There are no guarantees of success, and the risk of government endeavors in economic development is often higher than among other types of government activities. Forces outside local government control are often more important than policy interventions. It is therefore important to understand the key drivers of local growth, both internal and external, and to maintain a cautious approach toward government interventions.

Facilitating Private Sector Collaborations for Collective Efficiency

A critical premise of the cluster approach is that businesses compete not as isolated units but rather within complex webs of interdependence. The cluster concept involves the following elements: (a) leading firms that export products and services outside the region; (b) a supply network that provides inputs to these leading firms; and (c) the business environment and economic foundations, including such elements as human resources, technology, financial capital, and infrastructure. Figure 2.2 is a classic example of a wine cluster in California, while figure 4.2, in chapter 4, shows the present-day footwear cluster in the Cariri region of Ceará.[5] The strength (or competitiveness) of the location is determined by the presence of this sophisticated, closely integrated network of private, public, and semipublic entities. Moreover, a competitive cluster is a network of such magnitude that its members continuously learn, innovate, and improve, resulting in a continual upgrading of quality. The sophistication of such a web and its ability for continued renewal and innovation are, in the end, the source of sustained competitiveness for a locality.

Clusters can be formed "naturally" without much government support (for example the Napa Valley wine cluster). In other cases, the formation of competitive clusters may be facilitated or accelerated through government

Figure 2.2   The Napa Wine Cluster

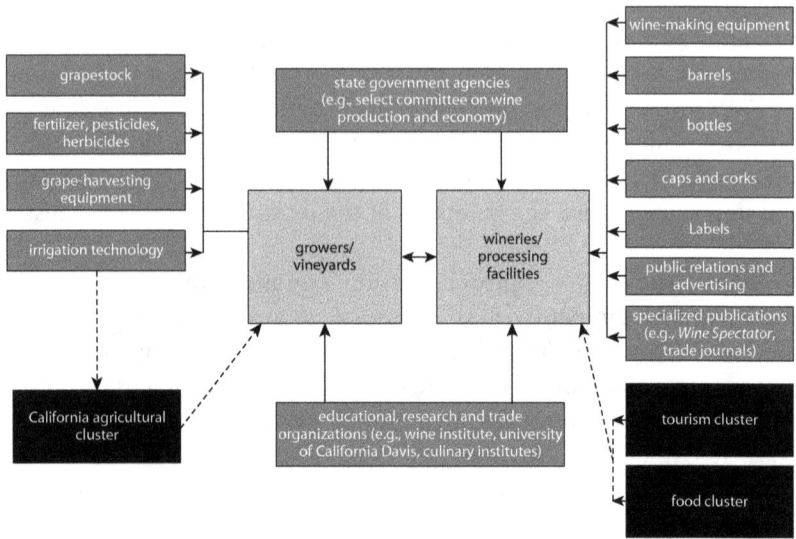

Source: California Wine Institute, California State Legislature. Based on research by 1997 MBA students R. Alexander, R. Arney, N. Black, E. Frost, and A. Shivananda, as cited in Porter (2000).

intervention. The essence of the cluster approach is not to create new clusters, although successful cases of cluster building exist, but to promote and exploit synergies, or to exploit interdependencies to leverage innovation. The cluster concept offers "a powerful framework for companies to organize, work together, and work with government to meet their needs and promote their interests" (Waits 2000).

A key task is to facilitate collaborative actions among private sector players that can lead to "collective efficiency," or the competitive advantage derived from external economies and the deliberate pursuit of joint actions (Schmitz and Nadvi 1999). For this purpose, it is important for local governments to strengthen networking and associative behavior of the local private enterprises (National Governors Association 2002). The relational assets (or "social capital") of a cluster depend on trust as well as on the frequency and depth of personal exchanges. To build a cluster is essentially to build relational assets and provide local collective goods.

The institutional forms of such relational assets, or "institutions for collaboration" (Porter 2000), include trade associations, entrepreneur networks, standard-setting agencies, quality centers, and technology networks. Cluster associations and alliances play a critical role. Successful examples often have the following features: government recognition of cluster identity; corporate status; strong business leadership; active recruitment of members; clear mission, goals, and plan; dedicated staff; an interactive Web portal; structure for membership fees or plan for revenue generation; real services; and frequent professional and social activities (National Governors Association 2002).

Such private networks can engage in a wide variety of activities to strengthen collaboration. Organized cluster networks in Colorado, United States, for example, had the following main tasks (Waits 2000):

- Cataloging the key components of the cluster and mapping interrelationships among firms
- Articulating an achievable vision of what the cluster can become over the next 10 to 20 years
- Identifying opportunities for growing the cluster in the desired direction by expanding existing companies, starting new companies, and attracting outside companies
- Identifying opportunities for more synergy within the cluster
- Identifying needs for specific economic foundations and proposed strategies.

There is no single formula or model that applies to the organization and activities of groups. The specific activities of clusters need to be conditioned on the nature of the cluster and the current status of group activities. In the case of Colorado, examples of group activities include:

- Co-informing: Identify cluster members and impacts, promote a heightened awareness of the industry, and improve communications among firms in the cluster
- Co-learning: Run educational and training programs
- Co-marketing: Carry out collective activities that promote the cluster's products or services abroad or domestically (for example, trade missions, trade shows, and advertisements)
- Co-purchasing: Strengthen buyer-supplier linkages within the cluster or jointly buy equipment that firms could otherwise not afford
- Co-producing: Form alliances to make a product together or conduct research and development (R&D) together
- Co-building economic foundations: Launch collective activities to build stronger educational, financial, and government institutions that enable firms to compete better.

Different types of clusters demonstrate different types of "collective efficiency needs." In a review of clusters in Latin America, Altenburg and Meyer-Stamer (1999) classify three types of "common" clusters: survival clusters of micro and small-scale enterprises; more advanced and differentiated mass production clusters; and clusters of transnational corporations. They propose the types of policies useful for each type of cluster, which are summarized in table 2.1.

The process of cluster organization is of great importance. The essence of a cluster initiative is to stimulate firms to cooperate, share information, and organize themselves for the common good. Building collaborative organizations requires building trust, often among competitors, and therefore it may take a long time and need considerable support. Cluster organization therefore is frequently characterized by an initial phase that requires intensive support.[6] Figure 2.3 shows a typical cluster process that the authors of chapter 5 recommended for São Luís, which can also be adapted to other situations. The important feature is the concurrent process of diagnosis, group process, and leadership actions, which constitutes a system of continual feedback among each of the elements. This indicates an action-oriented process, where the cluster members desire and expect quick results and actionable items, as opposed to waiting for prolonged diagnosis and planning without intermediate results.

Other important aspects of the cluster process are the roles of cluster leadership and facilitators. Strong leadership, by either a private or public sector leader, is crucial for cluster success. Moreover, an experienced cluster facilitator can be instrumental in determining the quality and effectiveness of the group engagement process. The facilitator should have the capacity to engage different actors, catalyze consensus, and be action oriented. At the beginning of the cluster process, it is often useful to have professional support and training in facilitation.

Examples of Specific Actions to Enhance Competitiveness

In pursuing competitiveness, each city must search for and formulate a unique set of strategies and actions that are suitable to its own situation and differentiated from those of other cities. No single action is applicable to all cities. In fact, the most important challenge is to propose a unique value proposition and formulate a strategy that differentiates the city from the rest. Nevertheless, certain actions have been used by many cities. This section summarizes a few examples of such actions from

Table 2.1 Different Policies for Different Cluster Types

Cluster type	Characteristics	Policies
Survival clusters of micro and small-scale enterprises	Most frequent type of cluster, they produce low-quality consumer goods for local markets, mainly in activities where barriers to entry are low. Many clusters are informal, and most need support.	Mixing general SME support and specific cluster policies with emphasis on promoting cooperation among SMEs by: • Encouraging the establishment of a local stakeholder dialogue to identify economically viable projects of collective action • Providing subsidies for groups of SMEs for joint activities, such as market surveys, feasibility studies, or participation in trade missions and fairs • Focusing on brokerage (mediation among firms) to build trust and identify common interests.
More advanced and differentiated mass production clusters	Production is mostly restricted to standardized consumer goods for mass markets, usually with little innovation and a high level of vertical integration. They often face "sandwich" situations, that is, competition from both the bottom (cost) and the top (innovation).	Stimulating firms to go beyond incremental adjustment efforts by: • Changing the role of business associations so as to organize collective action for self-help and articulate their demand through political actors • Professionalizing business associations • Enhancing local environment for private business through close consultation, removing unnecessary regulation, and improved bureaucratic efficiency • Promoting intensified interfirm cooperation in fields such as environment protection, measurement and testing, education and basic vocational training, technology development, design, and marketing • Providing information and advisory services (such as an international trade center) • Training • R&D and technology development.
Clusters of transnational corporations	Mostly dominated by large branch plants of world-class manufacturers; typically few linkages with domestic SMEs and institutions, therefore low degree of technological spillovers. Often fail to develop dynamic local entrepreneurship in knowledge-intensive areas.	Attracting additional FDI to deepen local production system, by: • Using selective promotion abroad and investment by government in dynamic locational advantages, such as a specialized workforce or R&D facilities • Encouraging local firms to upgrade their technological capacities to become suppliers for the transnational cluster, for example, subcontracting exchange schemes that matchmake supply and demand, even with specific support for potential suppliers • Making conscientious efforts to transfer technology to local firms.

Source: Author's summary based on Altenburg and Meyer-Stamer (1999).

Note: SME = small and microenterprise; FDI = foreign direct investment.

Figure 2.3   The Cluster Working Group Process

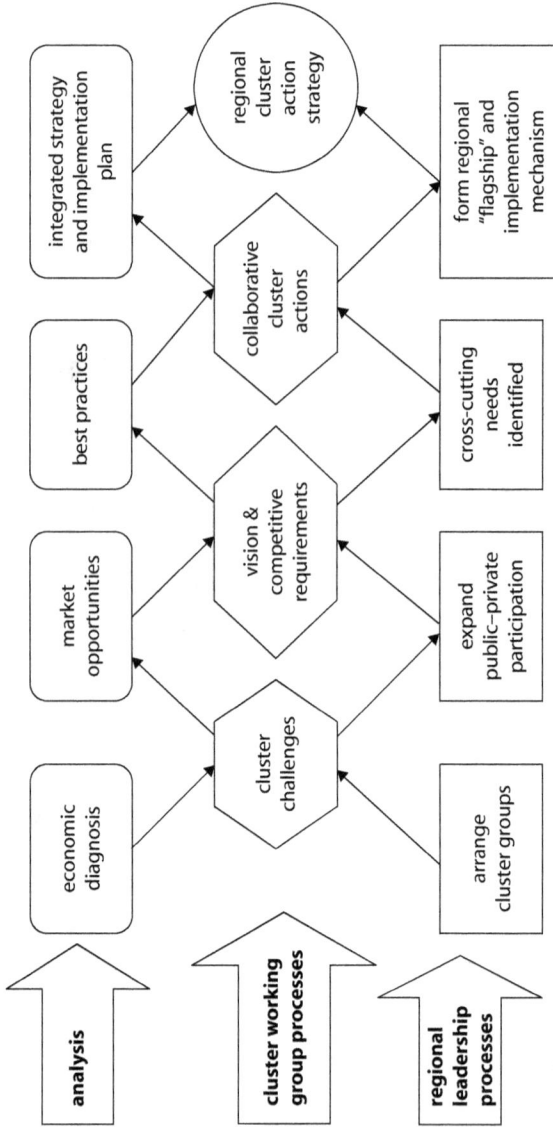

Figure 2.3 The Cluster Working Group Process

economic diagnosis

market opportunities

best practices

integrated strategy and implementation plan

regional cluster action strategy

cluster challenges

vision & competitive requirements

collaborative cluster actions

arrange cluster groups

expand public–private participation

cross-cutting needs identified

form regional "flagship" and implementation mechanism

analysis

cluster working group processes

regional leadership processes

Source: Chapter 5.

around the world. The list is by no means exhaustive, and the treatment of each topic in this chapter is necessarily very selective. The purpose is to provide examples of possible types of local policies and actions. Local policy makers need to bear in mind the specific characteristics of their own cities when assessing the applicability of specific actions and their potential for adaptation and use.[7]

Joint Marketing and Investment, and Export Promotion

This is clearly an area in which local governments can take the lead and undertake activities to expand the demand for local products and services, and attract external investments (foreign or domestic). Examples of actions that would bring general benefits to local businesses include market research, city branding, organization of characteristic local events, and active export and investment promotion.

Market research includes activities to identify potential markets for products and services from the city; analyze demand characteristics and standards for specific products manufactured in the city; acquire a better understanding of distributors and buyers; and identify key product intermediaries (Gausch 2007).

City branding aims to associate the city with a specific image or product or approach. Branding not only affects the success of marketing efforts, but also influences the overall strategy of the cluster, because it sends a signal about the vision of the cluster's products. The example of Chianti Classico (box 2.1) in Siena, Italy, is notable for the collective efforts by the cluster members to carefully nurture the brand image.

Organization of events to strengthen the local economy and increase awareness of local products and brands is another effective measure. The Olympic Games, for example, have played a critical role in the development of the local economies of Atlanta, Georgia; Barcelona, Spain; and Turin, Italy. Smaller cities can offer other types of events that correspond to unique local characteristics.[8]

Export or investment promotion can generate substantial returns, as shown by a review of export agencies (World Bank 2006). Although the review covered only national export promotion agencies, well-managed local or regional promotion should also bring significant benefits. Some of the key factors for success include a high level of private sector participation (for example, as directors of the board for export promotion agencies) and an emphasis on market research.

Box 2.1

Marketing and Branding Geographically Based Products: Chianti Classico, Siena, Italy

The Siena region is characterized by a culture of traditional agriculture. In such an area, granting locally produced agricultural products with "denomination of origin" or labels associated with product quality (or both) has become a successful branding and marketing tool for products such as Chianti Classico wine. In the early 20th century in Italy, geographic subdistricts were created to distinguish the "area of origin" of locally produced products. Chianti Classico is among the seven subdistricts of the Chianti wine district; today it is recognized as the oldest geographic area of origin. Through strong associative behavior and adherence to strict standards of quality and production, Chianti Classico wine producers earned the *Denominazione di origine controllata* (DOC) label in 1967 and the *Denominazione di origine controllata e garantita* (DOCG) label in 1984, enabling producers to brand and market the quality of their product to an international market. Consumers are increasingly aware of the stringent set of production standards imposed by the DOC and DOCG labels, giving impetus to the reputation of the Classico variety. Producers benefit immensely from the "Classico" distinction: a bottle of Chianti Classico sells for approximately three times that of a standard Chianti.

Among the major factors of success of the Chianti Classico variety are strong associative behavior among producers and efforts to market the relationship between the product and territory. Associative behavior began in the early 20th century with the formation of a consortium (legally sanctioned in 1930) to monitor product quality and production processes. As most producers are small scale, the Chianti consortium has served to bring producers together to devise a common marketing strategy, ensure the necessary collaboration between different actors of the value chain, and impose quality control systems to monitor the product from the cultivation of grapes to the bottling of the wine. More recently, the Chianti consortium began intensive research for improving the quality of the grapevines and cultivation practices. The ability of the consortium to experiment with new viticulture and winemaking techniques with minimal risk to individual producers confers a considerable competitive advantage on its members.

Another factor of Classico success is the producers' effort to market the relationship between the product and territory. The wine has adapted to the reputational changes of the territory over time; today, the wine is associated with the geographically isolated, small-scale nature of production, which are product features valued by most consumers.

Source: OECD (2002).

Value Chain Integration

A value chain is the sequence of activities required to make a product or provide a service. One important feature of today's global economy is the presence of global value chains, where the R&D, design, and manufacturing of different components, as well as marketing, are undertaken in a highly integrated fashion but from different locations (cities in different countries) and by different firms. For developing economies, one way to quickly catch up in productivity is to enter such a value chain, often starting with a less lucrative segment and then moving on to higher-value-added segments. Value chain analysis helps the policy maker identify bottlenecks in the productive chain and determine which bottlenecks deserve priority government attention, which can most likely be resolved by the private sector, and which require public–private partnership (Schmitz 2005). Examples of the value chain–based approach include the following:

- *Attracting additional investments as part of the value chain to achieve locational synergies.* The city government, in its investment promotion efforts, can target businesses that are closely linked to existing firms in the city, with either upstream (suppliers) or downstream (intermediate of final buyers) linkages. Box 2.2 gives an example of this in Guadalajara, Mexico, in the 1990s. This is particularly relevant where a single transnational firm operates in the city and its connection to the local economy is weak. While the presence of such a firm provides a critical advantage for other linked suppliers to locate in the same place, this is also advantageous to the current transnationals. Tapping the knowledge and assistance of those current transnationals is crucial for success, which has the potential to lead to the emergence of a real cluster rather than a single big business.

- *Strengthening weak linkages in the value chain by helping local firms enter the existing value chain.* This can be done by raising quality and consistency levels of local firms to supply leading firms in the value chain. Gaining the capacity to supply leading firms is a crucial milestone for local suppliers, because the requirements on cost, quality, and speed are often challenging; this accomplishment can raise local production standards to a much higher and perhaps internationally competitive level. The local government can aid the process by mobilizing collective actions of local small firms, facilitating the acquisition of technologies and skills, and encouraging the establishment of mutually beneficial relationships between leading firms and local suppliers. The

Box 2.2

Value Chain Integration: The Electronics Industry in Guadalajara, Mexico

Guadalajara, Mexico's second-largest city, is the "Silicon Valley" of Mexico. The city has successfully attracted electronics manufacturing firms, spearheaded by IBM, the first transnational firm to set up a personal computer assembly plant in the city. Other transnationals assembling and testing electronic equipment include Hewlett-Packard, Motorola, NEC, Philips, and Siemens.

At least three features distinguish Guadalajara from other geographic areas characterized by simple agglomerations of dislocated assembly plants. First, although R&D is still conducted at the parent plant, and production in Guadalajara involves only standardized processes, firms can move beyond simple assembly functions and engage in automated and more technologically complex production activities. Second, Guadalajara is increasingly attracting global contract manufacturers, such as SCI Systems, Inc., and Solectron, which provide a broad range of assembly services for brand-name corporations. Additional suppliers of inputs are expected to invest in the cluster. Third, collective action on the part of cluster firms is increasing. There are at least two active business associations at Guadalajara that transnational electronics firms use for information exchange, thereby adopting Silicon Valley–type traits. These associations also lobby local government to provide investment incentives for additional first-class suppliers from abroad. Yet another business development innovation is the creation of a Supplier Development Program by local government and business associations, with financing from transnational corporations. Although there are still very few Mexican suppliers, small strides have been made to integrate local suppliers into the value chain.

As a result of the initial formation of the electronics industry, the development of the software industry in Guadalajara has followed suit.

Source: Altenburg and Meyer-Stamer (1999, p. 1705).

Brazilian shoe industry in the early 1970s (box 2.3) and the Vietnamese garment industry in the late 1990s are good examples.

- *Identifying opportunities for added value in the chain, as certain activities enhance the value of the chain and are more lucrative than others.* In the case of São Luís (chapter 5), for example, opportunities exist for developing industries using currently exported commodities (minerals and agricultural products) as main inputs, and for coordinated government

Box 2.3

Linking Small Enterprises into Existing Supply Chains: Footwear Development in Rio Grande do Sul

The Program to Upgrade Small Suppliers, carried out by SEBRAE (Brazil Micro and Small Business Services) in the state of Rio Grande do Sul in the mid-1990s, was aimed at small firms that provided specialized components or services and that sought to raise their quality and delivery standards. To enable them to do this, it linked the small enterprises into existing supply chains. In the case of footwear, the entry point was large shoe manufacturers. Through these firms, contact was established with their small suppliers. Upgrading focused on training for the contractor and the small suppliers. Issues covered were both technical and behavioral, as it was recognized that improvements could only be made if both sides respected and trusted each other.

The issues covered in the training sessions were then tested by the fulfillment of existing orders. By doing this, the SEBRAE initiative avoided two common problems: that enterprises are offered assistance before they realize they need it, and that problems are only recognized by firms once orders have been lost. The cost of the program was shared between SEBRAE and the participating enterprises. A local business association and technology center helped in running the program. Judging from presentations at seminars of the business association, and from discussions with various stakeholders, this program was successful, particularly in reaching small providers of inputs and services.

Source: Schmitz (2005).

actions in terms of assembling land, acquiring licenses, reducing bureaucracy, and promoting investment.

Entrepreneurship Development and Support to SMEs

SMEs play an important role in local economic development. They often account for the majority of jobs in a city; they are frequently a source of innovation that brings new opportunities to the local economy; and they help nurture local entrepreneurship, which is a critical, though often hard to quantify, element in local economic competitiveness. However, SMEs regularly face numerous problems, such as lack of access to finance and modern equipment, lack of information about production methods and processes, and weaknesses in standardization and quality control, all of which hamper strong cooperative production chains. There is significant scope for public policies and actions to tackle market failures in terms of limited finance, weak business development services and training, paucity of industrial real estate, information problems faced by start-up enterprises, and noncompetitive market structures dominated by one firm or only a few. The challenge for local governments is to reach SMEs through a cost-effective enterprise development strategy. The following are a few possible actions that local governments can take to support SMEs (OECD 2003):

- *Ensure that microenterprises are given proper attention* in the system of enterprise support. For instance, the cluster enhancement process can give priority to SMEs because they can benefit more than larger firms from joint actions and government support.

- *Establish small business development centers* to support SMEs through management training, counseling/consulting, and research services (box 2.4). For example, studies suggest that microenterprises at times fail to grow because of problems associated with employee management and recruitment; training in such skills can help.

- *Reduce bureaucracy.* This is especially important for SMEs, as they do not have the resources and experience to overcome the red tape associated with opening a business, hiring employees, and acquiring space.

- *Facilitate SME access to existing financing opportunities.* Local governments may do this (as, for example, in Banco do Nordeste's CrediAmigo program) through promotion and assistance efforts. They may also bring together local financiers and major SME clusters to facilitate financiers' understanding of the particular businesses; provide seed capital for critical areas ("angel investment," which is widely used around the world); and develop the city's own SME financing program (in partnership with financial institutions).

- *Encourage small firms to use the Internet* by taking government online (e-government) and by promoting information and technology awareness.

- *Ensure the availability of business locations* offering affordable and flexible rents, for example, through incubators, or other specialized business accommodation services.

Support to Research and Development
R&D has become particularly important as economic competition becomes increasingly global. Often the only way for a firm to sustain a

Box 2.4

Creating State Entrepreneurship Centers in the United States

Physical incubators and entrepreneurship centers serve as one-stop resource centers for entrepreneurs in many states in the United States, providing many types of assistance, such as in navigating state regulations and on-site marketing counseling. The *Wisconsin Entrepreneurs' Network* (WEN), a partnership of the higher education system, a foundation, and a state agency, provides one-on-one consulting, educational workshops, executive-level programs, peer learning, and strategies to assess technologies and access capital. WEN conducts outreach in which counselors assess clients' intent to grow and their capacity to succeed. Promising clients are referred to one of the regional centers to evaluate further their management team, market size, competitive advantage, and other factors of success.

Other state entrepreneurship centers are more focused on a specific population or industry. Illinois launched the Chicago-based *Illinois Hispanic Entrepreneurship Center* (IHEC) to help spur innovation and job creation. The state pledged funds and agreed to partner with the Illinois Hispanic Chamber of Commerce to open the new center. The IHEC will offer financial awards and support services to help small- to medium-size businesses emerge as economically viable and sustainable companies in their communities and throughout Illinois. Iowa provided state grants to establish business accelerators to help more entrepreneurs become successful and attract and develop high-tech companies. Recipients of funding include entrepreneurial development centers and new venture centers.

Source: National Governors Association (2005).

competitive position is to innovate continually and consistently, and R&D is a critical source of innovation. The following are some of the actions that local governments can undertake to spur R&D:

- *Expand R&D expenditure* with a focus on applicable research. Social returns to R&D expenditure have proven to be very high. But local governments should also focus their limited resources on R&D specializing in highly localized, technology-related industries and scientific competencies, rather than implementing broad-based science and technology strategies. One successful example of focused R&D for specific clusters are the Technology Centers of

Spain and Peru (box 2.5) as public–private partnerships for technology and innovation.

- *Tap university resources* in the city and motivate universities to be involved in applicable research closely linked with competitive local industrial clusters. In this case, municipal governments can play the critical role of catalyst, as demonstrated in Finland by the partnership

Box 2.5

Technology Centers

CITEs (*Centros de Innovación Tecnológica*, or Technology Centers) are public–private partnerships that support innovation and technology transfer by providing specialized services to firms in existing or emerging sectors. Services are focused on a specific product or sector to strengthen value chains and SME development. Specific activities of CITEs include facilitating existing technology transfer to enterprises; addressing gaps in sectoral value chains; identifying bottlenecks and opportunities of product and process innovations; and supporting new product marketing. The mix of services depends on the needs of specific countries and sectors; some focus heavily on R&D while others mainly provide technical assistance.

CITEs are financed by public and private institutions, though they charge client firms for services to ensure commitment and the demand-driven nature of the activity; over time they are expected to become financially sustainable from the services they render. Private sector participation is paramount to the management structure because it enables the Technology Centers to respond to private sector needs.

CITEs in Spain. Private initiatives supported by regional governments gave rise to CITEs in Spain, which today are a key facet of the country's national innovation policy. R&D and technological services represent the majority of services provided and income generated by the centers. In addition to working with SMEs, many Spanish CITEs run incubators to encourage the creation of new firms according to the focus of the center. In terms of financial support, the national government represents 10 percent of all resources through grants and soft loans; regional governments represent 23 percent. Spanish CITEs have been increasingly successful in collecting for fee-based services; by 2004, about 59 percent of CITE income was derived from private funds. In 2004, Spanish CITEs worked with about 25,000 client companies.

(continued)

Box 2.5 *(Continued)*

CITEs in Peru. The first CITEs in Peru were created in 1998 as part of a technical assistance program with the Spanish government, and later they were also
supported by the World Bank. As of 2006, 12 CITEs operated across different sectors in Peru: 9 are private or mixed centers (overseen by chambers of commerce,
research institutions, or nongovernmental organizations [NGOs]) and 3 are public
(supported by the Ministry of Production with a private sector governing body).
The centers provide mainly technical assistance, services (quality improvements,
market information, design techniques, and more), and training, most often to
SMEs. Public CITEs generate 60 percent of their financing from government funds,
while private CITEs are expected to cover all their operational costs through fee-
based services, though most receive grants from international organizations.
Since 2001, public CITEs have trained more than 25,000 workers in Peru. In 2005,
the CITEs provided services to 1,743 client firms.

Source: World Bank project documentation.

between the City of Helsinki, the University of Helsinki, and local
businesses (box 2.6). In cases in which innovation and technology
themselves are to become a trademark for the city (for example,
Turin, Italy), the city should invest significantly to expand the capacity of the key universities.

- *Support innovation* through well-targeted and well-managed business
  incubators. Business incubation provides start-up and growing companies with expertise, networks, and tools to make their ventures successful. Incubators typically provide a managed work space with
  shared facilities; advisory, training, and financial services; a small management team with core competencies; and select on average 20–25
  start-up companies to enter the incubator (Scaramuzzi 2002). Brazil
  has a well-developed network of incubators that local governments
  can tap and support.[9]

- *Attracting talent and experts* who have trained in leading research centers abroad (or in other regions of Brazil) and who have acquired
  experience as well as contacts in some of the principal clusters outside
  the region is the most expeditious approach (Yusuf 2003, pp. 254–67).
  The use of hometown linkages and social networks, in combination

Box 2.6

R&D—The Helsinki Culminatum, Finland

Over the past two decades, the City of Helsinki and the University of Helsinki have worked together on innovations to support science-based enterprises, conduct transport and logistics planning, promote urban research, and market Helsinki as a destination for international students.

The two bodies have also collaborated to create a public–private organization, the Helsinki Region Centre of Expertise Culminatum Ltd. (the "Culminatum"). The organization is based on the triple helix model, meaning in this case that one-third of its shares are owned by local universities and research institutes; one-third by the City of Helsinki, neighboring municipalities, and the Uusimaa Regional Council; and one-third by the business community, financiers, and science park companies.

The Culminatum serves as a forum and basis for the development of collaborative projects. Its main objective is twofold: to oversee regional cluster-building activities in six sectors of the knowledge-based economy, and to develop the Helsinki region into an international center for innovation and R&D. On regional cluster building, the Culminatum promotes the exchange of knowledge and information between universities and technical institutions, thereby catalyzing knowledge-based initiatives and cluster-building activities. In this context, the Culminatum also supports the growth of spin-off companies of universities. Moreover, the forum has also led to increased interaction between SMEs and institutions of higher education.

In promoting the Helsinki region as a world-class system for innovation, an *ideopolis*, a common innovation strategy (*Yhdessä Huipulle:* Together to the Summit), was developed in 2005 by the partners of the Culminatum. The strategy includes 26 projects for innovation, on which universities, cities, and the business community collaborate, centered on four key objectives: (i) to increase the international appeal of local research and education; (ii) to develop strong clusters and create testing centers and living laboratories for product service development; (iii) to apply innovations to renew the welfare services provided by the cities and consolidate the role of the cities in the R&D; and (iv) to support university-driven business growth by, for example, developing a second-generation science park concept.

Source: OECD (2006a, p. 128).

with offering special incentives and business opportunities, may be useful in attracting such talent.

Skills Upgrading

Of all the factors that motivate and build clusters, none is more universally important than human resources. Two of the highest priorities of almost any cluster's plan should be the availability of experienced and skilled labor, and the customized and specialized education and training that produce, upgrade, and deepen skills and knowledge (National Governors Association 2002).

Brazil has a fairly well-developed skills training program, publicly funded through a 2.5 percent payroll tax. Local governments can strive to introduce targeted labor skills upgrading initiatives adapted to the needs of the local economy. Some of the measures that can be undertaken to scale up this important effort are outlined in the following sections.

Understand and Anticipate Local Skill Needs. Local governments can start by identifying the particular local skill shortages in light of the locality's unique economic composition and current status of its labor pool. In fact, local governments can use the clusters to identify these skill shortages. Cities in many OECD countries have established local or regional "observatories" to analyze and project demand, supply, and hence gaps in local skills. Examples include the Marchmont observatory in the United Kingdom, the German Baden-Württemberg agreement, and the Observatoires régionaux de l'emploi et de la formation (OREF) in France. In the United States, Workforce Investment Boards in states and at lower levels often undertake the main tasks of: (a) mapping workforce training schemes, such as group apprentice schemes, adult retraining, and new training initiatives to facilitate matching supply of and demand for skills training; (b) offering business support services that increase employment; and (c) providing shared facilities for training activities, general literacy and community education, and other activities for young adults. At least 50 percent of the boards' members come from the private sector.

Tailor the Design of Training Programs to Local Cluster Needs. To enhance local economic competitiveness, it is important that those with the particular skills needed for critical local clusters be highly trained. This is another useful source of local competitiveness. It is therefore often necessary to offer tailored courses as opposed to "off-the-shelf" college courses. Partnership between public training institutions and the key private sector firms, in terms of curriculum design and execution, hosting of training sessions (for example, at workplace or in community centers), and placement, can bring fruitful results.

Promote Employer Provision of, and Participation in, Labor Training. Local officials can try and persuade employers that investing in the training of their workforce will benefit their business, and expand the scope and level of employer-provided training. Local governments can also encourage the major clusters to include collective provision of training as a major cluster-competitiveness measure. Finally, close involvement of employers, even in public-sponsored training, will help ensure the effectiveness of labor training.

Adapt the Delivery of Training to the Target Group. U.S. workforce intermediaries, such as the Jane Addams Resource Corporation (box 2.7)

Box 2.7

Skills Training—The Jane Addams Resource Corporation, Illinois, United States

The Jane Addams Resource Corporation (JARC), a nonprofit organization, uses an approach combining workforce and economic development to help the retention and growth of local industry and jobs within the Ravenswood neighborhood on the north side of Chicago. In 1991, as demand for skills in metalworking grew, JARC opened its own training center, the Metalworking Skills Program (MWSP), in partnership with two metalworking companies. Begun as a pilot with only 7 workers, it has grown to serve as many as 280 workers and 30 companies in a single year. In 2003, 95 workers from over a dozen companies took part in the program. Most of the businesses are small establishments. The MWSP provides low-income, low-skilled employed workers with access to training that addresses basic skills upgrading and technical skills acquisition in a language and context that best meet their needs. Additionally, it seeks to change the way in which employers hire, train, and promote employees and assist companies as they strive to become more productive.[a]

One of the innovative aspects of MWSP is that training is demand driven. One business owner stated that he looked to JARC for training for several reasons,

(continued)

Box 2.7 *(Continued)*

such as the fact that JARC provides flexibility in the types of courses offered to employees and arranges times and places convenient to employees; that courses are contextual, in that they offer training on the same types of machines that the employees actually use in the workplace; that even the curricula for the basic literacy and numeracy courses are geared toward metalworking; and finally, that the cost of training is competitive, particularly when supplemented with funds from state and federal programs. The executive director of JARC has stated that "companies are in the business to make parts; it is not their job to be educators. . . . This is where JARC can step in."

Training is only one aspect of JARC's overall operations. JARC sees itself as a broker organization with the purpose of helping companies in their area remain viable business entities in order to maintain a strong employment base for the neighborhoods. JARC works closely with local businesses to identify their problems and then to help find the resources and tools that can best tackle those problems. Other activities include a real estate development venture that rehabilitates buildings to preserve quality industrial space in the area; a 14-week certificate course for under- and unemployed people that teaches the fundamentals of metalworking; and an adult learners' program.

Source: OECD (2006b, pp. 200–01).
a. JARC's Web site is at www.jane-addams.org.

and the Regional Wisconsin Training Partnership, prefer to recruit as course instructors "fellow tradespeople" (as opposed to instructors with high academic credentials) who possess the ability to convey technical skills and empathize with their fellow workers. Similarly in Canada, "job shadowing"—when a tutor goes to the field to assess how trainees are applying the learning to their job—has positive effects.

Train the Trainers and Improve Quality Standards in Provision.
Achieving and maintaining the quality of vocational training in an environment in which skill needs evolve quickly present a significant challenge to trainers, because their knowledge is rapidly rendered obsolete. Providers are thus under constant pressure to adapt their services to meet the requirements of the market. A policy of "training the trainers" is therefore paramount to the effectiveness of upskilling initiatives, both for pedagogical skills and vocational updates.

Economic Zones

Economic zones (or their variants, such as industrial districts and technology parks) have been widely used as a measure for local economic development. There are cases of very successful economic zones, but also many failures that have led to the waste of valuable financial and physical resources. The experiences with industrial districts in Brazil seem to be not very positive overall. Despite the popularity of the economic zone approach, a detailed empirical study of its effectiveness has yet to be conducted.

In theory, the economic zone approach offers a combination of benefits: it facilitates the land-assembly process for industrial development, which would be difficult for individual firms to accomplish by acting alone; provides specialized infrastructure needed by a group of firms (roads, telecommunications, power and water, and others); facilitates interfirm learning, exchanges, and collaboration through physical colocation of firms; and creates a cluster identity, facilitating marketing and investment promotion.

However, establishing economic zones is also risky. Investors may not come, resulting in wasteful investment. Locators that do use them may be attracted by the generous fiscal incentives offered for locating in the zone and may have relocated from other cities or even another part of the same city; such firms may not survive or thrive over time, particularly when the incentives end. The expected clustering of desired firms (for example, high-tech firms) may not occur when other locations are more attractive and competitive. In the early 1990s, some U.S. states invested heavily in cluster-specific technology centers. Chattanooga, Tennessee, tried, unsuccessfully, to develop an environmental technology cluster by creating the space, marketing it, and heavily recruiting firms to join. At the same time, the nearby Oak Ridge-Knoxville area did develop that type of cluster because the technology and expertise were already embedded in the nuclear industry (National Governors Association 2002). In Brazil, the extensive use of financial incentives for economic zones has resulted in waste of both financial and land resources, in some cases with very little to show in real economic development impacts.

There are enough cases of unsuccessful attempts with the economic zone approach to make one cautious. Particular attention should be paid to the market and demand side, and the following questions should be asked: Does the proposed economic zone address the particular needs of the emerging business potential in the city and region? Are there interested tenants with solid commitments? Will the proposed zone attract talent to the desired area? Is the zone built

on expanding the existing amenities offered by the city? R&D facilities and capacities can be as important as, or even more important
than, the physical infrastructure provided in the zone. The successful
Hsinchu Science Park in Taiwan, China, for example, only prospered
as a center for technology (specializing in semiconductors) with the
significant R&D efforts devoted by the government-sponsored
Industrial Technology Research Institute (Chen 2008). In China, where
economic zones have proliferated, it was found that while financial
incentives played a critical role in attracting firms to these zones, the
cluster process became important after the firms located and determined the sustainability of the zones' growth (Zheng et al. 2008).

Finally, professional, business-minded management of industrial parks
and districts is critical for the zone approach's success. The introduction
of the private sector through investments, cofinancing, or seats on the
boards of economic zones can play a significant role in providing market
expertise and discipline.

Specialized Infrastructure or Services

High-quality infrastructure, such as transport, power, water, and telecommunications, is in itself important for the local economy. In addition,
depending on the unique local competitive advantage, enhancing certain
types of specialized infrastructure or facilities may be important, and this
may play an instrumental role in the particular clusters or strategies that
a city pursues. Two particular examples, tourism and logistics infrastructure, are outlined below.

Tourism-Associated Infrastructure. Many communities give special priority to tourism, because developing local tourism often brings benefits
beyond the sector itself. Tourism can strengthen local identity with an
emphasis on "uniqueness"; provide a strong imperative to improve the
local environment with stricter environmental measures, such as for sanitation and garbage collection; and achieve higher visibility for the city.
Clearly, the improvements associated with tourism can also be enjoyed by
local residents. Depending on the type of tourism, communities often need
to develop special infrastructure, such as museums, art galleries, exhibition
and convention centers; special transportation facilities; urban landscape
improvements, including public parks; and sports facilities. For many communities, preservation and restoration of cultural and natural heritage are
critical tasks, as these assets present a unique characteristic of a city that no
other location can replace. Finally, soft infrastructure, such as local history,
culture, and events, is also an integral element of tourism infrastructure.

Logistics Infrastructure. This has become increasingly important with the rapid growth of trade. Technology advances have drastically increased the efficiency of logistics handling. Also, many companies are implementing lean initiatives and just-in-time processes, which means that raw-material supplies and warehousing facilities must be easily accessible, preferably nearby. Combined with the need for timely access to market, logistics has become a vital part of any firm's location or relocation decision. This would require cities to pay special attention to freight transportation needs, ease of intermodal connection, and the availability and quality of warehousing and distribution facilities.

Community Economic Development
In advancing the competitiveness agenda, municipal officials need to look for solutions to address the livelihood and job needs of their low-income communities. In Brazil, many of these communities are also informal settlements. While national, state, and municipal governments have been engaging in slum-upgrading activities to improve infrastructure, housing, and services in these neighborhoods, efforts at supporting economic development have thus far been limited. Some of the models used for community economic development in distressed areas in the United States and Europe, often based on nurturing and leveraging local entrepreneurship within the communities, can be of useful reference. Measures to support entrepreneurship and SMEs, discussed earlier, are especially relevant for these communities. The following approaches, rooted more strongly in the communities, are also particularly relevant.[10]

Community Development Corporations (CDCs). CDCs refer to nonprofit organizations that provide programs, offer services, and engage in other activities that promote and support a community, often focused on serving lower-income residents or struggling neighborhoods. First formed in the United States in the 1960s, CDCs have expanded rapidly in size and numbers. In 2006, 4,600 CDCs in the United States were developing over 86,000 units of affordable housing and 8.75 million square feet of commercial and industrial space per year. CDCs are involved in a variety of activities, ranging from day care centers, to employment and training, housing assistance, investment in real estate development, and taking shares in local start-up firms with experienced management. Successful CDCs tend to work with small investments and more closely with the private sector, especially with small businesses and the financial community. CDCs depend on full-time, professional staff.

Community Development Financial Institutions (CDFIs). CDFIs cover a variety of bodies with a community development mission, all of which provide credit, technical assistance, and other financial services that help low-income individuals, community development corporations, and other community-based entities pursue effective community wealth-building strategies. There are five key types of CDFIs: community development banks, community development credit unions, community development loan funds, community development venture capital funds, and microenterprise loan funds. In terms of funding, historically, mutual aid societies played a role in pooling capital for a wide variety of needs including insurance, medical care, and home loans. The modern CDFI industry follows the tradition set by mutual societies and other community efforts, including CDC business loan programs originating in the late 1960s, and has a variety of forms. CDFIs differ from traditional financial institutions in that they cultivate specialized knowledge about the communities in which they do business; offer below-market rate loans (through subsidies); and offer loans without the collateral or credit history that mainstream banks require (OECD 2005, p. 207–09).

Social Enterprises. Social enterprise refers to for-profit and nonprofit entities that operate businesses both to raise revenue and to further the social missions of their organizations. These businesses build locally controlled wealth, which both helps stabilize community economies and represents a shift in nonprofit operation toward a model of collaborating with "client" populations in community-building efforts. Social enterprise is particularly common in nonprofit entities with an employment training focus, since the businesses themselves can be integrated with the programs. Many types of nonprofit entities, however, use innovative business strategies.

Pulling It Together—Strategic Plan for Competitiveness

A strategic plan is always important for a city, but globalization and global competition have brought new urgency:

> Technology, globalization, and the increasingly footloose behavior of industries and of multinational corporations have made it imperative for cities to anticipate continuums of change. In those circumstances, it is becoming hazardous to assume that market forces will smoothly orchestrate structural changes across the competing urban centers and, on balance, engineer positive-sum outcomes. The more plausible inference is that the economic

integration and fluidity of movement introduced by globalization have made it more urgent for metropolitan centers to be closely tracking industrial changes, scrutinizing the actions of the competitors, and planning their own moves well in advance. Postindustrial cities now need their strategies (Yusuf and Nabeshima 2006, pp. 15–16).

The process of strategic planning is to identify the unique, hidden (intangible) capacities of a place, to achieve a broad-based agreement on the unique value proposition and direction for a city, and to arrive at an actionable road map for achieving a common vision. A clear and credible strategic plan (not to be confused with the traditional master plan or *plano diretor*) articulated by policy makers can send signals about government policy priorities and desired outcomes to the private sector, and therefore affect business investment and location decisions. At times, such interdependency leads to increasing returns as the strategic vision becomes a self-fulfilling prophecy: a credible plan leading to more private investments, which in turn make the plan look more realistic. By articulating a clear and broad vision, and sending clear signals, local policy makers might be able to influence such expectations.

To achieve such influence, local strategies must be more than just an aggregation of considerations and policy principles compiled in a document. The plan should identify the critical relationships among the many agents that are likely to shape the future economic, social, political, and environmental quality of the territory, and will need to secure answers to the following questions: How will the city be distinctive? What is the city's economic role in its region or neighborhood? In which clusters can the city build an advantage? What aspects of the business environment become crucial for the city to excel in relative to other locations? To attract investment, cities need to offer a unique mix of strengths in terms of business environment conditions and cluster positions; the mere absence of weaknesses is not enough.

But to develop a strategic plan is no easy task, especially in the context of a globalized market economy where technology and innovation advance rapidly. What often complicate the matter are the local and national political systems that make it hard to build consensus among different parties, or to have a long-term perspective. A number of guidelines for the strategic planning process are available. The World Bank's Local Economic Development Primer (Swinburn, Goga, and Murphy 2006), for example, outlines a five-step process: (i) organization of effort, (ii) local economy assessment, (iii) strategy making, (iv) strategy implementation, and (v) strategy review. The Cities Alliance, a global coalition of cities and their development partners, outlines a slightly different process: initiating the process, establishing the initial parameters and the scope of the city development strategies, making an initial assessment, formulating a vision, identifying strengths-weaknesses-opportunities-threats, setting strategic thrusts, building awareness, and starting implementation (Cities Alliance 2006).

Each city has to adapt the strategic planning process to its own particular circumstances, depending on factors such as urgency, scale of problems, and political context. The example of Turin's successful 2000 Strategic Plan (box 2.8), which has played an instrumental role in the

---

Box 2.8

Strategic Plan of Turin, Italy

In the early 1990s, the industrial city of Turin in northern Italy was facing a major economic and identity crisis. As Italy's dominant center of the automobile indus-try, Turin faced the challenge of the out-migration of auto manufacturing jobs that resulted in significant job losses; the presence of vacant or unused industrial land, about 5–6 million square meters in the center of the urban area; and an outdated infrastructure system that divided the city. Turin needed to find new ways to develop and restructure its role on the national and international level. In this context, the municipal government initiated a strategic planning effort in May 1998, resulting in the Strategic Plan of Turin, signed in February 2000. Turin became the first city in Italy to adopt a strategic plan.

The plan presented a vision of Turin as a European metropolis, an ingenious city that gets things done and does them right, and that knows how to choose its devel-opment path. The plan structured the vision for the future along 6 strategic lines, 20 objectives, and 84 actions. Flagship actions or groups of actions included:

- Development of the University of Turin and Polytechnic University of Turin, with the international research and enterprise training centers, to attract European and international youth to learn, study, invent, and apply
- Policies to consolidate the technology districts (auto-automation design, robotics, machine tools, aerospace, and information and communication technology [ICT])
- A new business incubator to support a new model of economic and social development

(continued)

Box 2.8 *(Continued)*

- Enhancement and expansion of the museum system
- Promotion of Turin as a prime destination for urban tourism, based on the quality of the city, and its cultural, entertainment, and commercial activities
- Development of new "centers"
- Implementation of the Agenda 21 sustainability program
- A new institutional structure of the metropolitan area of 1.5 million inhabitants
- A permanent roundtable of cooperation for internationalization
- Rail network renewal and airport upgrading.

While not all aspects of the plan have been fully implemented, judging by the economic, physical, and social transformations the city has undertaken since its launch, the strategic plan is judged a great success. Turin has been transforming its economy into one based on services and knowledge. The vacant industrial land is being converted into a variety of commercial, residential, cultural, and public uses under joint private and public efforts. Through the 2006 Winter Olympics and other international cultural events, Turin is establishing itself as a modern, innovative European metropolis with a rich cultural heritage.

What are the major factors that led to the success of Turin's strategic plan?

Strategic intention of the plan. The plan is not only technical, but was in fact strategically positioned to serve three functions: technical, mobilization of public opinion, and connection between the political players. It was not intended as a statutory document with binding prescriptions, but rather as a consensus-based, action-oriented road map for a new strategic direction. In the language of the plan itself: "In the first place, the strategic plan is an act of trust in ourselves and expresses the intention to build on the resources and innovative abilities of local society." "A strategic plan is not a list of requests sent by a community to its administrations; nor is it a book of dreams; it is rather a type of agreement between everyone responsible for a development path recognized as possible and shared, where everyone is held responsible for their own part."

Balanced combination of broad public participation and expert inputs. The plan involved almost 1,000 people who were organized into various working groups. The planning process was supported by the Scientific Committee (with Italian and foreign experts) and the Development Forum (with representatives of private and public interests). Through the Scientific Committee, expertise was tapped to provide in-depth diagnosis, experience, and strategic thinking. At the early stage of the planning process, the Scientific Committee published "Towards the Plan," which contained fundamental data on the present and future situation of the city.

(continued)

Box 2.8 *(Continued)*

Through the Development Forum, not only were the expert inputs verified and revised, but more importantly, innovative and pragmatic ideas were proposed, and ownership for the proposed measures was ensured, as many of these actors also later undertook responsibility for seeing them through. The planning phase was carried out by working groups along the strategic lines, jointly by stakeholders and experts.

Close integration of physical and urban renewal with economic and social transformation. The plan to reshape the outdated transportation infrastructure and to redevelop the vast, unused industrial land under an urban renewal program was tied closely to the economic restructuring objective of transforming the city into a premier knowledge economy in Europe. Even the facilities constructed for the 2006 Winter Olympics were planned to be used after the event for rental housing, student dormitories for the expanding universities, and new city parks. One benefit of the integration is the physical visibility of the entire transformation process: from the construction of new buildings to the revitalization of historical palaces and buildings, a new city is emerging with major signs—such as the new station of Porta Susa, the vast new civic library, the doubling in size of the Polytechnic University, the rebirth of the Palazzo del Lavoro (for the Science Centre), the reuse of the wholesale fruit and vegetable market (the media village for the Olympics)—all signifying a rich cultural and civic pride.

Careful consideration of implementation through joint public–private efforts in the plan. The plan indicated responsibilities for carrying out the proposed actions. The thematic working groups, built on the base of the strategic lines or objectives, were strong champions of their respective actions. The various projects included in the plan have been directly implemented through the work of agencies or dedicated associations. In addition, Torino Internazionale was formulated when the plan was signed, with responsibility for promoting strategic planning methods, monitoring the actions of the plan, and communicating to the public the opportunities for development created by the plan and encouraging the public's participation. Through this association, comprising 138 private and public sector partners, the stakeholders have continued to discuss the proposals of the working groups and have furthered their common base of knowledge. To this end, Torino Internazionale commissions research, creates channels of information, documents the actions' development, and follows projects as they are carried out.

Source: Author, based on information from Torino Internazionale, and Salone (2006).

physical, structural, and social transformation of the city in the last eight years, demonstrates some of the critical ingredients of a good planning process: strategic intention, balance between expert inputs and broad-based stakeholder participation, integration of physical plan and infrastructure renewal with economic restructuring, and careful consideration of plan implementation.

For cities where cluster organizations are active, it is also important to create a venue to bring the cluster leaders together regularly to identify the "transversal" or cross-cutting issues in order to focus local government priorities. These common cluster issues can be the key areas where the local government can maximize its impact on the local economy as a whole. The venue would also be important for bringing in other actors in the local economy, such as organizations representing the poor, so that any trade-offs in resource allocation can be openly discussed and addressed, and potential synergies among the different clusters and between the different sectors of the economy can be explored.[11]

Building Institutions and Capacity for Local Competitiveness

The task of promoting city competitiveness through the measures highlighted in this chapter poses severe institutional challenges to local governments, especially the ability to:

- Coordinate the efforts of the different departments within a municipal authority, because often government services to clusters are dispersed across different departments, making it difficult for businesses to access the services
- Involve and ensure strong commitment of a large number of stakeholders, particularly in the private sector, in the process of developing and implementing a common strategy
- Introduce business know-how, and sometimes even take informed business risks, which would require a different set of competencies and skills than the usual bureaucracies
- Coordinate—often—the efforts in a metropolitan region that includes several municipalities, as well as involve the state and national governments.

Various different models for building institutions and capacity have been used across countries, both public and private, and include the following:

- *Local economic development agencies.* A widely used concept in Europe and adapted in many other places, these are nonprofit associations with their own legal personality, usually having a governance structure that involves a wide range of public and private entities. They have an executive board that runs the agency and that is elected by a general assembly and are staffed by specially trained personnel. The agencies typically provide financial and technical assistance to SMEs, prepare plans for territorial economic development, offer special training programs, and conduct marketing and information campaigns.[12] One example in Brazil is the Economic Development Agency for the Greater ABC Region in metropolitan São Paulo (box 2.9), which covers multiple jurisdictions.

Box 2.9

Agency for Economic Development of the Greater ABC Region, São Paulo, Brazil

The Agency for Economic Development of the Greater ABC Region, created in 1998, seeks to contribute to the sustainable development of the region through regional economic development planning and SME development, marketing, and information sharing. The agency is a nongovernmental organization comprising the seven municipalities of the ABC region of São Paulo (represented by the Inter-Municipal Consortium of the Greater ABC), business associations, SEBRAE, petrochemical businesses, higher education institutions, and trade unions. Each of these segments has representation on the board of directors. The agency is the fruit of growing regional integration among municipalities and public and private institutions in the Greater ABC Region, and is a pioneer association of regional governance in Brazil.

The agency has six flagship projects to support local business development, including (i) two business incubators supporting SME development; (ii) a cluster development organization for automobile parts, computer hardware, and plastics; (iii) a microfinance program of the Banco Nacional de Desenvolvimento Econômico e Social (National Bank for Economic and Social Development, or BNDES) for SMEs; (iv) an export support program to strengthen SME participation in exports by offering information and assistance to access external markets; and (v) the Center for Information and Support for Plastics Technologies (CIAP), seeking to assist SMEs in the plastics sector to increase their competitiveness.

(continued)

Box 2.9 *(Continued)*

The ABC region is well known for its innovations in metropolitan governance, and the agency has been a key player in achieving such objectives. Nevertheless, institutional limits continue to pose obstacles to regional success. First, election cycles provide only a short period for projects and create bottlenecks for effective strategic planning. Because consensus among the seven municipalities is key for regional decision making, changes in political leadership can impose constraints on successful planning and project implementation efforts. Second, there is an apparent lack of scope, scale, and enforcement of regional agreements—a critical element for successful metropolitan governance. Finally, the ABC model has been more focused on strategic planning and lobbying than on service delivery, highlighting the need to strike a greater balance between the two elements.

Sources: http://www.agenciagabc.com.br; Klink (2007).

Public Limited Companies with Government Subsidy. Sevilla Global (Spain), for example, is a specialized municipal public limited company with a mandate by the Seville city council to implement a local public strategy to promote the urban economy and business development. It has five working areas: (i) business information and inward investment, (ii) business incubation, (iii) industrial land revitalization, (iv) innovation, and (v) business support to local clusters. The company mainly implements "projects" (such as technical assistance, sponsorship and other collaborative agreements, and consensus building) as determined by the city council, under arrangements of public–private partnership adapted individually to the project concerned. In 2006, Sevilla Global met 20 percent of its total budget from proceeds of its operations and services, while the rest was provided by the city council.[13]

Publicly Owned Commercial Companies. Greater London Enterprise Ltd., for example, is a commercial company owned by all 33 of London's boroughs, and has no public subsidy. Directed at small and medium enterprises, the company's businesses include business accommodation; facilitating financing and cash-flow management; start-up and early-stage business support; and consulting services offering information, funding, and strategic advice. Over 10 years, the company acquired and improved over 2 million square feet of business space accommodating over 950 tenants; it manages a £7 million loan fund that has provided finance to over 400 start-up and early-stage businesses; it operates London's leading Business Angels Network, with over 200 registered private business angel investors; and it now supports approximately 6,500 small companies each year. In 2006–7, the company had a profit of £9.3 million and a 21.8 percent return on assets, with net assets of £51.9 million. Because it has no subsidy, its success depends on the ability of management to ensure that the commercial aspects of the organization remain in good shape and that the work of the company remains relevant to the public policy agenda as perceived by its members.[14]

- *Regional development agencies.* Under the Regional Development Agencies Act of 1998, the United Kingdom created 10 such agencies to give greater emphasis to regional development and to transform England's regions through sustained economic development. Government sponsored, each agency has the statutory purpose of furthering the economic development and the regeneration of its region; promoting business efficiency, investment, and competitiveness; promoting employment; enhancing the development and application of skills relevant to employment; and contributing to sustainable development where it is relevant to the region to do so. A similar approach was adopted in 2007 by the Chilean government, with the creation of 13 regional productive development agencies.

- *Competitiveness councils.* The concept behind these councils is to have a body of leadership comprising public and private sector stakeholders in cities to guide the process of competitiveness strategy development and implementation. Councils are often formally headed by a local political leader (depending on the governance model in place) and a top business executive, and may include key representatives of the regional "triple helix" (public, private, and research sectors). They may also have a key role in developing an overarching economic regional strategy. Some councils guide working groups that focus on specific clusters and cross-cutting issues. In these working groups, specialists from companies, government agencies, universities, and other institutions identify specific actions and define responsibilities to execute them. The public sector's role in these councils should be carefully assessed, as experience suggests that the private sector should have a key operational role if a genuine partnership is to develop.

- *Reorganization and reorientation of government services.* Without creating new agencies, local governments can reorganize or reorient existing agencies to better cater to the service needs of local businesses. In

Arizona, United States, for example, state and regional organizations added cluster representatives to their boards and held special summits with clusters; government incentives, programs, and services were structured around clusters; and the state's department of commerce reorganized its services to fit the needs of clusters (Waits 2000).

The exact institutional form that each authority takes will depend on the local situation and should be adapted. Whatever the form though, there is also the issue of staff competency, because the requirements for economic development are different from the usual public sector skills. Recognizing this, local governments are usually cautious in recruiting staff for local economic development agencies, and seek people with business experience and expertise in dealing with the private sector. Partnership with the private sector is important in terms of bringing in expertise and discipline.

Moreover, the type and level of engagement by the local governments in competitiveness-enhancement measures need to be matched by local capacity. Some types of interventions entail greater risks than others, including business and market risks. It is therefore especially important to ensure sufficient capacity to analyze, assess, and prepare for the risks involved in the interventions. In fact, the more proactive policy approaches recommended for local governments in this chapter stress better governance and more competent management capacities at the local level.

Conclusions

Local Policies for City Competitiveness

To become and stay competitive, cities need to strive to reduce the cost of doing business by improving services and infrastructure and reducing bureaucracies. But for a middle-income country like Brazil, which needs to be economically competitive in a globalized environment, this is not sufficient. Cities also need to strive to add value to local businesses. A crucial part of the strategy should be to create and sustain an environment that stimulates local firms to innovate and learn from each other, to nurture and facilitate the creation of synergies generated by the presence of interconnected economic clusters in the city, and to provide incentives for all local players to continuously upgrade the level of competitiveness—to become better and the best.

With regard to the areas of policy interventions by municipal and state governments for enhancing local economic competitiveness, this report has focused on the cluster approach to competitiveness. As an expanded version of the widely used approach of *arranjos produtivos locais*, the cluster approach in essence is to facilitate private sector collaborations for collective efficiency: organizing and facilitating private and public institutions to arrive at a common cluster vision; identifying opportunities for growth and collaboration; promoting joint actions such as co-information, co-learning, co-marketing, and co-purchasing; and jointly building economic foundations such as R&D capacities, infrastructure, skills upgrading, and public–private sector support institutions.

While this report has provided many examples of actions that may be undertaken, it emphasizes the critical importance for cities to pursue a unique strategy based on their comparative and competitive advantages, rather than blindly applying different actions. Finally, the more active approaches discussed here will require the presence of stronger governance and management capacity at the local government level. Local governments should be fully aware of the market and governance risks involved in their actions, and should match the level of policy actions with the competence of local institutions and staff capacities.

Toward a National Policy Framework for City Competitiveness

The wide range of possibly powerful actions by local governments for city competitiveness and growth raises the question: "What is the proper role of the federal government in Brazil?" There is a case to move toward a national policy framework for city competitiveness, as has been done or proposed in China, the United Kingdom, the United States, and other countries. Some of the elements of that framework are:

- Guidance to municipal and state governments on how to compete and disseminate best-practice examples
- Performance measurements and benchmarking to enable cities to compare their performance in competitiveness in different dimensions
- Provision of the right incentives for competition, for example, discouraging fiscal wars and encouraging human capital enhancements and innovation efforts
- Provision of incentives on cross-jurisdictional efforts, especially for economic collaboration and integration of metropolitan regions, by establishing a metropolitan governance framework and channeling federal funding through cross-jurisdictional metropolitan entities.

Notes

1. See the series of articles on Northeast Ohio Clusters Project by Kleinhenz (2000); Hill and Brennan (2000); and Austrian (2000).

2. RAIS is the labor force database produced annually by the Ministry of Labor. It captures only formal employment.

3. "The fading lust of clusters," *The Economist*, October 11, 2007.

4. The cluster approach is broadly consistent with the approach of *arranjos produtivos locais* (local productive arrangements) widely used in Brazil. Their use has been focused mainly on small and medium enterprises, and in practice, *arranjos produtivos locais* have been often defined as a specific type of product. The cluster concept used in this chapter is to some extent an expanded version of this concept, and would include not only small and microenterprises (SMEs), but any private and public economic actors that are closely linked together in any sectors in a city.

5. This cluster concept is based on work by Alec Hansen of the Economic Competitiveness Group, Inc., a coauthor of chapter 5.

6. We are grateful to Kate Kuper, a peer reviewer, who highlighted this point during the review of the chapter.

7. Efforts are under way to establish a Web-accessible database for the different possible actions and examples of these actions being undertaken.

8. The example in box 4.1, in chapter 4, demonstrates the important role that an annual trade fair in Brazil has played in catalyzing the local footwear cluster.

9. Information is available through the Associação Nacional de Entidades Promotoras de Empreendimentos Inovadores.

10. The following summary is largely from www.community-wealth.org, which provides information about the broad range of community wealth-building activities.

11. The author is grateful to Kate Kuper for her suggestion on this topic.

12. World Bank Local Economic Development Web site.

13. http://www.sevillaglobal.es.

14. http://www.gle.co.uk.

CHAPTER 3

Benchmarking the Competitiveness of Brazilian Cities

Fernanda Ruiz Nuñez

This chapter presents an initial attempt to benchmark the competitiveness of Brazilian cities. Building a competitive index, large, medium, and small cities are ranked along four dimensions: urban, sociodemographic, institutional/fiscal, and economic. The methodology and results are very limited, but they can be improved in future work as more and better data become available.

This chapter is organized as follows: first, a description of the data available and the construction of the competitiveness index, and then a brief description of the methodology; next, a presentation of the ranking of cities and examples on how cities can be compared across the four components of the index; and finally, concluding remarks and recommendations for future work.

Index Construction and Data

The term "competitiveness" has often been used without a consensus on its meaning.[1] Begg (1999) makes an excellent review of the literature on the definition of competitiveness. He argues that "In practice, different definitions can be envisaged depending on the focus of interest." Based on a wide review of literature, here "competitiveness" is defined as the set of urban, sociodemographic, institutional/fiscal, and economic factors that attract investment and promote economic activities.

These four dimensions of city competitiveness are widely used in the literature because they represent the main components of the business environment. Firms seek to locate in cities with good economic and financial structures (economic), a skilled and productive labor force (sociodemographic), good infrastructure (urban), and with strong institutions and favorable fiscal policies (institutional/fiscal). Cabrero, Orihuela, and Ziccardi (2003) used these four dimensions to construct a competitiveness index for Mexican cities (figure 3.1).

Following Cabrero, Orihuela, and Ziccardi (2003), we compute such a competitive index for Brazilian cities using Brazilian population census data for 2000. The unit of analysis is the minimum comparable area (MCA). This definition was developed by the Instituto de Pesquisa Econômica Aplicada (Institute of Applied Economic Research, or IPEA), the Instituto Brasileiro de Geografia e Estatistica (Brazilian Institute of Geography and Statistics, or IBGE), and Universidade Estadual de Campinas (State University of Campinas, or UNICAMP) (2002), and it takes into account the changing definition and division of municipalities through the years, since the absolute number of municipalities increased from approximately 2,300 in 1960 to 5,507 in 2000. The resulting dataset represents 123 urban agglomerations, including a total of 474 minimal comparable areas (MCAs).[2]

Since there is significant diversity in city size, this study classifies Brazilian cities into small cities (between 50,000 and 100,000 inhabitants in 1991), medium cities (between 100,000 and 500,000 inhabitants in

Figure 3.1   Four Dimensions of the Competitiveness Index

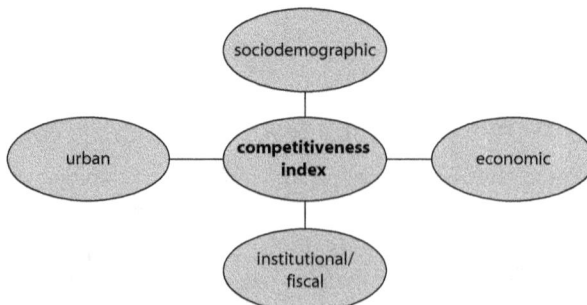

Source: Cabrero, Orihuela, and Ziccardi (2003).

1991), and large cities (above 500,000 inhabitants in 1991). Of the 474 MCAs, 277 are small cities, 172 are medium cities, and 25 are large cities.

Depending on their availability in the Brazilian data, the variables included in each component are an exact match to or a proxy of those of Cabrero, Orihuela, and Ziccardi (2003), and are summarized here:

- The urban dimension of the index tries to capture the urban infra-structure and the quality of urban services.
- The sociodemographic dimension attempts to describe the labor market conditions (skills and productivity) of cities.
- The institutional/fiscal dimension tries to capture the strengths of the government and the fiscal environment.[3]
- The economic dimension attempts to describe the economic and financial structure of the city.

The variables used are highlighted in table 3.1.

Table 3.1   Variables Used for the Four Dimensions of the Competitiveness Index

Urban	Sociodemographic
Urbanization rate	Per capita income
Number of people between 15 and 55 years old	% employment in primary sector, 1-digit
% of houses with garbage collection	% employment in secondary sector, 1-digit
% of houses with lighting	% employment in tertiary sector, 1-digit
% of houses with piped water	Population growth 1991–2000
% of houses with sewerage	% people receiving less than 3/4 of minimum wage
Number of banks	% of indigent
Number of banks per capita	Human Development Index
% of population with university degree	Years of schooling of people above 25 years old
Number of hospitals	Gini index
Number of workers in health	Life expectancy
Number of workers in health per capita	% of illiteracy
Number of hospitals per capita	Child mortality rate (up to 5 years old)
Number of homicides per capita	% people employed in total population
% of houses with computers	
% of houses with phone lines	
Number of persons who live in slums	
Transportation accidents by vehicle	
Expenditure on transportation	
If there is a port at the MCA	
If there is an airport at the MCA	

(continued)

Table 3.1   Variables Used for the Four Dimensions of the Competitiveness Index *(Continued)*

Institutional/fiscal	Economic
MCA total investments (excluding federal and state investment)	Average wage (monthly)
	Per capita GDP (R$1,000)
Current revenue of the MCA	% GDP primary sector
Expenditure of the MCA	% GDP secondary sector
Budget expenditure	% GDP tertiary sector
Municipal Participation Fund transfer amount	Long-term per capita savings (R$1,000)
MCA collected taxes	Government cash savings per capita (R$1,000)
MCA revenues	
Total tax revenue	Private sector cash savings per capita (R$1,000)
	% workers in high tech
	Assets per urban household (R$1,000)

Source: Authors, based on IBGE.

Methodology

To compute the competitiveness index, we followed the framework adopted by Cabrero, Orihuela, and Ziccardi (2003), and we applied principal component analysis (PCA). PCA is a simple nonparametric method often used to reduce multidimensional datasets to lower dimensions for analysis (box 3.1 gives a more detailed description of the methodology). PCA is very useful for computing indexes because it has three main advantages: it does not assign weights because the method will determine whether a variable is relevant or not; it allows disaggregation of the index into subindexes to better understand the areas of improvement; and it has been extensively used to build national competitive indexes, such as those featured in *The Global Competitiveness Report*, published by the World Economic Forum, and *The World Competitiveness Yearbook*, produced by the International Institute for Management Development.

This methodology has also important drawbacks, such as imposing linearity, and requiring the determination in advance of the number of factors to be used. However, we consider it to be a reasonably good approach for building an index to compare city performance.

We apply PCA to each of the four components, and after obtaining an index for each one, we reapply PCA to obtain an overall index. This allows us not only to rank cities according to an aggregate competitiveness index, but also to understand how those cities perform in the different dimensions of competitiveness.

Box 3.1

Principal Component Analysis

PCA is mathematically defined as an orthogonal linear transformation that transforms the data to a new coordinate system such that the greatest variance by any projection of the data comes to lie on the first coordinate, called the first principal component. The procedure transforms a number of (possibly) correlated variables into a (smaller) number of uncorrelated variables called principal components. The first principal component accounts for as much of the variability in the data as possible, and each succeeding component accounts for as much of the remaining variability as possible.

PCA can be used for dimensionality reduction in a dataset by retaining those characteristics of the dataset that contribute the most to its variance, by keeping lower-order principal components and ignoring higher-order ones. Such lower-order components often contain the "most important" aspects of the data.

Sources: Smith (2002); DIT and NCAER (2007).

Ranking of Cities

Applying PCA methodology, we computed the competitiveness index for the 447 MCAs. Tables 3.2–3.4 show the competitiveness ranking by component and by city size. The index has been rescaled to (–1) to (+1), with the best-performing city having an index of (+1), and the last in the ranking (–1).

The overall competitiveness index of large cities puts São Paulo, Rio de Janeiro, and Porto Alegre at the top.[4] Figure 3.2 compares the three top cities according to the four dimensions. São Paulo did better than the other big cities on the urban and institutional/fiscal dimensions, and it performs better than Porto Alegre and Rio de Janeiro on the economic dimension, but it still lags behind on the sociodemographic dimension.

The differences in performance across the 172 medium MCAs are more evident. Ribeirao Preto, Santos, and Florianopolis are at the top of the competitiveness index of medium cities. While Ribeirao Preto has the best institutional/fiscal performance, it is not in the top 10 in either the sociodemographic index or the economic index.

With respect to small cities, Jaragua do Sul, Cubatao, and Resende are at the top of the ranking. They are also in the top 10 of the economic and institutional/fiscal rankings. Jaragua do Sul is performing

Table 3.2 Competitiveness Index for Large^a Brazilian Cities in 2000

	Competitiveness index Ranking			Urban index Ranking			Sociodemographic index Ranking			Institutional/fiscal index Ranking			Economic index Ranking		
1	São Paulo	(SP)	1.00	São Paulo	(SP)	1.00	Porto Alegre	(RS)	1.00	São Paulo	(SP)	1.00	Brasília	(DF)	1.00
2	Rio de Janeiro	(RJ)	0.70	Rio de Janeiro	(RJ)	0.77	Curitiba	(PR)	0.89	Rio de Janeiro	(RJ)	0.64	São Paulo	(SP)	0.99
3	Porto Alegre	(RS)	0.48	Porto Alegre	(RS)	0.49	Campinas	(SP)	0.80	Belo Horizonte	(MG)	0.10	Porto Alegre	(RS)	0.61
4	Curitiba	(PR)	0.38	Belo Horizonte	(MG)	0.46	Rio de Janeiro	(RJ)	0.60	Salvador	(BA)	0.08	Rio de Janeiro	(RJ)	0.57
5	Campinas	(SP)	0.27	Curitiba	(PR)	0.35	São Paulo	(SP)	0.60	Curitiba	(PR)	0.06	Curitiba	(RJ)	0.38
6	São Bernardo do Campo	(SP)	0.13	Campinas	(SP)	0.26	Santo André	(SP)	0.55	Porto Alegre	(RS)	0.02	Campinas	(PR)	0.29
7	Goiânia	(GO)	0.07	Recife	(PE)	0.16	Belo Horizonte	(MG)	0.53	Fortaleza	(CE)	0.02	São Bernardo do Campo	(SP)	0.17
8	Salvador	(BA)	0.03	Goiânia	(GO)	0.14	São Bernardo do Campo	(SP)	0.49	Recife	(PE)	-0.18	Santo André	(SP)	0.10
9	Recife	(PE)	0.00	São Bernardo do Campo	(SP)	0.04	Brasília	(DF)	0.49	Manaus	(AM)	-0.35	Recife	(PE)	-0.03
10	Guarulhos	(SP)	-0.12	Salvador	(BA)	0.01	Goiânia	(GO)	0.41	São Bernardo do Campo	(SP)	-0.41	Salvador	(BA)	-0.04
11	Campo Grande	(MS)	-0.21	Fortaleza	(CE)	-0.10	Osasco	(SP)	0.40	Guarulhos	(SP)	-0.46	Goiânia	(GO)	-0.16
12	Fortaleza	(CE)	-0.22	Campo Grande	(MS)	-0.21	Campo Grande	(MS)	0.13	Campinas	(SP)	-0.55	Guarulhos	(SP)	-0.19
13	Belém	(PA)	-0.24	Osasco	(SP)	-0.25	Guarulhos	(SP)	0.02	Goiânia	(GO)	-0.57	Belém	(PA)	-0.34
14	São Gonçalo	(RJ)	-0.38	Natal	(RN)	-0.28	São Gonçalo	(RJ)	-0.01	Belém	(PA)	-0.72	Fortaleza	(CE)	-0.35
15	Natal	(RN)	-0.38	Guarulhos	(SP)	-0.28	Belém	(PA)	-0.06	Nova Iguaçu	(RJ)	-0.79	São Gonçalo	(RJ)	-0.36
16	Manaus	(AM)	-0.53	Belém	(PA)	-0.33	Salvador	(BA)	-0.12	Campo Grande	(MS)	-0.84	Natal	(RN)	-0.38
17	Nova Iguaçu	(RJ)	-0.59	Maceió	(AL)	-0.45	Recife	(PE)	-0.30	São Luís	(MA)	-0.87	Campo Grande	(MS)	-0.47
18	São Luís	(MA)	-0.61	Manaus	(AM)	-0.71	Nova Iguaçu	(RJ)	-0.39	Natal	(RN)	-0.90	Nova Iguaçu	(RJ)	-0.56

#															
19	Duque de Caxias	(RJ)	-0.64	São Gonçalo	(RJ)	-0.81	Duque de Caxias	(RJ)	-0.40	Maceió	(AL)	-0.92	Manaus	(AM)	-0.60
20	Maceió	(AL)	-0.78	São Luís	(MA)	-0.88	Natal	(RN)	-0.41	Teresina	(PI)	-0.95	São Luís	(MA)	-0.60
21	Teresina	(PI)	-1.00	Nova Iguaçu	(RJ)	-0.91	Fortaleza	(CE)	-0.41	Duque de Caxias	(RJ)	-0.96	Duque de Caxias	(RJ)	-0.64
22				Duque de Caxias	(RJ)	-0.94	São Luís	(MA)	-0.41	São Gonçalo	(RJ)	-0.99	Maceió	(AL)	-0.83
23				Teresina	(PI)	-1.00	Manaus	(AM)	-0.47	Osasco	(SP)	-1.00	Teresina	(PI)	-1.00
24							Maceió	(AL)	-0.94						
25							Teresina	(PI)	-1.00						

Source: Author's calculation.

a. Above 500,000 inhabitants in 1991.

Note: Some cities are not included in some of the indexes due to missing data in one or more of the variables considered.

Table 3.3 Competitiveness Index for Medium[a] Brazilian Cities in 2000

	Competitiveness index			Urban index			Sociodemographic index			Institutional/fiscal index			Economic index		
	Best 10 cities			*Best 10 cities*			*Best 10 cities*			*Best 10 cities*			*Best 10 cities*		
1	Ribeirão Preto	(SP)	1.00	Niterói	(RJ)	1.00	São Caetano do Sul	(SP)	1.00	Ribeirão Preto	(SP)	1.00	Macaé	(RJ)	1.00
2	Santos	(SP)	0.99	Vitória	(ES)	0.99	Niterói	(RJ)	0.79	Santos	(SP)	0.75	Florianópolis	(SC)	0.99
3	Florianópolis	(SC)	0.95	Santos	(SP)	0.91	Florianópolis	(SC)	0.71	São Jose dos Campos	(SP)	0.73	São Jose dos Campos	(SP)	0.85
4	São José dos Campos	(SP)	0.91	Ribeirão Preto	(SP)	0.88	Blumenau	(SC)	0.69	Vitória	(ES)	0.64	João Pessoa	(PB)	0.82
5	Niterói	(RJ)	0.91	Florianópolis	(SC)	0.84	Caxias do Sul	(RS)	0.67	Contagem	(MG)	0.58	Niterói	(RJ)	0.72
6	Jundiaí	(SP)	0.68	São Caetano do Sul	(SP)	0.74	Santos	(SP)	0.66	Sorocaba	(SP)	0.55	Santos	(SP)	0.67
7	Caxias do Sul	(RS)	0.63	São Jose do Rio Pret	(SP)	0.64	São Jose	(SC)	0.60	Campos dos Goytacazes	(RJ)	0.51	Jundiaí	(SP)	0.59
8	Sorocaba	(SP)	0.63	Aracaju	(SE)	0.61	Joinville	(SC)	0.60	Barueri	(SP)	0.50	Joinville	(SC)	0.58
9	João Pessoa	(PB)	0.60	Londrina	(PR)	0.60	Americana	(SP)	0.59	Caxias do Sul	(RS)	0.44	Blumenau	(SC)	0.54
10	Joinville	(SC)	0.59	Juiz de Fora	(MG)	0.59	Estrela	(RS)	0.58	Florianópolis	(SC)	0.42	Cosmópolis	(SP)	0.49
	Bottom 10 cities			*Bottom 10 cities*			*Bottom 10 cities*			*Bottom 10 cities*			*Bottom 10 cities*		
163	Vitória de Santo Antão	(PE)	−0.50	Marabá	(PA)	−0.47	Juazeiro	(BA)	−0.46	Uruguaiana	(RS)	−0.81	Piracuruca	(PI)	−0.65
164	Juazeiro	(BA)	−0.50	Porto dos Gauchos	(MT)	−0.51	Timon	(MA)	−0.46	Alegrete	(RS)	−0.83	Porto dos Gauchos	(MT)	−0.68
165	Arapiraca	(AL)	−0.51	Palmeira dos Indios	(AL)	−0.52	Ouro Preto do Oeste	(RO)	−0.47	Sapucaia do Sul	(RS)	−0.86	Arapiraca	(AL)	−0.70

166	Santarém	(PA)	-0.52	Piracuruca	(PI)	-0.56	Altamira	(PA)	-0.50	Santa Luzia	(MA)	-0.88	Santarém	(PA)	-0.72
167	Timon	(MA)	-0.61	Santarém	(PA)	-0.59	Arapiraca	(AL)	-0.51	Araguaína	(TO)	-0.89	Caxias	(MA)	-0.77
168	Ouro Preto do Oeste	(RO)	-0.62	Timon	(MA)	-0.60	Palmeira dos Indios	(AL)	-0.66	Niilópolis	(RJ)	-0.92	Palmeira das Missoes	(RS)	-0.78
169	Piracuruca	(PI)	-0.64	Altamira	(PA)	-0.61	Piracuruca	(PI)	-0.73	Palmeira dos Indios	(AL)	-0.95	Codó	(MA)	-0.79
170	Palmeira dos Indios	(AL)	-0.71	Codó	(MA)	-0.66	Caxias	(MA)	-0.78	Alagoinhas	(BA)	-0.99	Palmeira dos Indios	(AL)	-0.90
171	Codó	(MA)	-0.74	Ouro Preto do Oeste	(RO)	-0.72	Codó	(MA)	-0.93	Timon	(MA)	-0.99	Santa Luzia	(MA)	-0.96
172	Santa Luzia	(MA)	-1.00	Santa Luzia	(MA)	-1.00	Santa Luzia	(MA)	-1.00	Vitória de Santo Antao	(PE)	-1.00	Itaituba	(PA)	-1.00

Source: Author's calculation.
a. Between 100,000 and 500,000 inhabitants in 1991.

Table 3.4 Competitiveness Index for Small[a] Brazilian Cities in 2000

	Competitiveness index			Urban index			Sociodemographic index			Institutional/fiscal index			Economic index		
	Best 10 cities			**Best 10 cities**			**Best 10 cities**			**Best 10 cities**			**Best 10 cities**		
1	Jaraguá do Sul	(SC)	1.00	Botucatu	(SP)	1.00	Brusque	(SC)	1.00	Cubatão	(SP)	1.00	Jaraguá do Sul	(SC)	1.00
2	Cubatão	(SP)	0.93	Catanduva	(SP)	0.90	Jaraguá do Sul	(SC)	0.99	Cabo Frio	(RJ)	0.73	Resende	(RJ)	0.91
3	Resende	(RJ)	0.79	São João da Boa Vista	(SP)	0.86	Valinhos	(SP)	0.88	Jaraguá do Sul	(SC)	0.72	Cubatão	(SP)	0.84
4	Cabo Frio	(RJ)	0.73	Jau	(SP)	0.85	Birigui	(SP)	0.87	Caraguatatuba	(SP)	0.70	Araucária	(PR)	0.70
5	Valinhos	(SP)	0.73	Barretos	(SP)	0.76	São Bento do Sul	(SC)	0.86	Araucária	(PR)	0.56	Valinhos	(SP)	0.64
6	Araras	(SP)	0.68	Araras	(SP)	0.74	Sapiranga	(RS)	0.82	Angra dos Reis	(RJ)	0.55	Cabo Frio	(RJ)	0.63
7	Catanduva	(SP)	0.65	Assis	(SP)	0.71	Esteio	(RS)	0.82	Itabira	(MG)	0.52	Nova Lima	(MG)	0.63
8	Araucária	(PR)	0.63	Lins	(SP)	0.68	Jaú	(SP)	0.80	Barretos	(SP)	0.50	Paulo Afonso	(BA)	0.60
9	Barretos	(SP)	0.57	Pouso Alegre	(MG)	0.66	São Joao da Boa Vista	(SP)	0.79	Resende	(RJ)	0.45	Bebedouro	(SP)	0.55
10	Caraguatatuba	(SP)	0.53	Resende	(RJ)	0.65	Itatiba	(SP)	0.79	Araras	(SP)	0.45	Simões Filho	(BA)	0.50
	Bottom 10 cities			**Bottom 10 cities**			**Bottom 10 cities**			**Bottom 10 cities**			**Bottom 10 cities**		
268	Barra do Corda	(MA)	-0.77	Chapadinha	(MA)	-0.81	Sapé	(PB)	-0.76	Quixadá	(CE)	-0.88	Monte santo	(BA)	-0.92
269	Euclides da Cunha	(BA)	-0.77	João Lisboa	(MA)	-0.83	São Joao do Piaui	(PI)	-0.77	Sapé	(PB)	-0.89	Zé Doca	(MA)	-0.94
270	Alenquer	(PA)	-0.78	Viana	(MA)	-0.84	João Lisboa	(MA)	-0.79	Floriano	(PI)	-0.90	Turiaçu	(MA)	-0.94
271	Grajaú	(MA)	-0.82	Carutapera	(MA)	-0.85	Ouricuri	(PE)	-0.83	Tauá	(CE)	-0.90	Carutapera	(MA)	-0.95
272	João Lisboa	(MA)	-0.83	Alenquer	(PA)	-0.86	Vitória do Mearim	(MA)	-0.84	Arcoverde	(PE)	-0.91	Alenquer	(PA)	-0.97
273	Chapadinha	(MA)	-0.85	Turiaçu	(MA)	-0.91	Zé Doca	(MA)	-0.86	Serrinha	(BA)	-0.91	Grajaú	(MA)	-0.97
274	Carutapera	(MA)	-0.86	Vitória do Mearim	(MA)	-0.91	Carutapera	(MA)	-0.88	Limoeiro	(PE)	-0.92	Barra do Corda	(MA)	-0.98
275	Turiaçu	(MA)	-0.86	Ourém	(PA)	-0.95	Turiaçu	(MA)	-0.90	Santo Amaro	(BA)	-0.94	Cametá	(PA)	-0.99
276	Barreirinhas	(MA)	-0.96	Barreirinhas	(MA)	-0.97	Barreirinhas	(MA)	-0.94	Cajazeiras	(PB)	-0.98	Barreirinhas	(MA)	-0.99
277	Monte Santo	(BA)	-1.00	Monte Santo	(BA)	-1.00	Monte Santo	(BA)	-1.00	Timbaúba	(PE)	-1.00	Ourém	(PA)	-1.00

Source: Authors.

a. Between 50,000 and 100,000 inhabitants in 1991.

Figure 3.2   Comparison of São Paulo, Rio de Janeiro, and Porto Alegre along the Four Dimensions of Competitiveness

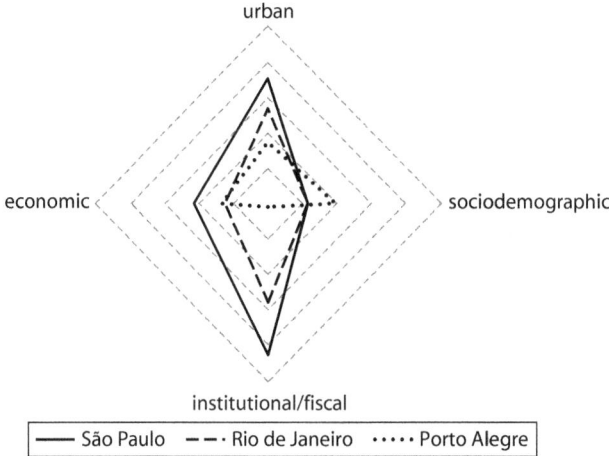

well in sociodemographic aspects, but it is not at the top of the urban index. Cubatao is neither at the top of the urban index nor the sociodemographic index.

The disaggregation of the competitiveness index by component allows identification of the areas for improvement. Even though a city may be at the top of the overall ranking, it is not necessarily performing well across all components.

The competitiveness index computed in this exploratory analysis is very limited because it only allows for a static analysis, that is, comparing competitiveness across cities in a specific year (2000). Comparing cities over time would be a very powerful tool to measure progress. Using data for 1991, we applied the same methodology to compute the competitiveness index for that year. Unfortunately due to data limitations, the index was unavailable for all cities and all four dimensions. As a result, the comparison was very incomplete, and therefore of too little value to be included here.

To illustrate the potential dynamics of the index, we compare three components of the index (urban, sociodemographic, and institutional/fiscal) for the city of Teresina in 1991 and 2000 (figure 3.3).

Interestingly, although Teresina improved substantially along the institutional/fiscal dimension in 10 years, it only slightly improved along the sociodemographic dimension, and presented no improvement along the urban dimension. This illustrates how a city, which is at the bottom of

Figure 3.3   Comparison of Teresina between 1991 and 2000 for Three Dimensions of the Competitiveness Index

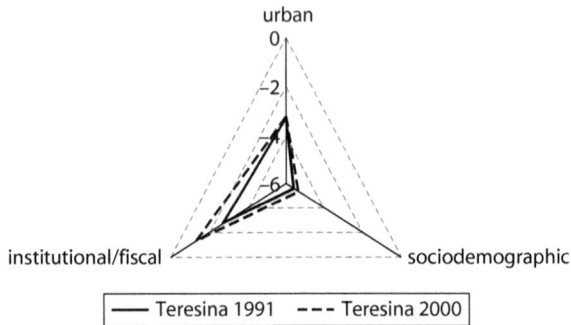

Source: Authors' calculations.

the overall competitiveness ranking of big cities, may be improving its performance over time, something that is not captured in the computed cross-sectional ranking.

Conclusions

Cities increasingly compete to offer a better business environment, and the measurement of their performance is a key management tool. Indicators of competitiveness performance have become in greater demand globally, and Brazilian cities are no exception.

In this exploratory exercise, we have presented a first attempt at measuring city competitiveness in Brazil. We have built a competitive index and ranked large, medium, and small cities according to four dimensions. The lack of data has prevented us from performing a more dynamic (time-based) analysis. Nevertheless, we were able to shed light on the best performers among Brazilian cities, and the areas of potential improvement.

Future efforts to improve the index could include:

- *Dynamic analysis.* This requires completing the database for past years (1980 and 1991), and including more recent data. (The next Brazilian census is scheduled for 2010).
- *Institutional dimension.* Data on institutions at the MCA level were unavailable during the preparation of this chapter, but there are some data on municipal institutions (Perfil dos Municipios Brasileiros) that could be used in the future if they become available at the MCA level.

- *Fiscal dimension.* There are also fiscal data that could be used to measure how municipalities comply with requirements under the Fiscal Responsibilities Law (*Lei de Responsabilidade Fiscal*), which is currently at the municipality level and not at the MCA level.
- *Unit of analysis.* The exercise was carried out using data at the MCA level mainly due to data availability. However, if a more forward-looking approach were to be used, performing the analysis at the municipality level could be more useful and offer a more fitting management tool for municipal governments.

Notes

1. For the definition used in this book, see chapter 1.
2. For the rest of this chapter the term "MCA" is used interchangeably with the term "city."
3. Although institutional data were not available during the preparation of this chapter, the category "institutional/fiscal" is maintained.
4. Interestingly, the states where these cities belong are not at the top of the *Doing Business in Brazil* ranking: São Paulo ranks 11 out of 13 Brazilian states, Rio de Janeiro 8, and Rio Grande do Sul in Porto Alegre, 6. *Doing Business* mainly reflects the complexity of business regulations (starting a business, registering property, getting credit, paying taxes, and enforcing contracts), and this dimension was not considered in the competitiveness index computed in this chapter.

CHAPTER 4

The Cariri Region of Ceará and the Footwear Cluster

Monica Amorim and Daniel da Mata

This case study on the Cariri region of the state of Ceará, Brazil, is divided into two parts. The first presents an economic analysis of the structure and evolution of the Cariri economy in recent years, based mainly on data from the Relação Anual de Informações Sociais (Annual Records of Social Information, or RAIS), produced by the Ministério do Trabalho e Emprego (Ministry of Labor). The analysis tries to isolate the key drivers of regional and municipal economies and to identify the main clusters of the local economy. The second part of the case study looks at the most important cluster of the region, the footwear cluster, and presents its main features, development challenges, and strategies.

An Economic Analysis of Cariri

The first part of this chapter discusses formal employment pictures of three Brazilian municipalities: Barbalha, Crato, and Juazeiro do Norte (for brevity, hereafter just Juazeiro). These three cities form the urban core of the "Cariri region" in the state of Ceará in the Northeast region. In this chapter, the terms "Cariri region" or "Cariri" are used as a synonym for the aggregation of these three municipalities.[1] Therefore, the other municipalities that make up the "official" Cariri region are excluded.

The following section shows formal employment changes and numbers from 1995 to 2005, based on RAIS data. Because these data are on
the formal sector, they tend to particularly underestimate primary sector activities. Secondary sector activities tend to be more formal in
Brazil and therefore RAIS data are appropriate for analyzing that sector. The tertiary sector is more heterogeneous, as some of its activities
are largely formal, such as architecture and engineering, whereas others,
such as small retail sales, are not, so retail establishments and jobs tend
to undercount.

Employment Structure

Table 4.1 shows formal employment data at the RAIS 2-digit level for
Barbalha, Crato, and Juazeiro. The first important characteristic is that,
overall, they have a similar employment structure. Manufacturing, commerce, and the public sector are responsible for approximately two-thirds
of all formal employment. Health- and education-related services are also
relatively important.

Manufacturing is the most important sector and represents much of the
formal employment in all three cities. Table 4.1 shows that manufacturing
employment growth was especially high in Crato and Juazeiro. Over the
period 1995–2005, manufacturing employment increased almost fourfold
in Crato and twofold in Juazeiro. Barbalha showed growth of just 3 percent
during the period. Because of Barbalha's weak performance, Crato sur-
passed Barbalha in the number of manufacturing jobs and had nearly twice
as many in 2005.

Commerce has also experienced a high formal employment
growth rate: roughly 80 percent in Crato, 260 percent in Barbalha,
and 160 percent in Juazeiro. While construction is not an important
sector, real estate activities show strong employment growth in all
three cities. Transportation growth is uneven: positive in Barbalha and
Crato and negative in Juazeiro. Similarly, public sector employment
grew in Barbalha and Crato, but not in Juazeiro. Noteworthy is that
there was a steady drop in finance sector employment in all three
municipalities.

For the region as a whole, manufacturing, utilities, commerce, real
estate, and education were key sectors, and these sectors also maintained
strong formal employment growth from 1995 to 2005. In contrast, there
is a clear tendency of decreasing public sector importance accompanying
the trends of a strengthening in private-based activities, though it is still
the region's third-largest sector.

Table 4.1 Formal Employment Share and Growth in Cariri, 1995–2005

2-digit sector	Employment share, 2005 (%)				Employment growth, 1995–2005 (%)			
	Region	Barbalha	Crato	Juazeiro	Region	Barbalha	Crato	Juazeiro
Agriculture and forestry	0.4	0.1	1.1	0.1	137	–86	1,100	21
Fishing	0.0	0.0	0.0	0.0	—	—	—	—
Mining	0.2	0.6	0.3	0.1	–67	–87	–27	475
Manufacturing	29.1	41.4	30.2	26.0	158	3	380	217
Utilities	0.6	0.0	0.5	0.8	156	–85	–29	—
Construction	2.3	1.9	1.5	2.9	–16	9	–55	6
Commerce	26.2	10.6	18.4	33.5	139	267	76	161
Food and beverage retail sales	2.5	2.2	2.4	2.6	183	163	234	165
Transportation, warehouses, and communication	3.0	1.3	1.3	4.3	27	111	–54	70
Finance services	0.9	0.7	0.9	1.0	–61	–32	–21	–70
Real estate services	2.5	0.4	2.8	2.7	222	467	147	283
Public services	15.6	17.7	19.3	13.3	2	21	54	–22
Education services	6.6	4.4	10.5	4.8	149	70	208	118
Health services	6.5	16.8	5.9	4.7	28	88	–6	30
Other services	3.5	1.8	4.8	3.1	139	–9	184	153
Domestic services	0.0	0.0	0.0	0.0	250	–50	—	—
Multilateral organizations	0.0	0.0	0.0	0.0	—	—	—	—
Total employment (number and % for growth)	**39,028**	**4,474**	**12,120**	**22,434**	**75**	**23**	**96**	**80**

Source: RAIS, Ministry of Labor.

But within manufacturing, commerce, and public service, what are the most important subsectors in terms of formal employment? Table 4.2 gives the most important 4-digit subsectors for the Cariri region (with the matching value for each of the three municipalities). Twenty-four sectors out of 600 are listed, and account for 64 percent of total formal employment. Public services–related activities have bigger employment numbers. Within manufacturing, manufacture of rubber and plastics footwear, of rubber products, and of footwear from other materials are among the top five. Manufacture of leather footwear is also relatively important. Services such as basic and college education as well as hotels are in the list as well. Several activities related to retail sales (commerce) are included, such as retail sales of pharmaceutical and food products. This reflects the role of the Cariri region as a regional sourcing center.

Labor Force Quality
The Cariri region has been an important base for education in Ceará's interior, but as revealed by table 4.3, much is needed to be done to improve labor force skills. Virtually half the formal workers in the Cariri region have completed high school. However, 1 percent are illiterate, 36 percent have completed basic schooling only, and only 13 percent have a degree equivalent to college level or higher. Workers with only a basic education are found mainly in manufacturing, commerce, and public sector activities, whereas college degree workers are more often in public services, education, and health. Lack of skilled workers in manufacturing can present a severe restriction for the region's attempts to move to a more innovation-driven economy.

Location Quotient Analysis
A widely used measure of economic activity concentration within urban areas is the location quotient (LQ). This indicator compares the share of local employment in a sector to the share of national employment in that sector. An LQ of zero means that there is no employment in the particular sector in the area. An LQ lower than 1 indicates that the area is less specialized than the nation in the particular sector. An LQ higher than 1 indicates that the sector is highly concentrated in the area. LQs are therefore useful as a primary tool in identifying clusters and highly concentrated sectors.

Yet in determining the dynamism of a particular sector in a region, LQ is only one piece of information. To determine whether the sector can provide a stable or growing base for the future, other measures

Table 4.2 Formal Employment for the Cariri Region, Barbalha, Crato, and Juazeiro do Norte, 2005

4-digit subsector	Cariri region	Barbalha	Crato	Juazeiro do Norte
General (overall) public service activities	6,063	763	2,330	2,970
Manufacture of rubber and plastics footwear	3,374	336	2,327	711
Hospital activities for in-patients	1,442	570	492	380
Manufacture of rubber products n.e.c.	1,143	212	0	931
Manufacture of footwear from other materials (except athletic footwear)	1,078	272	1	805
Basic education	993	60	424	509
Retail sales of household goods, disks, and similar products	963	0	77	886
Retail sales of products n.e.c.	836	15	105	716
Retail sales of pharmaceutical, medical, and orthopedic products	722	48	197	477
Retail sales of food and beverages in stores smaller than 300 square meters	718	82	276	360
Building of residential and business constructions	676	74	137	465
Retail sales of apparel and allied products	674	13	179	482
Retail sales of construction materials, tools, and hand tools	662	12	181	469
Retail sales of fabrics and allied products	640	16	117	507
Activities of other membership organizations n.e.c.	554	20	247	287
Manufacture of cut-and-sew apparel n.e.c.	550	156	132	262
Manufacture of leather footwear	536	0	0	536
College education	515	0	515	0
Retail sales of footwear, leather products, and luggage	497	24	109	364
Sale of motor vehicle parts and accessories	439	23	60	356
Retail sales of automotive fuel	406	65	145	196
Manufacture of pharmaceuticals for human use	403	402	0	1
Human health activities n.e.c.	401	87	12	302
Hotels	397	72	75	250

Source: RAIS, Ministry of Labor.
Note: n.e.c. = not elsewhere classified.

Table 4.3   Formal Employment and Schooling in the Cariri Region, 2005

2-digit sector	Illiterate (%)	Basic school (%)	High school (%)	College or higher (%)	Total (number)
Agriculture and forestry	19	48	29	5	166
Fishing	0	0	0	0	0
Mining	4	45	48	3	92
Manufacturing	1	51	46	3	11,359
Utilities	1	31	47	21	251
Construction	2	70	25	4	912
Commerce	0	30	64	5	10,221
Food and beverage retail sales	2	48	47	3	972
Transportation, warehouses, and communication	0	52	41	6	1,177
Finance services	0	1	29	69	360
Real estate services	2	49	37	11	959
Public services	3	27	44	26	6,100
Education services	0	7	34	59	2,558
Health services	1	18	67	14	2,521
Other services	1	34	50	15	1,373
Domestic services	0	86	14	0	7
Multilateral organizations	0	0	0	0	0
Total (number)	**426**	**13,981**	**19,483**	**5,138**	**39,028**
Percentage	**1.09**	**35.82**	**49.92**	**13.16**	**100.00**

Source: RAIS, Ministry of Labor.

should be considered, such as the total number of workers and employment growth.

Figure 4.1 illustrates the interaction between LQ and employment growth to determine the importance of a particular sector to the local economy. The first quadrant (upper right) represents key sectors to the local economy, since they have a high LQ and growing employment. Local economic development strategies may choose those sectors to create or maintain adequate business dynamism. The second quadrant (upper left) shows sectors with an LQ above 1 and declining employment growth. These sectors appear as opportunities to strengthen important areas of the local economy. The third quadrant (lower left) presents sectors with a low LQ and below-average employment growth. They are some of the least promising targets for local cluster strategies. Finally, the fourth quadrant (lower right) shows sectors with an LQ below 1, but with fast-growing

Figure 4.1   Location Quotient and Employment Growth

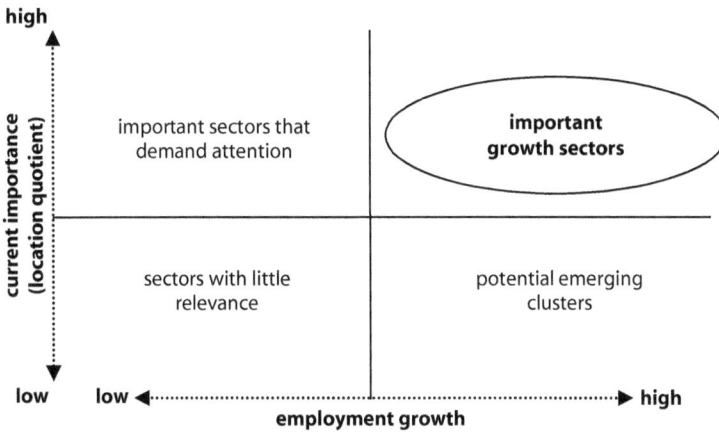

Source: Authors.

employment. These sectors represent possibilities as growth generators in the local economy and as potential emerging clusters.

In this analysis, a sector is identified as having increasing employment if it presents a performance above national employment growth. Table 4.4 reveals sample results of the LQ versus employment growth at 4-digit subsectors for the Cariri region. Generally, sectors that appear in each quadrant are as follows:

- **High importance, high growth:** Manufacturing (leather footwear, plastic products, furniture, underwear and nightwear, among others), some retail sale activities, radio activities, health, and motor vehicle sales activities
- **High importance, low growth:** Manufacturing of leather, banking, cement manufacturing, legal and accounting services, and leisure and entertainment activities
- **Low importance, low growth:** Logging, mining, some manufacturing activities (paper and software), telecommunications, and some high-tech activities
- **Low importance, high growth:** Transportation, some manufacturing activities (for instance, hardware such as doors, windows, and locks), and real estate.

Table 4.4   LQ and Employment Growth: Sectors in Each Quadrant in the Cariri Region

High importance, low growth	High importance, high growth
Distillery, purification, and bottling of liquor	Manufacture of bakery products
Manufacture of leather products n.e.c.	Manufacture of soft drinks
Printing services n.e.c.	Manufacture of cut-and-sew underwear and nightwear
Manufacture of cement	Manufacture of cut-and-sew apparel n.e.c.
Manufacture of brooms, brushes, and mops	Manufacture of luggage, bags, and purses
Building of residential and business constructions	Manufacture of leather footwear
Wholesale of general merchandise	Manufacture of plastics products n.e.c.
Transport of nonurban passengers by road	Manufacture of furniture from other materials
Savings and loan banking	Sale of motor vehicle parts and accessories
Legal activities	Sale of motorcycles and related parts
Accounting, bookkeeping, and auditing activities	Wholesale of footwear
Photographic activities	Retail sales of footwear, leather products, and luggage
Motion picture projection	Retail sales of office and computing equipment
Dramatic arts, music, and other arts activities	Lending by credit cooperatives
Other recreational activities n.e.c.	Medical and dental practice activities
Human health activities n.e.c.	Radio activities
Low importance, low growth	*Low importance, high growth*
Logging	Farming of cattle
Mining of iron ore	Manufacture of hardware
Mining of aluminum	Road construction
Mining of manganese ore	Wholesale of textiles and fabrics
Slaughtering and processing of animals	Retail sales of food products n.e.c.
Manufacture of manioc and derivative products	Transport of urban passengers by road
Manufacture of carpets and rugs	Transport of freight by road
Manufacture of paper	Cargo warehousing, handling
Reproduction of software	Activities related to air transport n.e.c.
Manufacture of textile machinery	Data processing
Transport by interurban railroads	Architectural and engineering activities and consultancy
Transport by air	Advertising

(continued)

Table 4.4   LQ and Employment Growth: Sectors in Each Quadrant in the Cariri Region *(Continued)*

High importance, low growth	High importance, high growth
Telecommunications	Transport via pipelines
Commercial banking	Transport by air, scheduled
Computer hardware consultancy	Cargo handling
Computer-related activities n.e.c.	Real estate activities

Source: Authors' calculations.
Note: n.e.c. = not elsewhere classified.

The presence of the (entire) footwear chain in the high-high category, from manufacturing to sales (both wholesale and retail), comes out as a striking feature and emphasizes the importance of footwear to the local economy. This is a leading cluster because its industries export to other regions in Brazil. Some activities that provide foundation to the footwear chain are also in evidence, such as lending credit cooperatives (high importance, high growth), whereas the following related activities are considered to have growth potential (low importance, high growth): farming of cattle; wholesale of textiles and fabrics; transport of freight by road; cargo warehousing handling; advertisement; and cargo handling. Though a more detailed analysis is required to analyze the proper links among these dynamic sectors, it is clear that they are all parts of a single larger chain and must be considered together in a local economic development strategy. For instance, designing efficient public policies for transportation can directly improve the competitiveness of the footwear cluster.

The low-importance, low-growth category contains several high-tech activities. Innovation is one of the main components for a successful local-level growth path and high-tech industries are some of the most innovative. Therefore, it will be useful for the state and municipal governments to pay greater attention to innovative sectors within the Cariri region footwear chain, for example, design and computer-aided technologies.

Table 4.5 indicates the high-high sector for each municipality. In Barbalha, manufacturing and retail sales activities prevail, but health-based activities are also important.[2] In Crato, some farming and research activities are high-high, in addition to traditional sectors (manufacturing, commerce, and health).[3] Juazeiro has a more extensive list of high-importance, high-growth sectors, comprising a wider range of manufacturing and retail sale activities.[4]

Table 4.5   LQ and Employment Growth: High-High Sectors in Barbalha, Crato, and Juazeiro

Barbalha	Juazeiro
Manufacture of bakery products	Manufacture of bakery products
Distillery, purification, and bottling of liquor	Manufacture of soft drinks
Manufacture of rubber and plastics footwear	Manufacture of cut-and-sew underwear
Manufacture of footwear from other	and nightwear
materials (except athletic footwear)	Cutting, tanning, and finishing of leather
Manufacture of pharmaceuticals	and hides
for human use	Manufacture of luggage, bags, and purses
Manufacture of rubber products n.e.c.	Manufacture of leather footwear
Manufacture of furniture from	Manufacture of soap and synthetic detergents
other materials	Manufacture of rubber products n.e.c.
Retail sales of automotive fuel	Processing and manufacture
Retail sales of footwear, leather products,	of precious metals
and luggage	Manufacture of prefabricated metal
Retail sales of liquefied gas	structures and components
Hospital activities for in-patients	Manufacture of metal structures and plates
Diagnostic and therapeutic human	Etching and engraving of precious
health activities	stones, metals, and jewelry
Human health activities n.e.c.	Manufacture of musical instruments
Social work without accommodation	Manufacture of miscellaneous goods n.e.c.
	Recycling of nonmetal waste and scrap
Crato	Sale of motor vehicle parts and accessories
	Sale of motorcycles and related parts
Farming of animals n.e.c.	and accessories
Processing and canning of fruit	Wholesale of processed cereals, flour, corn oils,
Manufacture of plastics products n.e.c.	and other cereals
Manufacture of nonrefractory structural	Wholesale of food products n.e.c.
clay products	Wholesale of footwear
Processing and manufacture of aluminum	Retail sales of food and beverages
Manufacture of domestic appliances	Retail sales of cookies and crackers
Wholesale of processed cereals, flour,	Retail sales of beverages
corn oils, and other cereals	Retail sales of fabrics and allied products
Wholesale of beverages	Retail sales of apparel and allied products
Wholesale of fuels	Retail sales of footwear, leather products,
Retail sales of food, meat, and beverages	and luggage
Retail sales of cookies and crackers	Retail sales of pharmaceutical, medical,
Retail sales of footwear, leather products,	and orthopedic products
and luggage	Retail sales of household goods, disks,
Retail sales of books, newspapers, journals,	and similar products
and stationery	Retail sales of construction materials,
Retail sales on streets and through mobile	tools, and hand tools
sales posts	Retail sales of liquefied gas
Catering	Retail sales of products n.e.c.
Research and experimental development	Renting of personal and household goods
on natural sciences	n.e.c.
Diagnostic and therapeutic human	Radio activities
health activities	
Social work without accommodation	

Source: Authors' calculations.

Note: n.e.c. = not elsewhere classified.

Shift-Share Analysis

Shift-share analysis is applied as an alternative method for identifying leading and lagging economic sectors. Shift share disaggregates local employment growth into three components:

- *National shift:* changes in the local economy due to changes in the national economy
- *Industrial mix shift:* changes in the local economy due to the mix of industries
- *Local shift:* changes in local employment due to local factors or local/city/municipality competitiveness.

Shift share disaggregates total employment growth according to the following equation:

$$\text{total employment change} = \text{national shift} \\ + \text{industrial mix shift} \\ + \text{local shift}$$

The interpretation of the shift-share results is straightforward. National growth share tells what part of local job growth is simply because of growth in the national economy. Industry mix represents the effect on particular industry performance and trends on local employment. Local shift emphasizes local/city/municipality factors' effects on local employment change.

For instance, shift-share analysis shows how much of the total employment increase in Cariri's manufacture of leather footwear subsector was due, individually, to Brazilian economic dynamics, to the national manufacturing leather footwear sector, and to Cariri region economic competitiveness and dynamics. In this case, almost all employment creation was due to the Cariri region's economic competitiveness and dynamics, which is consistent with its recent GDP growth.[5]

Table 4.6 shows the four leading subsectors in terms of employment growth as a consequence of local economic competitiveness and dynamics. While the footwear chain is clearly among the most dynamic segments, local growth of trade and commerce is also important, reflecting the role of Cariri as a regional commerce center in the interior. Some of the commerce activity growth is also related to the footwear sector boom.

What the Economic Structural Analysis Reveals

The structure of the Cariri region's economy is relatively diversified, although manufacturing, commerce, and services related to education and

Table 4.6   Shift Share: Leading Four-Digit Subsectors of the Cariri Region, 2000–05

Top sectors (local dynamics)	2000	2005	Growth	Shift share		
				National shift	Industrial mix shift	Local shift
Retail sales of household goods, disks, and similar products	122	963	841	33	86	723
Retail sales of food and beverages	249	718	469	67	104	298
Manufacture of leather footwear	219	536	317	59	4	255
Sale of motorcycles and related parts and accessories	42	208	166	11	45	110

Source: Authors' calculations.

health play an important role. Public services, while still significant, lost employment share in the period 1995–2005. In contrast to other regions in Ceará, agriculture does not seem to play a major role in driving the economy, despite the fact that the region is endowed with good soil and water resources.[6] Within manufacturing, footwear shows considerable dynamism in terms of job creation and the capacity to drive (via spillover effects) some other industries such as wholesale, retail, and transport. It is clear that footwear has formed a cluster, and this fact should be a key consideration in regional development strategies (Nogueira and Lopes 2008). In addition, the area is clearly a trade and commerce center of regional significance, as demonstrated by the importance of retail and wholesale and the fast growth of business services such as transport, data processing, and advertising. Also, a significant part of commerce activities are related to tourism, particularly religious pilgrimages.

The analysis suggests that there is potential for the footwear industry to develop as a vibrant cluster, fostering related businesses, investment, and growth. Clustering, however, is not just about industry concentration and proximity. It depends on social relationships, economic connections, and joint initiatives. The next section attempts to describe how these assets function and how they have helped strengthen the Cariri footwear cluster.

The Cariri Footwear Cluster

The footwear industry is a major economic activity in the Cariri region, second only to trade. As the most vibrant manufacturing industry in the region, associated employment has grown roughly 350 percent in the last 10 years, more than doubling the job growth of regional manufacturing. The industry accounts for nearly 45 percent of manufacturing jobs in the region. Though footwear production started as a leather-processing activity, the industry is now dominated by synthetic products, mainly plastic-injected women's sandals.

Regardless of these features, the Cariri footwear cluster faces several significant challenges if it is to move from a low-cost base to innovation in a very competitive sector. First, it must quickly enhance labor skills to achieve product quality improvements, value-added growth, and gains in labor productivity. Second, the cluster must overcome technology bottlenecks (for example, lack of laboratories and modern equipment) to improve quality standards and meet the demands of more sophisticated markets. Third, also related to its markets, the cluster has to reach out to world markets to increase sales. Fourth, it needs to solve issues of sourcing, including attracting input suppliers and creating appropriate mechanisms to finance inputs. Finally, the cluster needs to expand its social capital to allow for more collective initiatives to achieve economies of scale, improve innovative capacity, and boost competitiveness. The following sections attempt to throw some light on the development challenges faced by the footwear cluster.

A Brief History of the Cariri Footwear Cluster

The footwear cluster of Cariri has its origins in the early 19th century, when the municipality of Juazeiro do Norte was established, reflecting the volume of pilgrims coming to the region to pay their respects to the legendary Catholic priest and the city's first mayor, Father Cicero. The priest encouraged newcomers to engage in production activity, especially small manufacturing and handcrafts. A number of small workshops emerged that specialized in processing wood, agricultural and animal products, as well as metals and minerals. Juazeiro saw its influence growing not only as a religious center, but also as a major regional commercial power.

One of the prominent incoming groups was the cowboys (*vaqueiros*), a common character in the Northeast hinterland and a symbol of the major role of cattle raising in the 19th and 20th centuries in Ceará's economy. The numerous cattle and *vaqueiros* made the raw material (leather) available, and created demand for cowboy costumes and utensils for cattle ranchers. In particular, a simple and low-cost type of sandal soon became popular among the poor pilgrims and the low-income, rural,

Northeast population. Juazeiro shoemakers, encouraged by Father Cicero, became the major suppliers of such products to the Northeast region.[7]

Production of footwear in Cariri went through a significant change in the early 1960s, with the introduction of plastic (PVC[8]) material in the footwear industry. In 1962, a large firm in southern Brazil (São Paulo) bought from a Japanese company a license to produce plastic sandals. Supported by huge national advertising campaigns, these "Japanese sandals" became popular all over the Northeast. In 1963, a producer in Juazeiro do Norte also bought the license and started local production. Initially, the firm acquired parts from suppliers in the South, and assembled the sandals in Juazeiro. Years later, the firm integrated production vertically by producing the plastic components at its own plant in Juazeiro. In addition, some of the plastic inputs were sold to local assemblers.

The plastic sandals gradually replaced the leather-made ones produced in the region. Consumers preferred the new products, with their exuberant colors, low cost, and easy care. Mass-produced new sandals soon replaced the traditional types and many small artisan shops went out of business.

Recent Developments
Following the pioneer producer, a few other local companies began to mass-produce plastic sandals in the Cariri region. Supply of plastic inputs came originally from producers established in southern states and later from a Northeast state (Bahia), more than 1,000 kilometers away. Two decades later, a local firm began the production of plastic inputs, especially laminated plaques, the most important components for plastic sandals. This revitalized the micro and small footwear workshops because they could then buy plastic inputs in retail amounts and make similar, low-cost products. Mostly because of this event, in the last two decades the Cariri industry has experienced significant growth, both in jobs and number of firms. Table 4.7 gives data for the last decade.

Since the introduction of plastic, the Cariri footwear industry has changed trajectory, becoming more and more specialized in plastic and other synthetic material, such as fake leather. Today, although the cluster produces a range of products, more than 60 percent of output consists of female sandals, made primarily of synthetic leather (da Costa 2007). The region currently accounts for nearly 10 percent of Brazil's jobs in plastic and synthetic footwear, while the state of Ceará has nearly two-thirds of these jobs. Table 4.8 shows this specialization by LQ for the three municipalities calculated with employment data produced by RAIS for 2004,

and in comparison with the state of Ceará and with Brazil. LQs are calculated separately according to the main input (leather or plastic) used by
the cluster.

Production of footwear is concentrated in Juazeiro, but is also significant in the other two neighboring municipalities. Official data indicate
that 140 formal footwear firms in Cariri are responsible for nearly 6,000
formal direct jobs, equivalent to 45 percent of regional manufacturing jobs
(table 4.9; from RAIS 2006 data). Unofficial data, however, indicate the

Table 4.7   Footwear Industry in Cariri, 1996 and 2006

| | 1996 | | 2006 | | % change | |
Municipality	Firms	Jobs	Firms	Jobs	Firms	Jobs
Juazeiro	93	691	130	2,839	39.8	310.9
Crato	4	487	1	2,277	−75.0	367.6
Barbalha	1	77	9	503	800.0	553.3
Total Cariri	98	1,255	140	5,619	42.9	347.7
Ceará	298	10,755	361	51,095	21.1	375.1
Total Cariri as % of Ceará	32.9	110.7	38.8	11.0		

Source: RAIS, Ministry of Labor.

Table 4.8   Cariri Footwear Location Quotient

| | Leather footwear | | Plastic footwear | |
Municipality	Compared to Ceará	Compared to Brazil	Compared to Ceará	Compared to Brazil
Crato	4.04	18.15	6.41	2.98
Barbalha	1.89	8.51	5.82	2.71
Juazeiro	1.75	7.86	2.27	1.05

Source: Amaral et al. (2006).

Table 4.9   Cariri Footwear and Manufacturing Industries, 2006

Municipality	Footwear jobs	Manufacturing jobs	Footwear as % of manufacturing
Juazeiro	2,839	7,294	38.9
Crato	2,277	3,544	64.2
Barbalha	503	1,762	28.5
Total	5,619	12,600	44.6
Ceará	51,095	195,288	26.2

Source: From RAIS data.

existence of 270 formal firms accounting for nearly 12,000 direct jobs.[9] This greater magnitude is easily seen on a visit to the region, especially in Juazeiro, where footwear workshops can be found in industrial zones, downtown, family backyards, and even improvised tents under trees.

Cariri is now one of the largest producers of footwear in the country. Annual production amounts to some 70 million pairs of shoes, equivalent to 9 percent of Brazil's estimated total.[10] Though exports are not significant, they are rising. The main markets include Latin American countries, Portugal, Spain, France, the United Kingdom, Italy, Greece, and the United States.

Footwear Cluster Features

Agglomeration, proximity, specialization of a large number of firms operating in the business, and a certain level of interdependence among them are allowing the footwear business in Cariri to function as an emerging cluster, rather than a set of isolated firms (de Souza 2003; da Costa 2007). According to official data, 140 formal firms are engaged in footwear manufacturing, excluding suppliers or service providers. SMEs account for the majority of manufacturing firms. RAIS data for 2006 indicate that 97 percent of firms have fewer than 100 workers (table 4.10).

Agglomeration of specialized firms in the region enables them to often complement each other, which facilitates production efforts. As production takes places in a range of places, locals learn different tasks involved in footwear production almost immediately. Basic skills are disseminated through community and family connections. It is common for an entire family to be involved in the footwear business, often each member owning a shop. Likewise, an entire street can be filled with footwear workshops, a result of neighbors influencing each other to join the business.

The Cariri footwear cluster is fairly dense and the main players include footwear producers, input and equipment suppliers, providers of services, as

Table 4.10   Cariri Footwear Firms, by Size

Size	Number of firms	%
Large (more than 500 workers)	1	0.72
Medium (100–500 workers)	3	2.14
Small (20–100 workers)	3	2.14
Micro (fewer than 20 workers)	133	95.00
Total	**140**	**100.00**

Source: Based on RAIS data.

well as a range of support agencies. Figure 4.2 illustrates how the cluster is organized. Geographic proximity encourages the easy flow of information, which becomes a collective good, because it circulates at no cost from one firm to another (Prochnik 2005). In many circumstances, proximity and networking enable managers to quickly learn, for example, which firm is replacing old equipment for new—hence creating a secondary market for equipment—or which firm is hiring which professional and for how much.

The presence of supply and demand players in the cluster makes the region conducive for footwear production. On the one hand, availability of inputs, information, machinery (including secondhand), and a pool of low-cost labor (though mostly unskilled) reduce barriers to entry; on the other, both local and outside buyers have been important elements ensuring business, especially for SMEs who cannot afford to have sales representatives outside the region or to travel to distant markets.

Informality plays an important role in the cluster. It is often the door to the business. Availability of raw materials, components and, especially, used equipment, makes it relatively easy to open a footwear business in the area. Access to markets is usually through subcontracting. Established firms often use informal businesses to fulfill orders, as a strategy both to reduce costs and to meet seasonal peak demand without investing in plants. Alternatively, informal shops sell production at local fairs or to informal merchants who travel to other states to market low-cost footwear and garments.

Leading Firms and Followers

Operations differ according to a company's size, and bottlenecks affect larger and smaller firms in different ways. Large and medium firms lead the cluster, as they drive production volumes, control sourcing, and define product styles. They manufacture synthetic leather footwear and are organized as mass production vertical plants, producing most components, including the injected plastic soles (the most expensive part).[11] Subcontracting is limited, but may be used for the more labor-intensive tasks. Because they are more capital-intensive operations, large and medium firms produce the more expensive products, which are often imitated by other firms as soon as they are disclosed to local vendors. Average prices for typical products are in the range of US$10–20 per pair (though some firms also produce cheaper products, including some made of recycled plastic). Most of these firms have developed prestigious brand names and sell their output to larger and more distant national markets, such as the north and northeast regions and some states in the southern part of the country.

124

Figure 4.2 Cariri Footwear Cluster

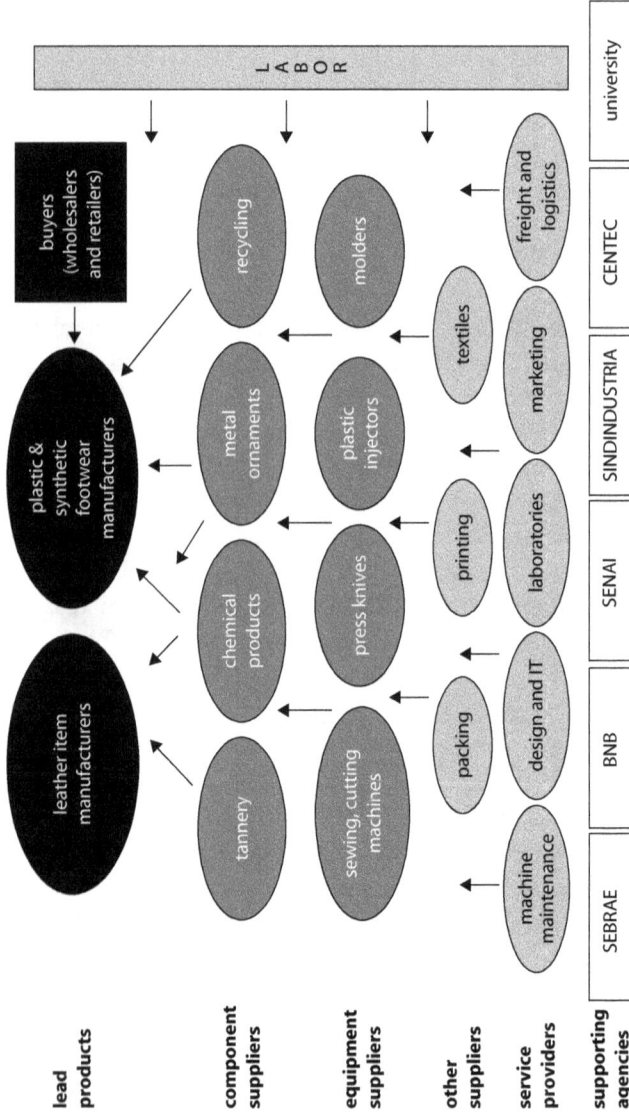

The diagram is organized into rows labeled on the left:

- **lead products**
- **component suppliers**
- **equipment suppliers**
- **other suppliers**
- **service providers**
- **supporting agencies**

A horizontal bar labeled **LABOR** spans the top with arrows pointing down.

Lead products: buyers (wholesalers and retailers); plastic & synthetic footwear manufacturers; leather item manufacturers

Component suppliers: recycling; molders; metal ornaments; plastic injectors; chemical products; press knives; tannery; sewing, cutting machines

Equipment suppliers: textiles; printing; packing; design and IT; machine maintenance

Other suppliers / service providers: marketing; laboratories; freight and logistics

Supporting agencies: SEBRAE; BNB; SENAI; SINDINDUSTRIA; CENTEC; university

Source: Authors.

Note: SEBRAE = Brazil Micro and Small Business Services; BNB = Northeast Development Bank; SENAI = National Industrial Training Service; SINDINDUSTRIA = Cariri Footwear Industry Association; CENTEC = Technology Center Institute of Cariri.

Large firms have their own machine tool section, as well as design staff. They complain about the lack of specialized laboratories in the region, which forces them to depend on facilities located either in the state of Paraiba (350 kilometers away) or in southern Brazil. Large and medium firms suffer from low skills among the local labor force, compounded by limited training and few other skill-enhancing activities for workers. Specific skill areas most lacking include sewing, product assembly, operation and maintenance of machinery, design and computer use (for example, computer-aided design and computer-aided manufacturing), in addition to production supervision. At the firm level, needs for training include environmental management and quality and cost control.

SMEs also produce synthetic footwear items, but use low-cost and low-quality components, such as less expensive soles and cheaper metallic parts. Production depends heavily on local supply of raw materials and shoe components. Products prices are typically US$4–15 per pair. These firms tend to lag behind the more sophisticated and larger ones, producing copies of items created by the latter. In general, SMEs are more labor-intensive operations, mixing mass production methods with handcraft procedures and using obsolete equipment. Some of these firms are in family homes, though recently several of them have moved into more appropriate production facilities. As much of this segment is informal, its real size is not reflected in the above formal data.

SMEs' real challenge is obtaining the working capital needed to purchase inputs and produce independently from inputs financed by suppliers. They have difficulty in procuring supplies in bulk, and rely on input retailers— at steep cost—to supply the necessary components (discussed further in the section on demand and buyers below). SMEs have needed a centralized procurement system a for long time, but as yet that need is still unfulfilled.[12]

As long as SMEs can deal with these financial constraints, they have significant flexibility to manufacture, change product styles, and expand volumes. They have often worked together and shared orders, primarily because of family connections or neighborhood ties. Likewise, equipment sharing or exchanging is common among SMEs. Over the last two decades, SMEs have developed a network that allows many of them to expand production, reach new markets, and improve quality standards.

Inputs and Suppliers

Inputs such as plastic components and other synthetic items, metallic parts, textiles, and chemicals are supplied by a few local plants and many retailers.[13] A local tannery provides some of the leather. Also locally available are equipment merchants, providing, for example, sewing machines and press knives. Two independent firms specialize in producing molders for plastic shoes and serve some local medium-size footwear plants. Other businesses provide packing material, such as paper boxes, cardboard, and other heavy-duty paper-based products. Various printing shops supply labels, tags, stickers, and similar items. Firewood, supplied locally, is used as the basic fuel by firms that process plastic material.

Synthetic plastic inputs come from as far as 1,500 kilometers away. Despite this limitation, Cariri footwear firms have specialized in processing plastic inputs and Cariri has become one of Brazil's most important plastic footwear producers, exceeding regions that have their own chemical inputs and a well-developed footwear industry, such as Rio Grande do Sul and Bahia.[14] Access to plastic raw materials has improved due to recycling. Some firms have recently created a special line of equipment to recycle plastic material. They both produce footwear made of recycled plastic and sell the surplus from recycled plastic plates to other footwear firms.[15] The availability of recycled material has cut down production costs and reduced entry barriers to the industry, especially to informal firms. However, products made of recycled material are cheaper and less attractive, since most of them are black.

Though at an emerging stage, a few workshops have specialized in providing maintenance services for machinery on the shop floor. Additional services such as freight, logistics, and marketing are available in the cluster. However, other specialist services, such as design creation, product branding, quality-enhancement systems, and laboratories, are largely missing. Only a few design professionals serve the low-rank medium and small firms, and on a contract basis. The larger firms and the top medium firms have their own permanent designers.

SMEs face difficulties in accessing key, but expensive, equipment to perform tasks such as cutting and folding, as well as creating the different sizes for each product design. Lacking this type of equipment, firms either use manual techniques or pay other better-equipped firms to perform the tasks. Either of these alternatives has different limitations. In the first case, quality is of a low standard mainly because of poor finishing. In the second case, difficulties in synchronizing operations with the firm that owns the equipment are a major problem, and occur because the better-equipped firm will only perform operations for SMEs after they have met their own needs and when their equipment is idle.

The Cariri footwear cluster enjoys a high supply of low-cost labor, though the majority of workers are low skilled or unskilled. They lack training in manufacturing procedures such as equipment maintenance, machinery operation, quality control, and waste prevention. Skills are often acquired informally on the shop floor ("learning by doing"). Many workers are hired with no previous experience in industrial facilities, with exposure only to agriculture production, and therefore lack the ability to perform more complex tasks and operate specialized machinery.

Though labor costs in Brazilian footwear production may represent only 15 percent of total production costs, low labor costs stand out as a significant advantage of the Cariri footwear cluster (Brandão and Rosa 1997; Une and Prochnik 1999). The majority of workers earn the minimum wage, roughly US$240 per month.[16] Those with specialized skills on the shop floor (such as equipment maintenance) may earn twice as much. Indeed, the low cost of labor in the Northeast has been one of the main reasons for the intense migration of southern (Rio Grande do Sul and São Paulo) footwear firms during the 1990s (Santos et al. 2002).[17]

Demand and Buyers

Demand for Cariri footwear is mostly from the north and northeast regions and comes from retail stores, department stores, and individual merchants operating at regional trade fairs or door-to-door sales. Given the low prices of products, the focus is on medium- and low-income consumers, though a few firms have recently been successful in reaching higher-scale markets, as they have managed to improve product design, quality control, and have developed prestigious brand names.

Buyers have a strong presence in the cluster. They operate year round, are clearly visible and accessible in the region, and play an important role in spurring production and opening markets for small firms. As a small entrepreneur who has operated in Cariri for more than a decade explains: "Marketing products is relatively easy in the cluster, as buyers are seen everywhere and knock on firms' doors constantly." The region attracts buyers from different parts of the country, given its reputation as a low-cost footwear production site.

There are two main types of buyers. The first are local agents, who usually run input retail businesses. They perform a dual role, simultaneously ensuring supply of footwear inputs, as well as expanding the market for footwear products. These buyers place orders with footwear firms and make part of the payment upfront, supplying the necessary inputs to enable production. Prices paid for products in this case are lower than the usual levels when such in-kind inputs are not provided. Firms often complain about this arrangement, as they see their profit margins compressed. Given their ordinary financial constraints, SMEs are often the target of these transactions.

The other type of buyers are outside agents who come to Cariri to do business regularly. These buyers are circulating the region continuously to negotiate orders, buy in bulk, observe producers, and identify business opportunities. They are either purchasing agents of footwear retail stores or independent agents who purchase footwear products to resell to retailers. Prices paid may be higher than with the first type of buyer as production finance is not part of the deal. Payments, however, are often made in two or three installments, a situation that again requires firms to draw on considerable amounts of working capital.

Support Agencies

The cluster is connected to key private and public institutions, which provide some technical, managerial, and financial assistance. The services provided, however, are often limited or inadequate.

Training for the footwear cluster is mostly provided by the Serviço Nacional de Aprendizagem Industrial (National Industrial Training Service, or SENAI), which is partially funded by industry associations. Over the last 20 years, SENAI has made an important contribution in improving workers' skills and firms' productivity. The agency organizes courses, performs some basic laboratory tests, and for a short time, carried out some on-site consultancy on production organization (for example, shop-floor layout and quality control procedures). There is no direct charge for training, because SENAI uses its own budget to fund it. However, due to obsolete and limited equipment, courses do not fulfill the industry's current needs, either in quality or quantity. In 2007 for example, SENAI trained only 30 workers, while demand was at least 10 times as high. In addition, training is also limited to a 200-hour schedule, an arrangement that does not go well with cluster reality. This is too long a period for workers to be absent from production for most firms, particularly for SMEs, which do not have the flexibility to reallocate workers to make up for leave. Short-term training on a continuous base is a missing element in the cluster and such initiatives would help improve cluster productivity and competitiveness.

Serviço Brasileiro de Apoio às Micro e Pequenas Empresas (Brazil Micro and Small Business Services, or SEBRAE) is the most active institutional actor in the cluster and has contributed to improving cluster organization while strengthening cluster cohesion. The agency has supported firms in organizing into associations; in expanding markets by taking part in industry events and by organizing important events in the region; and in assisting firms to enhance management and innovation capacity. For example, the agency has brought nationally known consultants to Cariri to disseminate state-of-the-art industry information on product styles, trends, markets, and business strategies. However, despite their importance, these are one-time events, as they take place only on specific dates, whereas firms need to have such support on a continuous basis. This is a major problem because the footwear industry needs to be constantly aware of changes in, for example, fashion, market profiles, consumer preferences, technology, machinery, and inputs.

The Banco do Nordeste do Brasil (Northeast Development Bank, or BNB) is the main credit agency for productive activities in Cariri.[18] It has branches in Crato and Juazeiro do Norte. The bank accounts for nearly 80 percent of the long-term credit that benefits the region. Out of the credit committed to manufacturing, 60 percent goes to footwear firms. In 2007, nearly 67 percent of BNB long-term credit targeted SMEs, with large and medium firms accounting for 33 percent.[19] However, BNB credit lines seem more accessible to large and medium firms than SMEs. While some firms in the former group have recently built new production facilities, bought modern equipment, or improved management and marketing strategies as a result of access to BNB credit, SMEs face difficulties in access for lack of collateral.[20]

In addition to the agencies above, the Instituto Centro de Tecnologia do Ceará (Technology Center Institute of Cariri, or CENTEC) and the Universidade Regional do Cariri (Regional University of Cariri, or URCA) have begun initiatives aimed at fostering technology improvement in the footwear cluster. However, they both lack specialized equipment and have been unable to provide individual and prompt on-demand assistance to firms, because they have limited staff and, needless to say, give priority to teaching and other academic activities.

Organization and Social Capital

The cluster's environment has stimulated some firms to cooperate, share information, and organize themselves as a group. But this is not the standard pattern because many firms prefer not to engage in cooperative arrangements, but rather to produce in an isolated environment, and so fail to take advantage of cluster benefits. Initiatives to promote social capital hence emerge as an opportunity to promote cluster competitiveness through economies of scale and more efficient operations stemming from collective action.

Cooperation and rivalry are, therefore, seen simultaneously in the cluster: firms may cooperate to subcontract. But they also act as rivals, stealing the best workers from each other, copying others' designs, fighting over scarce inputs, and engaging in industrial espionage of competitors' production plans. Indeed, the role of rivalry is as important as the role of cooperation in driving product quality and cluster learning, as firms step up their efforts to keep their best workers, imitate best practices, introduce more efficient technologies and components, and replicate competitors' innovative designs, while also learning how to upgrade their in-house "style" ("learning by imitating"). For example, some firms, including small ones, have built new production facilities to improve working conditions on the shop floor and to maintain workers' health and well-being.

The ability to initiate and engage in collective projects has been a salient feature of the cluster's evolution. Cariri footwear firms are organized in three entities: the Associação dos Fabricantes de Calçados (AFABRICAL), the Cariri Footwear Industry Association (SINDINDUSTRIA), and the Sindicato da Indústria de Calçados de Crato (SINDCALC). AFABRICAL, the oldest (created in 1986), covers largely artisans and microenterprises, the majority of them informal. At the start of this century, AFABRICAL had more than 180 members and was for many years the most important regional footwear business association. After a period of dynamic involvement in the footwear cluster, the entity is now facing a severe crisis due to a failure to pay back a loan contracted with BNB for members of the association, using AFABRICAL equipment as collateral. Out of 70 members involved in this credit operation, 3 failed to pay what they owed to BNB, which was forced to take action against AFABRICAL.

AFABRICAL had a major role in strengthening the footwear cluster, especially in facilitating the launch and operation of new SMEs. For example, for more than a decade AFABRICAL operated a service center containing key equipment (for example, cutting and finishing machinery), which associates could use and pay for by the hour. This was an important initiative because it enabled beneficiaries to have access to specialized equipment (more appropriate for volume production) and to improve product quality, without having to find the resources to purchase the equipment themselves and without incurring idle capacity and inefficiency. Having such a service center that allowed time and cost sharing according to firms' actual needs was an important endeavor to improve small firms' competitiveness and reduce barriers to entry. AFABRICAL is, in fact, the sponsor of several of today's medium firms that began operations as microenterprises. During the initial phase of their business, these firms counted on AFABRICAL's support to expand production, improve quality, and increase competitiveness. Access to machinery, loans, and business events facilitated by AFABRICAL were important elements in their graduation from microenterprises to medium firms.

SINDINDUSTRIA was created in 1997 and is now the largest and most active footwear business association in Cariri. It has expanded its membership from fewer than 50 to 72, all of them in the formal sector, and predominantly SMEs. In the Cariri region, SINDINDUSTRIA represents the powerful state industry association, Centro Internacional de Negócios do Ceará (FIEC), which is headquartered in Fortaleza, the state capital.

SINDINDUSTRIA is active in encouraging business development, reaching out to support agencies, and mobilizing local footwear firms to act collectively. Among other initiatives of the last 10 years, it has, with SEBRAE, organized a major annual footwear trade fair (FETECC— Ceará Footwear Technology Trade Fair; see box 4.1) in the region. SINDINDUSTRIA has put strong emphasis on improving the quality of footwear items made in Cariri. Some of these initiatives include organizing lectures and seminars and producing printed material on key elements, such as quality control and lean production, new materials, innovative design and technologies, and ergonomics. In addition, SINDINDUSTRIA organizes missions to major footwear centers in the country (box 4.1), and coordinates the participation of Cariri footwear firms in the most important Brazilian specialist trade fairs (Couromodas and Francal in São Paulo, and Fenac and Fimec in Rio Grande do Sul).

SINDCALC is the newest organization, with three member firms operating in Crato. It is led by the second largest firm (with more than 1,100 workers) in the cluster, which relocated to Cariri in the 1990s, encouraged by low wages, fiscal incentives, and other advantages granted by the Ceará state government.

Innovation

Though the volume of Cariri footwear production is impressive, cluster innovation capacity is limited, because the majority of firms do not have the ability to create original designs. Only the larger (and some medium) firms have a design unit, with specialist professionals and equipment. As plastic soles are an important element of product design innovation, large firms are in a privileged position because they tend to possess both plastic injectors and the machine tools to manufacture the plastic molders for soles. These firms are leading product styling.

Box 4.1

FETECC—Ceará Footwear Technology Trade Fair

FETECC is Brazil's second-largest footwear technology trade fair, after the annual FIMEC (International Fair of Leather, Chemicals, Components, and Equipments for Footwear and Tanneries), held in Novo Hamburgo (Rio Grande do Sul), home of Brazil's largest footwear cluster. An annual event, currently in its 11th year, FETECC is held during three days in August, in Juazeiro do Norte. Exhibiting firms come from other states and a few from other countries, such as China. FETECC is jointly organized by SINDINDUSTRIA and SEBRAE.

FETECC is the most important event for the Cariri footwear business and its impact goes beyond commercial promotion. Having started mainly as a marketing tool to promote cluster sales, FETECC has served as a learning opportunity to local firms, because it brings new technologies, inputs, and machinery to Cariri, which most local producers would not otherwise have a chance to see. As a specialized trade fair, FETECC is a natural place to go for those in the footwear industry: it brings together suppliers, buyers, local producers, and support agencies. As Mirela Duarte, commercial director of Inbop, a large footwear firm in the region, puts it: "FETECC is one of the best opportunities to do business during the year, as well as being an essential tool for sales promotion, marketing, and networking initiatives. The event allows participants to be in close contact with clients and to secure visibility on the local and national scene."

As a consolidated trade fair in the national calendar of the footwear industry, FETECC is a much more anticipated event in the Cariri region, not only by those in the footwear industry but also by those in business-support activities, as well as the tourism sector—the fair contributes significantly to business for hotels, restaurants, and other tourist services (for example, stand assemblers, public relations businesses, catering, and decoration). Nearly 300 people are directly involved in assembling the trade fair exhibition area.

FETECC numbers are remarkable. During the first fair in 1998, 54 firms took part, and it resulted in sales of approximately US$6 million. At FETECC 2007, nearly 120 firms took part, including some from other states in Brazil, and from as far away as Latin America and China. That year, business volume was US$77 million and visitors reached 12,000.

Source: Authors.

In terms of product design, SMEs function as followers, and produce items imitating those originally created by the leading firms. Copying, therefore, is a common phenomenon. SMEs have become skilled at quickly reproducing designs created by larger firms and adapting them to low-end markets, using cheaper and lower-quality components. Also, footwear designs shown on television, in magazines, and in publicity material have served as a source of inspiration to small firms as they readily copy these models and produce similar items for the local market.

Independent professional designers are rare in the cluster, a fact that has prevented firms from creating original designs and from enhancing the value added of their products. A design school is still needed. Institutions such as SEBRAE, SININDUSTRIA, and SENAI have tried to help by bringing in professional designers from other regions to give lectures and short training sessions, but these initiatives are fragmented and have not been enough to create solid design capacity in the region.

In plastic footwear production, molds are key elements for sole manufacture. Easy access to mold production helps in innovation because these pieces are responsible for the shape of plastic-injected items. Together with design capabilities, molding allows for creation of innovative products. Yet Cariri molder production is far from satisfactory. Only one independent firm can perform this work for the footwear cluster. A few large and medium firms have the appropriate equipment to make molders, but do this only for their own product lines. Support agencies such as SENAI and CENTEC do not have such capacity. As a consequence, most firms face great difficulties in innovating and creating new product styles. The ones that manage to do so order molds from firms in Fortaleza, 600 kilometers away.

In terms of product quality, the Cariri footwear cluster faces significant challenges. Improvements in products and in production processes depend heavily on specialized laboratory facilities, which are rare in the region. Most firms have problems in performing laboratory tests (such as those for input resistance, rigidity, and stability, and other physical and mechanical tests) as they attempt to improve and to monitor product quality. These tests are also important for enhancing firms' bargaining power in relation to input suppliers, as well as for enabling firms to sell to more demanding markets, which often require product quality certification. Laboratory support, including equipment, personnel, and footwear industry–related research, is a major gap in cluster competitiveness enhancement. In response, SENAI has acquired a mobile mechanical laboratory, which will serve cluster firms on a subsidized-fee basis.

Branding is another strategy that firms may use to innovate and add value; it aims to encourage market acceptance of specific businesses or products. Effective branding needs to be linked to product excellence, though, hence the interdependence of this strategy with laboratory improvements. A few Cariri footwear firms have developed a quality brand name. As a result, the market value of their products has risen to twice as much as apparently similar items produced by less sophisticated firms. As some local footwear brands gain a reputation, they tend to be imitated by other SMEs. It is therefore common for SMEs to have names similar to those of more successful firms.

Vision of the Future: The Cluster Road Map

Cluster organization involves encouraging actors to interact and join efforts to continuously advance the cluster agenda. Aware of the importance of the footwear cluster and its potential to strengthen the regional economy, the Ceará state government initiated in-depth discussions with local actors on the design and implementation alternatives of a series of complementary interventions to foster cluster competitiveness. Getting cluster actors together and creating opportunities for them to discuss common issues proved to be a fruitful starting point for devising a cluster development strategy. The necessary step in formulating this strategy included a cluster organization process that started by getting actors together to produce a cluster diagnosis, followed by forging a cluster vision of the future. Following these two elements, actors moved on to formulate a strategy to achieve the envisaged future, with further discussion to identify necessary measures to reach desired goals. During the process, leadership, collaboration, and trust are important elements to bind mutual interest, to ensure continuous stakeholder mobilization, and to maximize results.

Cluster Process

Cluster organization is a process of developing genuine relationships with actors. The organization process should ensure participation, unite voices, promote synergies, and foster continuous steps toward cluster goals. The process may involve informative meetings and seminars, hands-on and participatory events, networking and information-sharing activities, training, identification of and undertaking of group activity opportunities (for example, joint purchases), and other forms of dialogue and relationship building. In this process, two cluster actors play strategic roles: the champion and the facilitator. They bear the greatest responsibility to ensure that shared plans are transformed into actions and subsequently into concrete and positive results to ensure cluster competitiveness gains, business expansion, and enlargement of the cluster employment base.

The champion has the role of leading the cluster, encouraging group cohesion, keeping attention to the agreed-on cluster vision of the future, while also focusing on immediate gains to reinforce actors' confidence in the strategy. The champion should ensure continuous connection among actors and ensure that collective actions are geared toward fulfilling cluster needs. In the Cariri footwear cluster, this function is fulfilled by a private sector representative, the president of SINDINDUSTRIA. The cluster facilitator has the role of mobilizing actors, motivating participation, and conducting activities defined as essential to achieve short- and medium-run goals. In the Cariri case, it is planned that this role will be filled by an experienced professional, hired by the cluster.

From 2005 to 2008, under the leadership of the state government (Secretariat of Cities), following initial visits and interviews with cluster stakeholders, small group meetings were held with cluster actors to identify cluster-specific bottlenecks, growth opportunities, and concrete proposals for a cluster development joint-action plan. Cluster representatives then visited other Brazilian footwear clusters (Sinos Valley in Rio Grande do Sul and Campina Grande in Paraiba) to see how other footwear clusters operate. Also, a team comprising Ceará state government officials and a representative of the Cariri footwear cluster visited Peru to assess the experience of industry-specific technology innovation centers, known as CITEs, including one focused on leather and footwear (see box 2.6 in chapter 2). Finally, a more formal and comprehensive consultation took place with cluster actors with the purpose of settling on a consensus agenda focused on enhancing cluster competitiveness.

Vision of the Future

In strategic planning, a vision defines a target in the future, showing where the organization wants to be at a certain time. A vision conveys an optimistic prospect for the organization. In cluster organization strategy, a vision portrays some form of achievement, and functions as a source of inspiration, allowing decisions to be made effectively and enhancing coordination.

In the Cariri footwear cluster, the above elaboration of the vision of the future energized actors and gave rise to optimistic expectations. Having experienced a number of group meetings before, actors were quick and assertive to point out clear directions and future status for the cluster. They agreed to work together to improve cluster competitiveness and transform the Cariri footwear cluster into the "World's leading producer of synthetic footwear." It is expected to take 10 years to reach this ambitious goal. Accomplishing the goal will require cluster cohesion, strong leadership, clear strategy, capacity to act continuously without losing focus, and a fostering of public–private collaboration.

Strategy and Actions

On the basis of the cluster diagnosis and with the vision of the future in mind, Cariri footwear actors identified four key areas in which the footwear cluster would be strengthened: cluster organization, technology upgrading, marketing initiatives, and enlargement of the cluster sourcing base. For each one, actors agreed on a series of initiatives to which both private and public sectors needed to cooperate. Table 4.11 presents the road map for improvements to which actors are committed over the next few years.

The cluster organization process started with identifying the cluster champion. Significant, too, is that the cluster actors realized there is a need for a facilitator to encourage collaboration and effective joint action, and to promote synergy. Also, part of the organization process are initiatives to promote cluster social capital to encourage synergies and joint initiatives (promotional activities, shared industry infrastructure, buyer-supplier relationships, and others) to facilitate economies of scale and other efficiency gains.

The Cariri cluster organization process and the proposed interventions have been incorporated into the state government's regional development agenda. The state government's aim is to promote key drivers of the Cariri regional productive system, with initial priority given to footwear and tourism.[21] The interventions will complement private sector initiatives, as well as others implemented by support agencies (for example, SENAI and SEBRAE). The key issues to be addressed include innovation and continual upgrading of design and technology; enhancement of human resources, especially labor skills; strengthening collective actions; business environment streamlining; marketing outreach; environmental protection; and infrastructure improvement. Specifically, the focus will be on improving the functioning of value chains, facilitating access to domestic and international markets, strengthening social capital, and promoting collaborative activities, as well as enhancing stakeholders' implementation

Table 4.11 Cariri Footwear Cluster Road Map

Phase/area	Cluster organization	Technology and design innovation center	Marketing initiatives	Sourcing base
1st year: Concept and alliance	–Define cluster champion –Define cluster vision –Construct a work program for short, medium, and long run –Hire a cluster facilitator	–Design and plan the facility (government agency and cluster productive actors)	–Strengthen FETECC –Organize technical missions to competing states/countries –Promote visits to key trade fairs –Promote information-sharing workshops	–Work with government agencies to define incentives to attract suppliers' manufacturing plants
2nd year: Setting up	–Draw up a cluster work program and calendar of activities –Private actors work together with government agency to strengthen cluster	–Construct, establish, and organize facility –Define financial arrangements	–Bring in buyers (national and international) –Train sales agents (to visit strategic markets to promote Cariri footwear) –Organize and disseminate information gathered at each event/mission	–Attract plants for thermoplastic resins, pigments, adhesives, footwear soles, insoles, metal ornaments, molders, and packing items –Attract specialized services (equipment maintenance, styling, fashion bureaus, and others)
3rd year: Into operation	–Promote cooperation, collective actions, and trust –Create specialized working groups to face specific challenges	Initial activities: –Design support –CAD/CAM service center –Laboratory tests and analyses –Short-run training –Subsidized services	–Organize information on industry trends and competitors' strategies (industry observatory) –Develop a certificate of origin (for example, "Cariri Footwear") –Set up Internet sales	–Have local representatives or production facility of all suppliers of footwear components –Focus on expanding cluster value added

(continued)

Table 4.11 Cariri Footwear Cluster Road Map *(Continued)*

Phase/area	Cluster organization	Technology and design innovation center	Marketing initiatives	Sourcing base
Medium run: 5–7 years	–Private actors lead the work (encourage local suppliers; facilitate production; attract private investments, including FDI; stimulate R&D, technology transfers; link university to firms; promote regional growth) –Encourage organization of other clusters	–Market price services –Establish an information bureau –Prospect new materials –Develop new equipment –Establish a product development facility –Initiate a high-level course on new materials and industrial design –Become sustainable	–Consolidate the Cariri footwear brand as a monitored production –Attract major footwear traders –FETECC consolidated as an international footwear event –Organize major specialized events during the year focusing on technology, design, marketing, and seasonal collections	–Attract makers of footwear equipment –Become a center for suppliers –Suppliers to develop research facilities in the region –University to create college courses on footwear production and graduate courses on quality control and product development
Long run: 7–10 years	Cluster acts as a regional developing agency	Be recognized as a center of excellence in synthetic footwear	Become the world's leading producer of synthetic footwear	Consolidate sourcing base

Source: Authors.

Note: The first year of the road map is scheduled to be 2009/10. CAD = computer-aided design; CAM = computer-aided manufacturing.

capacity—the ability to move from ideas to actions and to concrete results (Hansen 2008).

Technology upgrading will include the establishment of a public–private technology and design innovation center focused on the footwear industry, which is based on the successful Technology Center model developed in Spain (Centros de Innovación Tecnológica [CITEs]) and replicated in Peru. The main functions of the facility will incorporate:

- Assistance in design development, with a special focus on enhancing product value added and productivity gains
- Production and diffusion of information on market trends in reference to style, fashion, and consumer preferences, including international markets
- Introduction, dissemination, and leasing of modern equipment to small footwear firms
- Demand-driven training and capacity enhancement activities to allow for product improvement, including short-term courses
- Laboratory support for input and product analysis
- Branding strategies.

The design, launch, and running of the technology and design innovation center will be carried out in close consultation with cluster stakeholders, especially SINDINDUSTRIA. The center will be governed by a board of representatives of the state government and members of the private sector in the cluster. Services will be charged according to cost, although initially some subsidy will be included. The idea is that this benefit will be gradually phased out, after which service fees are expected to cover full operational costs.

Marketing initiatives include actions to consolidate the position of FETECC, both nationally and internationally; benchmarking studies; and organization of missions to leading world footwear centers and trade fairs. Cluster actors plan on developing a certificate of origin—"Cariri Footwear"—which will be associated with quality and sustainability. Also part of this marketing plan is establishing a matching fund to cofinance participation of private sector cluster members to take part in missions, trade fairs, and other promotional events.[22]

Enlarging the cluster source base is key to cluster competitiveness. Cluster actors intend to work with the state government to boost input production in the region, and this may include attracting suppliers currently based in the south of the country. Local sourcing is particularly challenging for inputs such as thermoplastic resins, pigments, adhesives, soles, insoles, metal ornaments, molders, and more sophisticated packing items. Another target is to locally source improvements related to specialized services, such as machine maintenance, computer-aided design and manufacturing, styling, and fashion bureaus. In the long run, cluster actors intend to attract footwear equipment plants.

This whole initiative is an innovative approach for the state of Ceará. It relies heavily on private sector actors to ensure successful implementation and the accomplishment of final objectives. Despite the fact that the state government will fund most of the investment, the demand-driven approach and the public–private partnership adopted early on are important elements that should contribute to greater impact. In this context, an important challenge lies in ensuring enhancement of cluster social capital. This element will influence how effective the actors will be in organizing themselves to face tasks, join forces, share responsibilities, and work collectively in pursuing agreed goals (as seen in the cluster road map).

However, the Cariri footwear cluster is not starting from scratch. The strength shown by SINDINDUSTRIA in mobilizing actors, expanding its membership base, holding events such as FETECC, and, in particular, taking the initiative to reach out to small firms, are all significant evidence that the cluster has already accumulated a considerable stock of social capital. Still, further enhancement of social capital will be critical for future cluster growth.

Final Remarks

The Cariri footwear cluster provides points of interest for development planning, in particular related to cases where the challenge is to move from a simple, low-cost base to innovation in a very competitive sector. First, the emergence of the cluster is somewhat surprising. Local development strategies are often based on natural resources. Processing of existing local raw materials emerges as a natural step as regions attempt to enhance the local productive base and promote their economies. Building on what is already available may reduce the risks, costs, and barriers related to starting a business or building a regional industry. In addition, this approach tends to require fewer efforts and resources to produce an economic impact than one that starts from scratch. The history of the Cariri footwear cluster differs from this trajectory of growth based on local resources, as the cluster emerged and then developed the processing of synthetic inputs produced far from the region. It was able to do this by drawing on its inhabitants' previous experience as traders, when they learned how to access sourcing centers and market products, and thus developed a network of strategic contacts.

The Cariri footwear business is also remarkable because it developed spontaneously as a cluster, rather than scattered businesses. As skills and business contacts were disseminated, workshops emerged, production boomed, and the region acquired a reputation as a footwear pole. Footwear buyers and brokers emerged to do business with local shops and the industry later attracted suppliers of inputs and equipment and service providers. This array of actors contributed to further expanding the industry by making it relatively easy for locals to open a footwear workshop as both supply and demand were at hand. Currently, the Cariri footwear cluster is made up of an interweaved network of actors that, though still facing some important weaknesses (for example, coordination, technology support, innovation capability, and skill enhancement), has been an important element expanding businesses and driving cluster competitiveness.

A cluster approach is mostly about coordination of efforts. But in designing a cluster development strategy, it is important to bear in mind that each case is different, and there is no uniform solution. Relationships are important features of industry clusters, and the nature and intensity of the links between different actors determine how effective they can be in promoting the actors' common interests. The structure of the cluster networks differs from one to another and each cluster needs to be assessed and properly addressed. In the case of Cariri, the cluster road map reflects how actors perceive the business in relation to competitors, as well as cluster assets in terms of social capital.

It is also striking that the Cariri footwear cluster managed to establish itself as a major national player in a highly competitive business dominated by some of the most industrialized Brazilian states (for example, Rio Grande do Sul and São Paulo). Located in the poor Northeast, far from Brazil's industrial base, facing difficulties in accessing technology and inputs, the Cariri plastic footwear industry has taken advantage of an abundant labor force and low wages, and focused on the low end of the market, in addition to drawing on firms' flexibility to quickly adapt to industry standards developed in the south of the country.[23] This flexibility includes the promptness and ability to fulfill and share orders, follow trends, copy designs, adapt technology, and reduce costs, as well as using recycled materials.

Moreover, the Cariri footwear cluster stands out as an initiative driven initially by the private sector and market incentives, and less by public policy. Only recently, encouraged by state fiscal incentives, have a few southern firms opened footwear plants in the region. Despite the region's scarcity of capital, the industry was built and developed by locals, rather than outsiders (da Costa 2007). Many firms now of medium size (fewer than 500 workers) opened as workshops in backyards. The ability to draw on local factors (local demand, business networks, a pool of workers, a secondhand equipment market, and others) was an important ingredient for industry growth.

Finally, this case illustrates the importance of the cluster organization process, including the design and implementation of cluster-based economic strategies. Through this process, actors in the Cariri footwear cluster have been able to identify and agree on key steps to plan for business development, including vision, strategies, and actions. The process also shows the importance of the cluster facilitator role in ensuring continuous cluster mobilization to implement and follow through on the approved development strategy.

Notes

1. The three urban municipalities had approximately 400,000 inhabitants in 2000.

2. Barbalha is the center of the Cariri health sector and is home to the region's largest hospital.

3. Farming in Crato reflects the size of the municipality (1,009 square kilometers, or nearly twice the size of Barbalha and more than four times the size of Juazeiro). The importance of research activities relates to the fact that Crato is home to the Regional University of Cariri (URCA), a state-funded institution.

4. Juazeiro emerged in the early 20th century as a regional commercial center, as well as a manufacturing location for basic products.

5. During 2002–05, average GDP growth for the three municipalities was 43.9 percent, compared to 41.6 percent for the state of Ceará.

6. As RAIS captures only formal employment, employment numbers for agriculture are underestimated. This is less common in Cariri, where agriculture is mainly a family business, rather than a firm undertaking.

7. The Northeast region is made up of nine states, totaling 1.5 million square kilometers, and equivalent to roughly 18 percent of Brazil's territory.

8. PVC (full form polyvinyl chloride) is a thermoplastic polymer. EVA (ethylene-vinyl acetate) is a polymer used to absorb physical shock and is used in athletic materials and shoe soles.

9. Estimate by the local SEBRAE accounts for an additional 200 informal firms.

10. Abicalçados (the Brazilian Footwear Industry Association) estimated national footwear production at 800 million pairs in 2006. http://www.abicalcados.com.br/estatisticas.html.

11. The cost of this equipment is approximately US$560,000.

12. In the early 1990s, the SME association (AFABRICAL) established a centralized supply facility. But this closed after a short period of operation because of poor management and individual defaults.

13. Retailers of inputs are locally known as *casas coureiras.*

14. Rio Grande do Sul is Brazil's largest footwear manufacturer and specializes in leather items.

15. The volume of plastic material recycled by local footwear firms is approximately 600 tons per month; material comes from as far away as Belém, 1,600 kilometers from the Cariri region.

16. Excluding mandatory fringe benefits, which average 85 percent of the wage amount.

17. Labor costs in the South, at the beginning of this century, were nearly three times as high as in the Northeast.

18. The government-funded Banco do Brasil is also an important financial agency in the region, but focuses on short-term credit and banking services to municipal governments, management of public transfers (for example, pension funds and federal government transfers to municipalities), commercial businesses, and individual accounts.

19. BNB criteria for firm size are different from the ones used in this chapter, as they relate to annual gross revenue. For micro, small, medium, and large firms, correspondent values are, respectively, below US$141,000, below US$1.4 million, below US$20.5 million, and greater than US$20.5 million.

20. SME representatives report that collateral requirements may reach 150 percent of loans, and that firms have difficulty in providing the mandatory legal papers certifying property. BNB argues that it is forbidden by law to lend money without requiring legal property documents of assets offered as collateral.

21. Ceará Regional Development Project (Cidades do Ceará), proposed to be partially funded by the World Bank.

22. Resources for the fund will come out of a World Bank loan to the State of Ceará (Cidades do Ceará).

23. Wages paid by the Cariri footwear industry are estimated to be half those paid by the industry in Brazil's southern states.

CHAPTER 5

São Luís Cluster Development Strategy: An Initial Assessment

Ming Zhang, Daniel da Mata, Alec Hansen,
Enrique Asturizaga, and Kim Cuenco

Background

This case study presents an initial assessment of São Luís, Maranhão, in terms of its potential and strategies for economic competitiveness. It was written after a local economic development mission to the city in January 2008, made by a team of World Bank staff and consultants. Additional limited data analysis was conducted after the mission. The chapter is divided into five parts: after introducing the municipality and its recent policy initiatives on local economic development, it analyzes the economic structure and its evolution in recent years, using data analysis to understand the key drivers of the regional and municipal economies and to identify the main clusters of the local economy. This is followed by initial analyses and strategies for two identified priority clusters: the port-industrial cluster and the tourism cluster. The chapter concludes by outlining an overall cluster strategy and the next steps.

São Luís Municipality

The municipality of São Luís, the capital of the state of Maranhão, is located on the island of São Luís in the extreme north of the

Northeast. The "island" is, in fact, an archipelago of 62 islands com-prising 720 square kilometers of land and an additional 150 square kilometers of mangrove swamps. The archipelago contains the metro-politan region of São Luís, which is divided into four municipalities with a total metropolitan population of more than 1 million, of which over 900,000 people reside in the São Luís municipality. The metro-politan region is home to a significant industrial sector with potential to expand, and its Itaqui seaport is an important driver for develop-ment, given its strategic location, depth, and modern facilities. The city is of historical significance, and the United Nations Educational, Scientific, and Cultural Organization (UNESCO) has declared its colonial center a UNESCO World Heritage Site. The archipelago is distinguished by ecological diversity, encompassing mangroves, ripar-ian forests, and patches of Amazonian forest, which, in combination with over 30 kilometers of beaches, offer substantial potential for ecotourism.

Despite this potential, São Luís is located in one of the poorest and least developed states of Brazil; Maranhão ranks close to last in per capita household income, access to services, and health indicators. The major-ity of the state's population supports itself through subsistence agricul-ture, but there is a trend toward higher-productivity activities, including manufacturing and transportation. This is stimulating migration to cities generally, and to São Luís in particular.

Municipal Initiatives for a Development Strategy

In recent years, the municipal government of São Luís has taken several steps to enhance economic and employment development, including:

- *Creation of the Secretary of Planning and Development (SEPLAN) and Sub-Secretary of Sustainable Development (SAGED).* In 2005, the position of SEPLAN was created with the aim of initiating a highly participative process to achieve sustainable development for São Luís. The process started in March 2006, with a workshop to set an agenda for sustainable local economic development. The post of SAGED was created to propose and promote municipal policies for local economic and employment development. SAGED develops and supports specific projects to create favorable conditions for eco-nomic development and job and income generation, and, with other secretaries and main municipal stakeholders, articulates activities for local economic development.

• *Permanent Forum for Sustainable Development and "São Luís + 400 Years."* The municipal authorities created the Permanent Forum for Sustainable Development in April 2006, with the participation of all main stakeholders of the municipalities, including representatives of the poor, the private sector, government institutions, and other civil institutions. The main goals of the forum are to balance the needs of promoting growth and development, protecting the environment, reducing poverty, fostering environmental sustainability, and setting forth the conditions for a sustainable future. The forum has been quite successful not only in attracting the most important institutions in São Luís, but also in participating in key issues such as the municipal development strategy "São Luís + 400 Years." This strategy aims to become a key instrument for improving the living conditions for the population, especially the poor. It has a time span of 20 years, with a particular focus on 2012, or São Luís' 400th anniversary. The first draft, main directions, and long-term vision were delivered on September 4, 2007. The strategy addresses likely scenarios, devises guidelines for participatory management of the city, and guides the municipal administration's decision making.

• *Socioeconomic Mapping and Development of the Local Economic and Employment Program.* The municipal government has launched an important process to understand the economic and social aspects of the municipality. It is developing an indicator framework based on four pillars (local economic structure, human resources, local endowments, and institutional capacity) and is in the process of identifying primary and secondary sources for data collection and analysis. This framework will be used to identify strengths, weaknesses, threats, and main opportunities for sustainable local economic development. Moreover, under a World Bank–financed project, the municipality has allocated US$6.2 million for its local economic and employment program. It will support capacity building for job and income generation, and the development of a local economic development and competitiveness strategy, which includes a competitive upgrading strategy for critical clusters, simplification of business processes, and other actions that are recommended from the cluster enhancement process.

Analysis of Economic Structure

Advantages and Disadvantages

In the last few years, São Luís has experienced high GDP growth. From 2002 to 2005, the annual real GDP growth rate was 10.2 percent (table 5.1). The difference among the selected regions is significant. São Luís outperformed the other regions and saw a rate of growth almost twice as fast as the national average. As in the Brazilian economy, the service sector in São Luís accounts for more than 60 percent of total GDP, and industry about 23 percent.

São Luís has shown a steady increase in its per capita income as well (table 5.2). The annual growth rate during the 1990s was 3.2 percent, according to the 1991 and 2000 population censuses. For this indicator, the Maranhão and Northeast growth rates were higher than that of São Luís.

A comparison between per capita income growth rates and GDP per capita growth rates is important, even though we are dealing with different periods of time. Since estimated population growth in 2002–05 was 2.09 percent (table 5.3), GDP per capita growth in São Luís was around 8 percent during that period, compared to 3.2 percent income per capita growth in 1991–2000. These trends may suggest that returns to the factors of production did not stay entirely in São Luís. In other words, what

Table 5.1   GDP, Selected Regions, 2002 and 2005

Regions	2002 (R$)	2005 (R$)	Annual growth, 2002–05 (%)
São Luís	5,613,502	7,514,838	10.2
Maranhão	15,448,774	20,374,787	9.6
Northeast region	191,591,603	225,667,141	5.6
Brazil	1,477,821,769	1,727,465,239	5.3

Source: IBGE.
Note: Deflated to 2002 values.

Table 5.2   Monthly Per Capita Incomes, Selected Regions, 1991 and 2000

Regions	1991 (R$)	2000 (R$)	Annual growth, 1991–2000 (%)
São Luís	189	252	3.2
Maranhão	80	110	3.6
Northeast region	114	155	3.4
Brazil	230	297	2.9

Source: IBGE.

Table 5.3   Population Trends for Selected Regions

Regions	1991	2000	Annual growth, 1991–2000 (%)	Annual growth, 2002–05 (%)
São Luís	666,433	870,028	3.01	2.09
Maranhão	4,930,275	5,651,475	1.53	1.37
Northeast	42,497,643	47,741,711	1.30	1.19
Brazil	146,825,807	169,799,170	1.63	1.45

Source: IBGE.

is being produced in São Luís does not reverberate in salaries or profits to the municipality. And given that São Luís' per capita income is below the national average, it becomes more important to pursue policies to boost local income growth and to encourage local economies to benefit more, proportionally, from the economic growth.

With regard to the distribution of growth in the 1990s, income has grown in every income bracket, but the rate of growth among the poorest segments was slower than among other income groups. Therefore, despite an average per capita income increase, income inequality widened in São Luís. Indeed, according to IBGE data, the Gini index (a measure of income inequality) rose from 0.61 in 1991 to 0.65 in 2000.

The population is also increasing faster in São Luís than in the other regions (table 5.3). Populations can grow (or decline) through three factors: fertility rate, mortality rate, and migration. Once the fertility rate and mortality rate do not vary much across regions, population growth is attributable to migration. The 3 percent annual population growth rate in the municipality for 1991–2000, compared to the Brazilian and Maranhão rates of roughly 1.5 percent, suggests intense immigration to the city. This strong pattern stands out even more when one remembers that the Northeast's population growth rate is smaller, as the region has had a historical propensity to net out-migration.

On the one hand, immigration shows that the city is indeed attractive to people, otherwise migrants would go elsewhere. A more detailed analysis is required, but it is clear that income and GDP growth rates are driving migrants' decisions. On the other hand, these new "citizens" demand public services, pressuring for efficient public policies.

The characteristics of migrants are also important indicators of the local economy. Those with several years of schooling generally have more positive outcomes (both for themselves and for the city), because they are likely to be more productive. Therefore, any city should include measures

Table 5.4   Migration to Selected Regions, 1995–2000

Regions	Ratio of out-migration to immigration	Ratio of out-migration to immigration (skilled)
São Luís	0.971	1.096
Maranhão	1.279	0.816
Northeast region	1.380	0.917

Source: IBGE.

in its strategic planning to attract qualified migrants—those with greater skills and education attainment. In the decision to migrate or not and where to relocate, the qualified migrant ponders several city characteristics (da Mata et al. 2007). Labor market, climate, and quality of public services and other amenities are important factors in attracting (or repelling) this category of migrants.

Table 5.4 shows that São Luís receives more immigrants than it loses emigrants (since the outmigration to immigration ratio there is less than one). The opposite is the case in Maranhão and the Northeast region. However, São Luís is not attracting skilled migrants: worse, it is suffering from a "brain drain." In sum, the city is attracting migrants, but not skilled ones.

Employment Structure

Table 5.5 shows formal employment growth from 1995 to 2005 at the 2-digit level, according to the Classificação Nacional de Atividades Econômicas (National Classification of Economic Activities, or CNAE).[1] Commerce and some retail activities experienced a formal employment growth rate of more than 60 percent for the whole period, or more than 5 percent per year. Construction and real estate activities were also important growth sectors, since they had an increase of roughly 50 percent in employment. Manufacturing lost around 2,000 formal workers in the period. More recently, from 2000 to 2005, finance services appeared to be a high-growth sector.

A notable feature was the fall in formal public sector employment (figure 5.1). In 1995, São Luís had 45 percent of its formal labor force in public sector activities, a proportion that fell to 35 percent in 2005. The decrease took place mainly after 2000. In contrast, finance and real estate, as well as commerce and construction, expanded their shares.

Most formal workers in São Luís have no more than high school education (59 percent in 2005, table 5.6), 24 percent have received basic schooling, and only 16 percent have college degrees or higher. Those who

Table 5.5   Formal Employment Trends, 1995–2005

2-digit sector	Formal employment share (%)			Growth (%)	
	1995	2000	2005	1995–2005	2000–2005
Agriculture and forestry	2.2	0.2	0.4	−81	124
Fishing	0.0	0.0	0.0	−68	631
Mining	0.1	0.1	0.0	−56	−32
Manufacturing	5.0	4.1	3.4	−32	−17
Utilities	2.2	1.2	1.0	−55	−20
Construction	5.1	8.2	7.5	48	−9
Commerce	10.3	12.4	16.7	63	35
Food and beverage retail sales	1.5	2.1	2.7	86	30
Transportation, warehouses, and communication	6.3	5.8	7.0	11	21
Finance services	2.1	1.3	2.5	21	96
Real estate services	7.2	8.0	10.4	44	30
Public services	45.7	44.5	34.9	−24	−22
Education services	3.3	4.1	3.0	−9	−26
Health services	4.0	4.0	5.3	32	33
Other services	3.7	4.1	5.0	37	24
Total employment (number and % for growth)	**161,435**	**172,478**	**180,928**	**12**	**5**

Source: RAIS, Ministry of Labor.

have been educated to the high school and college level (or higher) are more attracted to finance and education services.

In 2005, according to table 5.7, , banking activities, electric power generation and distribution, and transportation paid the highest mean salaries to formal workers, at least twice as much. The total wages (*massa salarial*) in São Luís' formal sector amount to more than R$190 million, or an average wage of R$1,056 (around US$580).

The cross-tabulation of LQs (which show sector importance) and employment growth, as explained in the section "Location quotient analysis" in chapter 4 for the Cariri region, helps identify important sectors and clusters in the local economy. Table 5.8 shows results of the LQ versus employment growth at the 4-digit level. Generally, sectors that appear in each quadrant are as follows:

- **High importance, high growth:** Transportation, real estate, social capital, infrastructure, health, and culture and entertainment activities

Figure 5.1   Evolution of Employment Share (1995–2005)

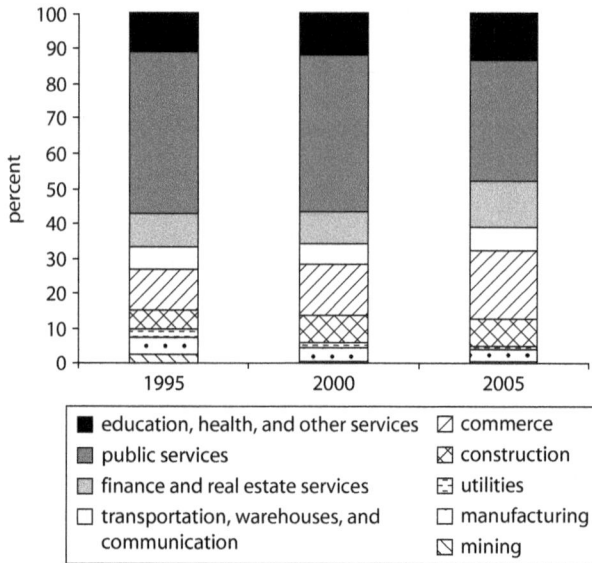

Legend:
- ■ education, health, and other services
- ▨ commerce
- ▦ public services
- ▧ construction
- ▤ finance and real estate services
- ▤ utilities
- ☐ transportation, warehouses, and communication
- ☐ manufacturing
- ◩ mining

Source: RAIS, Ministry of Labor.

Table 5.6   Formal Employment and Schooling, 2005

2-digit sector	Illiterate (%)	Basic school (%)	High school (%)	College or higher (%)	Total (number)
Agriculture and forestry	3	20	65	12	744
Fishing	0	30	70	0	23
Mining	2	53	37	8	89
Manufacturing	1	28	63	9	6,205
Utilities	0	15	57	28	1,787
Construction	1	48	47	4	13,591
Commerce	0	12	82	5	30,301
Food and beverage retail sales	0	28	70	2	4,924
Transportation, warehouses, and communication	0	25	63	12	12,635
Finance services	0	1	50	48	4,558
Real estate services	1	25	68	6	18,800
Public services	0	29	46	24	63,064
Education services	0	6	40	54	5,478
Health services	0	12	77	11	9,602
Other services	1	24	55	20	9,082
Domestic services	7	36	52	5	44
Total (number)	**535**	**44,048**	**107,095**	**29,250**	**180,928**
%	**0**	**24**	**59**	**16**	**100**

Source: RAIS, Ministry of Labor.

Table 5.7   Formal Employment and Top 20 Mean Wages, 2005

4-digit subsector	Total wages[a] (R$)	Average wage[b] (R$)	Share of mean wage (%)
Pipeline transportation	175,652	7,637	723
Electric power generation	997,067	5,601	530
Manganese mining	5,352	5,352	507
Forestry activities	25,759	3,680	348
Public banking	1,964,728	3,399	322
Commercial banking	179,151	3,257	308
Defense	713,862	3,173	300
Multiple banking[c]	3,798,164	3,034	287
Other financial activities	5,887,568	2,980	282
Industrial gas manufacturing	45,226	2,827	268
Justice and public order	6,522,531	2,717	257
Oil (wholesale)	387,874	2,502	237
Electric power distribution	1,524,474	2,447	232
Coastal transportation	208,249	2,422	229
Nonmetallic mineral mining	2,334	2,334	221
Interurban rail transportation	5,181,892	2,108	200
Pension funds	145,431	2,108	200
Aluminum production and processing	41,631	2,082	197
Agriculture-related services	666,984	2,046	194
Support activities for cargo transportation	942,429	1,988	188
All employment	**191,065,378**	**1,056**	**100**

Source: RAIS, Ministry of Labor.
a. The sum of all salaries in the 4-digit subsector.
b. The mean wage of a representative formal worker.
c. Banks that have functions of commercial banks and investment banks.

- **High importance, low growth:** Social capital activities (unions), banking, beverage manufacturing, real estate, health, culture and entertainment activities, and hotels
- **Low importance, low growth:** Agriculture, fishing, mining, some manufacturing activities, some high-tech-related activities, and consulting activities
- **Low importance, high growth:** Publishing, some manufacturing activities (for example, hardware), food services, and professional services (legal, medical, dental, architectural, advertising, and engineering).

Activities related to tourism appear mostly in the high-importance, low-growth quadrant (mainly culture and entertainment activities and hotels), and although important, have not grown as much in recent

Table 5.8   LQ and Employment Growth: Major Sectors in Each Quadrant

High importance, low growth	High importance, high growth
Distillery, purification, and bottling of liquor	Building of complete constructions n.e.c.
Manufacture of stout and beer	Construction of dams for hydroelectric power generation
Manufacture of soft drinks	Wholesale of tobacco products
Manufacture of organic chemicals n.e.c.	Retail sales of furniture and other residential-use products
Collection, purification, and distribution of water	Retail sales of books, newspapers, journals, and stationery
Building of complete residential and business constructions	Transport by interurban railroads
Assembly of structures	Transport of passengers by inland water ways
Air conditioning and refrigeration system installations	Activities related to water transport n.e.c.
Wholesale of pharmaceutical, medical, and dental products	Activities related to air transport n.e.c.
Transport of urban passengers by road, scheduled	Activities of transport and freight-handling agencies
Transport by coastal water	National post activities
Savings and loan banking	Pension funding, open funds
Pension funding, closed funds	Health insurance
Real estate management for third parties	Renting of construction and civil engineering machinery and equipment
Hospital activities in emergency rooms	Investigation and security activities
Other human health activities by health professionals	Diagnostic and therapeutic human health activities
Human health activities n.e.c.	Social work without accommodation
Other entertainment activities n.e.c.	Sewage and refuse disposal, sanitation, and similar activities
Retail sales of food and beverages in convenience stores	Activities of other membership organizations n.e.c.
Hotels	Television activities
Low importance, low growth	**Low importance, high growth**
Agriculture and fishing activities	Manufacture of foods n.e.c.
Mining of iron ore	Manufacture of textile products from fabrics
Mining of aluminum	Knitting of textile products n.e.c.
Mining of manganese ore	Publishing and printing of other products
Manufacture of fruit and vegetable juice	Manufacture of hardware

Several food manufacturing activities
Manufacture of fruit and vegetable juice
Manufacture of textile goods n.e.c.
Manufacture of leather products n.e.c.
Manufacture of paper
Reproduction of software
Manufacture of cement
Manufacture of construction machinery and equipment
Computer hardware consultancy
Data processing
Computer-related activities n.e.c.
Business and management consultancy activities
Dramatic arts, music, and other arts activities

Manufacture of general-purpose machinery n.e.c.
Manufacture of medical and therapeutic apparatus
Demolition and construction site preparation
Building of large constructions and art work
Sale of motor vehicles
Wholesale of industrial machinery and equipment
Restaurants and bars with complete service
Luncheonettes and similar eateries
Cargo handling and warehousing
Legal activities
Architectural and engineering activities and technical consultancy
Advertising
Medical and dental practice activities
Activities of professional and political organizations

Source: Authors' calculations.
Note: n.e.c. = not elsewhere classified.

years. Food services, another important sector for tourism, comes out in the low-importance, high-growth quadrant, and is therefore a potential emerging cluster.

Several transportation subsectors—the necessary foundations for a port cluster—come out in the high-importance, high-growth quadrant. Several other subsectors of the transportation sector appear in the high-low quadrant. These outcomes suggest that transportation and port sectors are relevant to a local development strategy. In addition, transportation is a sector that pays one of the best salaries in the São Luís economy.

Another result was the classification of high-tech sectors as low employment growth and low LQ. Innovation is one of the main components for a successful growth path and high-tech industries are one of the most innovative. Its extremely limited presence should be a concern in terms of sustained growth potential.

Again, as with the Cariri region, shift-share analysis was applied as an alternative method for identifying leading and lagging economic sectors. Shift share disaggregates local employment growth into three components:

- *National shift:* changes in the local economy because of changes in the national economy
- *Industrial mix shift:* changes in the local economy due to the mix of industries
- *Local shift:* changes in local employment due to local factors or local/city/municipality competitiveness.

Shift-share disaggregates the total employment growth according to the following equation:

total employment change = national shift
+ industrial mix shift
+ local shift

The interpretation of the shift-share results is straightforward. National growth share tells what part of local job growth is simply because of growth in the national economy. Industry mix represents the effect on particular industry performance and trends on local employment. Local shift emphasizes local/city/municipality factors effects' over local employment growth (or decline).

For instance, shift-share analysis shows how much of the total employment increase in the São Luís' "wholesale of hardware, construction and equipment and tools" sector was due to Brazilian economic dynamics, how much to the national wholesale hardware sector, and how much to São Luís economic competitiveness and dynamics. In this case, according to table 5.9, almost all employment creation was due to São Luís economic competitiveness and dynamics, consistent with its recent GDP growth rates.

Table 5.9 shows the 10 leading sectors in terms of employment growth as a consequence of local economic competitiveness and dynamics. All these sectors are considered dynamic, indicating that the local factor contributed more to job growth than either the national factor or the sector factor. Table 5.10 presents the 10 leading sectors with more than 1,000 formal workers in 2005. The results show that some of the large sectors are dynamic while others are not. The idea is to control for national economic growth and industry performance nationwide. It is important to

Table 5.9   Top 10 Leading Four-Digit Subsectors, 2000 and 2005

Top 10 sectors (local dynamics)	2000	2005	Growth	National shift	Industrial mix shift	Local shift
	Employment			Shift share		
Activities auxiliary to financial intermediation n.e.c.	3	1,976	1,973	1	2	1,970
Social work without accommodation	507	2,132	1,625	136	32	1,457
Drilling and foundation building for civil construction	45	812	767	12	5	750
Transport by interurban railroads	1,446	2,458	1,012	386	47	578
Sewage and refuse disposal, sanitation, and similar activities	817	1,608	791	218	51	522
Building of large constructions and art work	46	514	468	12	2	454
Manufacture of prefabricated metal structures and components	99	428	329	26	18	284
Catering	309	832	523	83	195	245
Wholesale of food products n.e.c.	276	686	410	74	121	215
Wholesale of hardware, construction, and equipment and tools	34	276	242	9	20	213

Source: Authors' calculations.
Note: n.e.c. = not elsewhere classified.

Table 5.10 Top 10 Four-Digit Subsectors with More Than 1,000 Workers in 2000 and 2005

Sectors	Employment			National share	Industrial mix share	Local shift	Index[a]
	2000	2005	Growth				
Transport by interurban railroads	1,446	2,458	1,012	386	47	578	Dynamic
Social work without accommodation	507	2,132	1,625	136	32	1,457	Dynamic
Activities auxiliary to financial intermediation n.e.c.	3	1,976	1,973	1	2	1,970	Dynamic
Sewage and refuse disposal, sanitation, and similar activities	817	1,608	791	218	51	522	Dynamic
Retail sales of footwear, leather products, and luggage	646	1,051	405	173	77	156	Nondynamic
Activities of other membership organizations n.e.c.	2,559	3,763	1,204	684	445	75	Nondynamic
Retail sales of construction materials, tools, and hand tools	1,447	2,127	680	387	287	6	Nondynamic
Retail sales of furniture, lighting products, and residential-use products	1,385	1,955	570	370	174	26	Nondynamic
Building of complete constructions n.e.c.	1,042	1,881	839	278	540	20	Nondynamic
Retail sales of food and beverages in stores smaller than 300 square meters	538	1,094	556	144	225	187	Nondynamic
Retail sales of office and computing and telecommunications equipment	513	1,047	534	137	379	18	Nondynamic

Source: Authors' calculations.

a. Dynamic means a positive contribution of the local economy for job creation at a higher rate than the national economy and the national sector.

Note: n.e.c. = not elsewhere classified.

identify local sectors that were able to prosper in excess of, or despite, national performance.

Conclusions from Economic Data Analysis

The complete list of 136 "competitive" sectors reveals a similar scenario to the previous section's analysis of LQ versus employment growth. Activities related to transportation and tourism had a very powerful local competitiveness factor. Services, especially legal, medical, dental, architectural, advertising, and engineering, have lower local dynamics.

The analysis highlighted the following strengths of the local economy:

- Economic growth has been faster in recent years, almost double the speed of national average. Per capita income growth also grew faster than the national average.
- The city is attractive to people, with a population increase double the national and state averages.
- Private sector employment has shown a significant increase, reducing the share of public sector employment from 45 percent to 35 percent in 10 years.

Notable weaknesses include the following:

- Income generated within the region is not being captured by the region.
- The poorest did not benefit as much from recent growth as the overall population.
- Skilled migrants are not attracted to the city.
- Large migrant inflows have added high pressure to infrastructure and public services.

Economic structural analysis leads to the following conclusions:

- São Luís is a major regional commercial and political center, as demonstrated by the importance of real estate, health, infrastructure and public services, and social activities. Its role as a regional commercial center has strengthened in recent years.
- Transportation is a major cluster and fast growing, reflecting the importance of the ports of São Luís and other facilities.
- Overall, tourism does not seem to have been a main driver of the local economy in recent years. It covers a wide range of activities, some in the high importance, slow growth category (hotels, food retailing, and

entertainment) and others are in the low-importance, high-growth category (restaurants, bars, and eateries). However, tourism should be viewed in the context of São Luís as a regional commercial center; therefore business tourism, in addition to recreational tourism, should be considered seriously in the cluster and overall growth strategy.

• There appears to be an emerging cluster of business services (cargo handling and warehousing, advertising, engineering consultancy, and professional organizations), which is either related to the role of the ports or to the nature of the city as a regional commercial center. This cluster may well generate a future positive impact for business.

• Some manufacturing activities (food, textiles, hardware, machinery, and medical apparatus) also seem to be gaining ground and would seem to have potential in the city.

Initial Assessment of the Port-Industrial Cluster

Cluster Background

The potential for a cluster based around the ports in São Luís stems from two distinct but related agglomerations:

• The three major (and four smaller) deep-water ports, and their related suppliers
• Existing and potential manufacturing industries located near the ports.

Either one of these agglomerations alone would be enough to justify a cluster approach; both together represent a major opportunity for alignment of priorities and synergistic growth. Thus at this stage, the appropriate "cluster" from a collaborative strategy development perspective would include the transportation and logistics functions of a port-based cluster, combined with those in an industrial park or duty-free zone (*zona franca*). If this joint transportation–industrial nexus is established and takes off, the cluster can be disaggregated into separate port and (possibly several) industry clusters.

Overview of the Three Major Ports. The major ports share an approach channel that is 108 meters wide and 27 meters deep, with current depths of 19 meters at the municipal port and 23 meters at Vale's, which means that they can likely accommodate cargo vessels of any tonnage in the world. This seaport has the best natural physical conditions in Brazil and all of South America. All the ports are protected from winds and waves, and the region is not subject to hurricanes, like Caribbean ports. The region is in a good position to profit from the expansion of the Panama Canal. However, these ports are not well known, and need greater recognition worldwide. Of the three major deep-water ports, one is public (Itaqui) and two (for bulk handling) are owned and operated by private mining and metals-processing conglomerates (Alumar and Vale).

Porto do Itaqui—Maranhão's Municipal General Cargo Port. The port of Itaqui has 6 berths, with depths up to 19 meters and length of 480 meters, and has a plan to add another 12 berths to the south of the existing berths. Currently, there is limited container traffic—almost none goes out while inflows are mainly consumer and capital goods. Also, there are no specialized container cranes. However, dry cargos (for example, aluminum ingots from Alumar trucked to Itaqui and loaded onto vessels using pallets), liquid cargos (fuel), and bulk cargos (especially soybeans) are relatively common. Total shipments in 2007 amounted to 94 million tons.

Ponta da Madeira—Vale's Private Terminal. Vale is a diversified mining company producing a variety of metal products in São Luís, mainly iron, copper, and nickel. The São Luís facility currently processes 105 million tons of iron ore per year, and after the R$4 billion expansion due to be completed in 2011, it will be able to process 240 million tons, making it the largest iron ore and pellet processing facility in the world. The current employment level at the facility is 6,000. The port is 23 meters in depth, and accommodates vessels with drafts up to 22 meters. Each berth handles 45 million tons per year, with a maximum loading rate of 16,000 tons per hour. By 2010, Vale's logistics arm (a subsidiary separate from the mining operations) will complete the final section of a north–south railroad link to the interior of Brazil, which will greatly augment the importance of São Luís as a logistical hub.

Porto da Alumar—Alumar's Private Terminal. Alumar is one of the largest producers of aluminum in the world, with a major ownership share by Alcoa. The company brings in bauxite from the interior of Brazil (mostly by ship via the Amazon) and processes it at the refinery (to produce alumina) and then smelters it (further processing into aluminum) in São Luís. Alumar's port currently handles 4.9 million tons per year, but it is currently undergoing expansion that will allow three full berths, expected to handle 12 million tons a year. While all the bulk cargo is handled at

Alumar's own port, the actual processed aluminum is stacked on pallets and trucked from Alumar to Itaqui port and loaded onto ships using their cranes—about 440,000 tons per year. Total employment by Alumar in São Luís is about 2,000, but another 1,500 are estimated to be employed locally, indirectly, via subcontracting.

Each year, Vale hires some 50 mining engineers, 50 civil engineers, 30 mechanical engineers, 30 electrical engineers, 30 railroad engineers, and 20 port engineers. The local universities cannot produce enough engineers to meet this demand. However as the region positions itself to become a metals-processing and logistics hub, expansion of the engineering school in some of these specializations is probably justified.

Ports' Growth Potential. Transshipments through São Luís' ports are expected to expand significantly in 2010, with the completion of the north–south railroad. Locals point out that external demand may notch up again when the Panama Canal is widened, because this is one of the only deep-water port systems in the region, and Brazil's closest major port system to the canal. The depth and width of the various channels would accommodate the largest cargo vessels under consideration.

Existing Port-Industrial Cluster. During workshops held in São Luís in January 2008, participants, comprising cluster members and the municipal government, identified producers and service providers in the cluster. As shown in figure 5.2, there are other industrial users of the port system, such as Coca-Cola and Brasil Ecodiesel. In addition, the system offers many intermediate and final services, ranging from cleaning and maintenance to fueling.

Initial Diagnostics
Supply/Input Conditions. The existing port facilities are adequate for the current quantities of metals processed in São Luís. However, significant expansion is anticipated in the near future for all three major ports: Itaqui (from 6 to 18 berths), Vale (doubling of capacity), and Alumar (tripling of capacity). What this will actually create, especially near the public port, is an artificially generated shortage of land. The need for large tracts suitable for port-related warehousing and logistics will increase—even more so if São Luís is seen as an attractive location for related manufacturing activities (from steel mills to machinery production to food processing).

Human resources are another significant issue on the factor side. Workforce training is weak by Brazilian standards, with low education

Figure 5.2   Current Map of Port Cluster, São Luís

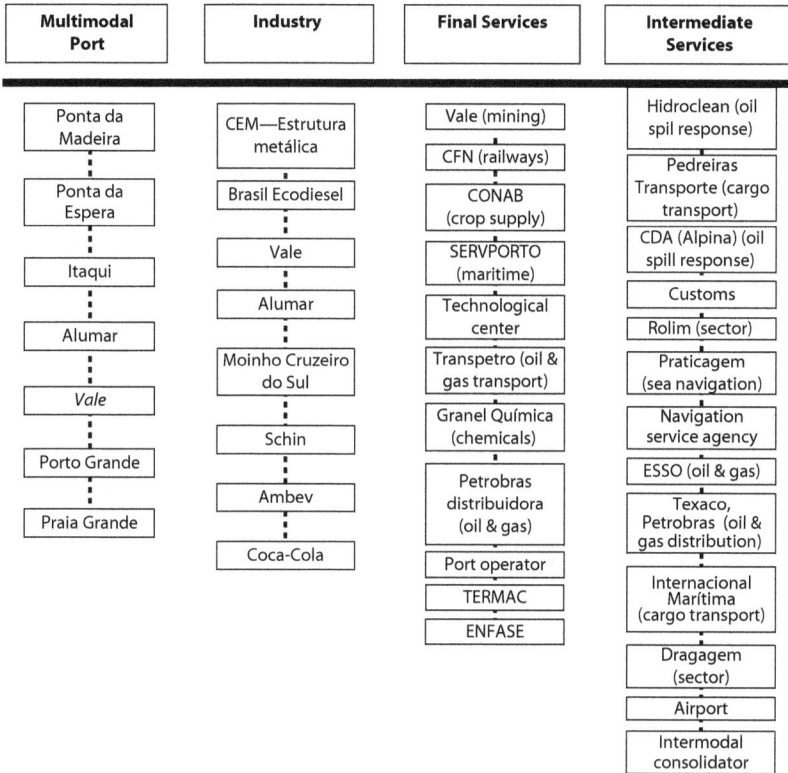

Multimodal Port	Industry	Final Services	Intermediate Services
Ponta da Madeira	CEM—Estrutura metálica	Vale (mining)	Hidroclean (oil spil response)
Ponta da Espera	Brasil Ecodiesel	CFN (railways)	Pedreiras Transporte (cargo transport)
Itaqui	Vale	CONAB (crop supply)	CDA (Alpina) (oil spill response)
Alumar	Alumar	SERVPORTO (maritime)	Customs
Vale	Moinho Cruzeiro do Sul	Technological center	Rolim (sector)
Porto Grande	Schin	Transpetro (oil & gas transport)	Praticagem (sea navigation)
Praia Grande	Ambev	Granel Química (chemicals)	Navigation service agency
	Coca-Cola	Petrobras distribuidora (oil & gas)	ESSO (oil & gas)
		Port operator	Texaco, Petrobras (oil & gas distribution)
		TERMAC	Internacional Marítima (cargo transport)
		ENFASE	Dragagem (sector)
			Airport
			Intermodal consolidator

Source: Workshop for cluster members and municipal government, São Luís, January 2008.

levels and relatively undistinguished local universities. This will require a long-term effort. Vale alone estimated in 2008 that it would need to hire 260 engineers per year over the next three years in various categories (electrical, mechanical, mining, civil, port, and railroad), and it appears that local universities are ill equipped to handle this demand at present.

Demand Conditions. On the whole, national and international demand are driving the cluster. The current trend of global demand for commodities and materials points to further increases in demand, if perhaps not in the immediate future. To the extent that the potential cluster represents an amalgam of a port (transportation and logistics) cluster with a heavy industry cluster, the existence of two large metals and mining firms has created local demand for port services. However, since both have their own ports, and only Alumar uses the municipal port (Itaqui) for exports (of aluminum ingots), even in this respect, local demand is not a significant factor driving innovation or excellence. There is potential for the port system to further tap the hinterland's potential, and this would require the construction of dedicated container berths.

Business Environment. Two factors related to the business environment are causes for concern—"red tape" and the industrial structure. For the former, the relatively antiquated regulatory structure will remain a serious constraint to private investment in the region. The lack of clear and predictable procedures on zoning, permits, and rights-of-way is hampering the region's ability to attract new manufacturing investments. This constraint can be improved significantly in a short time with better coordination among the different government agencies, and strong political leadership.

On the latter, the existence of a single, large public sector entity (the municipal port) and two large private sector entities (Alumar and Vale) does not lend itself to a healthy sense of rivalry nor a rich environment for spin-offs and start-ups. Nevertheless, the two private firms see the value of promoting more similar industries, such as steel mills and machinery manufacturers, if only to anchor their operations with greater local demand; therefore, they can be counted on to actively support the diversification effort. The two firms will feel the pinch in recruiting talented staff: currently they have the luxury of selecting only the best, but this may translate into an even greater commitment to improving the educational system at all levels. Both companies appear to be closely involved in community assistance projects, such as education and environmental protection, which augurs well for a wider cluster strategy commitment.

Related and Supporting Industries. Despite the current dominance by three large port entities (Vale, Alumar, and Itaqui), the cluster map shows that there are multiple smaller entities, both in industry- and port-related services. While linkages are currently weak, the potential for evolution of specialized service providers will grow if throughput at the port system expands. Similarly, the establishment of two or three new manufacturing entities would significantly expand the richness of the local environment and its ability to support innovative suppliers and new institutions for collaboration. In fact several large companies, including Petrobras, Vale, and Alumar, already have plans to make significant investments in São Luís and its vicinity in the next few years.

It is common in São Luís to conclude that, since agriculture on the island (that is, within the municipality), once quite a significant food producer in its own right, has now shrunk to only 3 percent of the land area, the food-processing industry will also necessarily shrink. However, with the island surrounded by agriculture-dominated regions, the potential for São Luís to become a significant center for food processing, which can in turn be tied into the tourism cluster's vibrancy, is significant. The potential linkage to tourism via a greater number of visits from cruise ships remains to be explored. The city's rich cultural heritage and the UNESCO designation of the historic district can be significant draws. Other activities, such as visits to the Lençóis Maranhenses National Park, need to be closely integrated.

Potential Expansion Path. The cluster members envisaged the "desirable" cluster composition in the workshops in January 2008. As shown in figure 5.3, by 2010, the port system should have consolidated its expansion. The two mining and metal giants have both announced major expansions, increasing throughput nearly 2.5 times current levels over the next three years.

Some steps in the direction of attracting and expanding other industries, and linkages to other types of transportation services (for example,

Figure 5.3   Potential Expansion of the São Luís Port System by 2010 and 2013

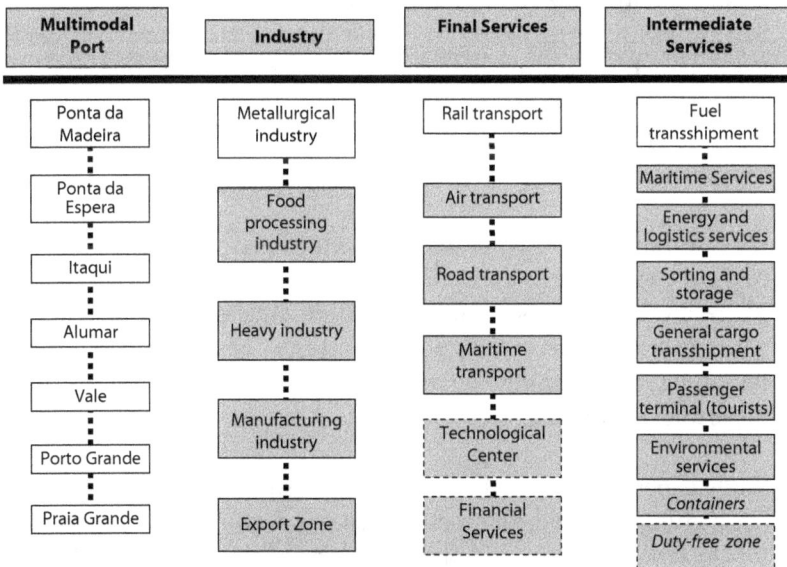

Multimodal Port	Industry	Final Services	Intermediate Services
Ponta da Madeira	Metallurgical industry	Rail transport	Fuel transshipment
Ponta da Espera	Food processing industry	Air transport	Maritime Services
			Energy and logistics services
Itaqui		Road transport	Sorting and storage
Alumar	Heavy industry		General cargo transshipment
Vale		Maritime transport	Passenger terminal (tourists)
	Manufacturing industry	Technological Center	Environmental services
Porto Grande			
Praia Grande	Export Zone	Financial Services	Containers
			Duty-free zone

Source: Workshops for cluster members and municipal government, São Luís, January 2008.
Note: All shaded boxes are due for expansion by 2010. All dashed boxes are due for expansion by 2013.

air transport and cruise ships) should also have been made by this time (shaded boxes in figure 5.3). In particular, the location is a logical one for a steel mill, and the obstacles to locating a mill there appear to be mainly institutional—lack of clearly defined zoning, rights-of-way, and environmental licensing.

Setting an ambitious goal, participants envisaged continued rapid expansion into additional sectors related to the port complex by the end of five years. By this time, the following could be under way: additional light industry (for example, food processing) and heavy industry (steel mill) located in one or more industrial parks; advanced port services in place; and the region moving toward establishing a duty-free zone (*zona franca*), as well as a logistics and distribution technology hub and financial services to further support and complement the high volume of transshipment and local production that could be taking place.

Priority Actions: Initial Recommendations
The following initial priority actions were agreed upon by cluster members and the São Luís municipality during the workshops in January.

- **Formalize cluster arrangements.** The first step for the cluster is to maintain the momentum from the initial work of the port-industrial cluster and formalize cluster arrangements, in terms of defining membership (with participation of public, private, and nongovernmental institutions), structure, and short-term actions. It is important to include state government agencies in the process, as many of them have direct responsibilities in the cluster (management of Itaqui port and industrial districts, for example).

- **Hire or train staff in cluster development.** To successfully adopt some of the recommended approaches, having qualified staff will be crucial. There are several opportunities for short courses and conferences to get exposure to these techniques, and the concept of clustering is becoming more commonly taught in business schools and economics departments in Brazil.

- **Study experiences with similar clusters.** A small group of officials and business leaders could, for example, visit one or two regions with successful clustering activities and observe the process firsthand—such direct contacts seem to enhance the progress of cluster initiatives significantly, while also cementing important public–private relationships among the leaders who are traveling together. While not as helpful, a two- or three-day training course in clustering in São Luís may provide key examples as well as sensitize leaders to the issues, and could potentially include a larger number of participants at lower cost than a study tour.

- **Form a team to evaluate and take steps on the industrial parks.** One initiative that appears to have strong support among cluster members is the notion of providing ample space close to the port area for manufacturing activity, extended logistics and warehousing, or both. To attract investments of related industries in the area, it is critical that land be made available to potential investors without excessive bureaucratic processes. While the economic justification has been clear, the main obstacles appear to be on the institutional side. Clearer zoning and regulatory policies including environmental licensing, appropriate transportation, and access to utilities are necessary for such a site to be developed, otherwise only smaller parcels are available, which are not of interest to large investors.

Setting this as a clear priority and launching a visible process to address the issue with full participation of the private sector would not only solve a major impediment to the growth and diversification of the São Luís economy, it would also provide a strong signal to potential participants in the wider cluster process that breakthroughs are possible and that changes are taking place in São Luís.

Initial Assessment of the Tourism Cluster

Cluster Background
São Luís' tourism assets include:

- A UNESCO World Heritage Site, the Historic Center (*Centro Historico*) of São Luís. This is the largest colonial urban and architectural ensemble in Latin America, with over 4,000 buildings representative of its whole history
- The Lençóis Maranhenses National Park, less than four hours away from the city, with unique scenery including 1,000 hectares of sand dunes
- Thirty kilometers of beach
- Rich culture, in terms of dance, music, history, and festivities
- A convention center, museums, and many other cultural and business facilities.

Despite these assets, tourism growth has not been spectacular and has not been a major driver of the local economy. The municipal government has started to develop a tourism cluster strategy. Some initial analysis and recommendations, largely based on a World Bank mission conducted in early 2008, are presented here.

Initial Diagnosis

Figure 5.4 maps the key components of the tourism cluster.

Supply/Input Conditions. As a tourism destination, São Luís offers visitors a unique combination of cultural and historical experiences, as well as adventure and ecotourism, which can be packaged together to attract

Figure 5.4   São Luís Tourism Cluster Map

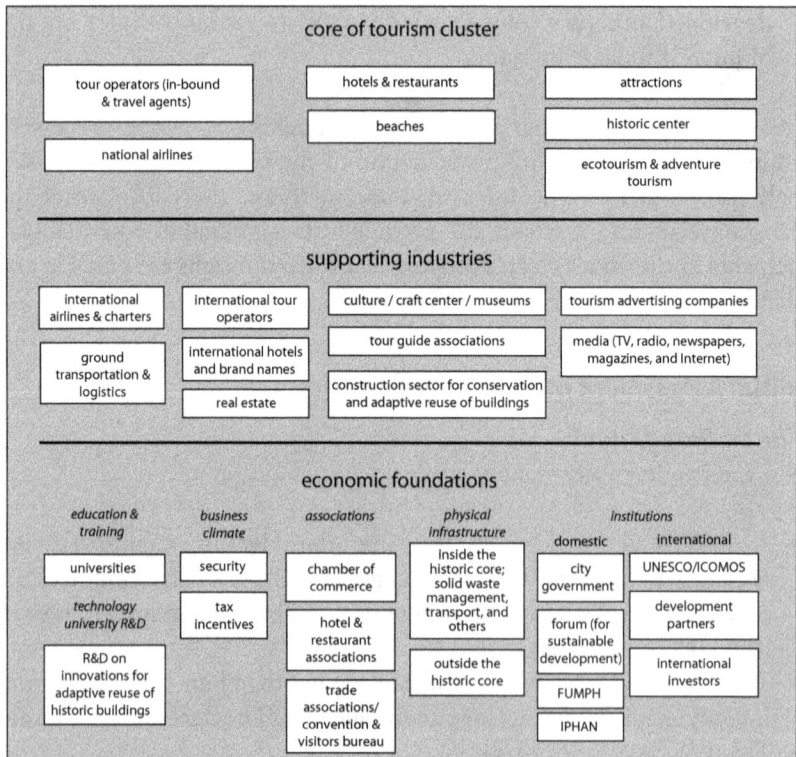

Source: Authors, based on workshops conducted in January 2008.
Note: ICOMOS = International Council on Monuments and Sites; FUMPH = Fundação Municipal de Patrimônio Histórico (Municipal Historic Heritage Foundation); IPHAN = Instituto do Patrimônio Histórico e Artístico Nacional (Brazilian National Historical and Artistic Heritage Institute).

both leisure and business travelers. Given its remote location, it is important that the destination be marketed whenever possible as a "package" destination, where visitors can experience both culture and adventure (ecotourism).

In terms of history and cultural attractions, the most important site is the Historic Center. The late 17th-century core of this historic town, founded by the French and occupied by the Dutch before coming under Portuguese rule, was listed as a UNESCO World Heritage Site in 1997. It is one of the finest examples of an Iberian colonial town with its original integral pattern of the streets and open spaces entirely preserved. There are many buildings that UNESCO considers as having high individual merit and that acquire a more significant quality when treated as an entire townscape. UNESCO also highlights the perfect integration of the urban landscape with its setting at the junction of two rivers. The Historic Center is one of the most significant examples of life in 18th and 19th century Brazil.

São Luís is also rich in cultural attractions, including regional gastronomy, handicrafts, night life, folk festivals and activities, as well as walking and boat tours. However, they must be developed for tourists and prepared for national and international markets. They also need to be integrated, organized, and promoted as part of the broad tourism portfolio.

About 30 kilometers from São Luís, by ferry across São Marcos Bay, is the small historic town of Alcântara. Founded by French explorers in the 16th century, Alcântara was later conquered by the Portuguese, who used the small village as a base to take São Luís from the Dutch in 1646. In the boom years of the 18th and 19th centuries, Alcântara was a regional capital for sugar and cotton trading. In 1948, the half-empty city was declared a historic site, primarily for its lovely collection of colonial houses covered in bright Portuguese tiles with ornately decorated doors.

As for parks and beaches, the Lençóis Maranhenses National Park—a desert with unique scenery of blue lagoons among the vast sand dunes—is less than four hours from São Luís. A trip to Lençóis can be combined with a more relaxing day-trip from Barreirinhas down the River Preguiças to Caburé, a tiny fishing village located on a piece of land where the river joins the sea. In addition, São Luís has more than 30 kilometers of beach.

Business and events tourism is facilitated by the new convention center on the outskirts of the old town, which boasts a 1,500-person capacity auditorium. Some hotels offer meeting venues for corporate and special events. The convention center is among 100 convention and visitors bureaus competing for a share of this market nationally.

In addition to the Itaqui seaport, São Luís has a medium-size airport (Marechal Cunha Machado), bus and rail stations, and two passenger ship terminals (one in São Luís and one in São Jose de Ribamar). The island can be reached by bridge or by rail. The airport of São Luís, the main gateway for national and international tourists to the state, allows the city to develop programs with a tourist focus, mostly combining itineraries with Lençóis Maranhenses.

Some of the key infrastructure challenges, for both tourists and local residents, include (a) water pollution, resulting from deficiencies in the sewage collecting network and from discharge of wastewater from the drainage systems; (b) lack of proper storm drainage defense mechanisms; (c) poor operation of the urban cleaning services and storm-drain cleaning (resulting in the presence of solid waste in the rainwater-collecting networks); and (d) discharge of solid waste into open-air ditches (causing offensive odors and sanitary risks).

Another challenge is that the municipality suffers from a lack of well-trained and skilled personnel in different sectors of the tourism industry. A 2007 survey of businesses conducted by the municipal Secretariat of Tourism (SETUR 2007) identified this as a major weakness. For example, there is a shortage of qualified tour guides in the Historic Center, and those that are available are limited to the Portuguese, Spanish, and English languages. Lack of skilled human resources also extends to the hotel and restaurant, transportation, travel, public relations/media, and other supporting sectors.

The wider area has several universities, such as the State University of Maranhão, which can be tapped to offer both short-term training and vocational courses, as well a degree program, in tourism. An inventory and assessment should be made of the training programs available with a view to developing a certification program for the different types of training. Accessibility to this training by the underemployed and poor residents of the historic town will also contribute to employment creation and address the larger social issue of retaining the original residents in the Historic Center.

Demand Conditions. At present, domestic demand is driving the tourism cluster. About 95 percent of tourists come from within Brazil, with the remaining mostly from Europe. Compared to other cultural and historic sites in Brazil, São Luís receives a small number of tourists.

The Secretariat of Tourism of São Luís has conducted research on tourism, which was updated by a survey of tourists in July 2007. The most common reasons given for visiting São Luís are leisure, visiting family or friends, and business or studies (table 5.11). In seasonal terms, leisure travel in particular increases during the high season, while the reverse is true for business travel. The trips related to visiting family and friends remain relatively inelastic.

The highest influx of domestic visitors comes from within the state of Maranhão (table 5.12), with 37 percent in the high season and 51 percent during the low season, when prices are lower. Seasonal variations were also apparent in the number of tourists depending on the state of origin.

For visitors, the main draw of São Luís is its natural resources, which attract close to 50 percent of visitors (table 5.13). These figures show the potential for linking ecotourism with culture and history to maximize the draw during both high and low seasons.

Table 5.11   Reasons for Travel, 2007

Reasons for travel	High season (%)	Low season (%)
Leisure	42.40	16.67
Visit family/friends	23.63	23.39
Business/studies	19.71	32.21
Health	10.21	14.57
Events	2.02	7.28
Sports	0.00	1.40
Others	2.02	4.48

Source: SETUR (2007).

Table 5.12   Domestic Tourist Origins, 2007

High season (%)		Low season (%)	
Maranhão	36.82	Maranhão	50.56
Pará	17.22	Pará	4.76
Federal District	6.29	Federal District	1.68
São Paulo	6.06	São Paulo	5.32
Ceará	4.63	Ceará	5.88
Rio de Janeiro	4.16	Rio de Janeiro	4.34
Piauí	3.92	Piauí	4.34
Minas Gerais	2.49	Minas Gerais	8.96
Amazonas	2.02	Amazonas	1.40
Goiás	1.31	Other states	0.56
Other states	10.81		

Source: SETUR (2007).

Table 5.13   Main Attractions, 2007

Reasons for travel	High season (%)	Low season (%)
Low prices	1.40	7.01
Historic Center	10.36	10.52
Cultural events	21.56	9.64
Natural attractions	49.29	46.49
Others	17.36	26.31

Source: SETUR (2007).

Most visitors stay with family and friends, 60 percent in the high season and 70 percent in the low season. The second preference is hotels, with 24 percent of tourists staying at such places during the high season and 21 percent during the low season.

Business Environment. São Luís has a relatively benign regulatory environment for conducting business compared to other Brazilian cities. Of 25 municipalities surveyed by the International Finance Corporation, São Luís ranked fifth. For example, in terms of the time needed to obtain a construction permit, São Luís and two other municipalities are the most efficient, taking fewer than 35 days to grant a permit. However, areas for improvement still exist, and a general improvement in the business environment (in terms of opening a new business, securing permits, paying taxes, and more) is important for tourism as the cluster involves many small businesses engaged in a wide range of areas.

There is a need to increase the level of competition in some market segments. In particular, tour operations are now dominated by one large operator, which is not healthy. The municipal and state governments have adopted a special incentives package for new businesses in the Historic Center. Innovative businesses there are to be exempt from a share of state and municipal taxes. This should help further revive the historical district as a place for living and doing business. However, it is important to have clear planning and restoration guidelines to ensure that the new businesses will preserve the cultural heritage.

Related and Supporting Industries. A cluster of supporting services includes:

- *Hotels.* The hotel network in São Luís is located in three principal sections of the city: at the Historic Center, around the airport, and close to the beaches. In total, there are 64 establishments providing 3,119 rooms with 6,472 beds. Overall, there is room to upgrade the level and quality of hotels in the city.

- *Events organizers and promoters.* There are 23 firms specializing in events organization and promotion. Some groups specialize in different sectors, such as reception, audiovisual, and media and dissemination. In September 2005, the São Luís Convention and Visitors Bureau was set up to hold national and international conventions and workshops as well as other meetings related to culture, technology, and science. In 2007, the bureau held 38 events.

- *Bars and restaurants.* There are 720 registered establishments, 180 of which are members of the Association of Hotels, Restaurants, and Bars (SINDHORBS) and 66 tied to the Brazilian Association of Bars and Restaurants (ABRASEL). There is a need to strengthen this subsector both by increasing the number as well as upgrading the quality of service to cater to both the domestic and international market.

- *Travel agencies and tour operators.* During the 1960s and 1970s, the city had only 3 agencies or operators; by the 1990s, more than 12 were operating in the city, and presently the number has reached 123. Of these agencies or operators, 43 are members of the Maranhão section of the Brazil Association of Travel Agents. However, it is estimated that 90 percent of the tourists visiting São Luís are not part of a package; trips organized by travel agencies and tour operators represent only 1 percent of the visitors to the city. This can be explained by the dominance of a single tour operator; aggressively attracting more travel agents will introduce competition and likely improve these numbers.

Collaboration within the Cluster. Various types of networks drive tourism activities in São Luís. Among the most important are entities involved in the promotion of local trade-related tourism activities.[2]

Several initiatives have recently been undertaken to strengthen the cluster of organizations around tourism. Among this is the biannual "round of business" for the different corporate entities, public agencies, and entrepreneurs who are interested in looking at potential markets in the city. Participants stay for two days and participate in a large promotional event with cultural presentations, food tasting, arts and crafts exhibits, as well as business meetings. However, these events have had little result, and have served primarily to plan for future events. On the other hand, there have been several agreements reached by establishments within the network of different institutions involved in the tourism industry that will benefit the whole cluster, such as the imposition of taxes on local hotels and restaurants to fund tourism promotion.

Another venue for collaboration is the Municipal Tourism Council, which consists of representatives from various government agencies, the private sector, and civil society groups. Its mission is to promote the development of the tourism industry and its productive sectors. With its broad stakeholder base, the council provides a vehicle for collaboration and closer integration among the different interest groups.

The creation of the Convention and Visitors Bureau is clear evidence of awareness of the need to collaborate and a mobilization of private initiative. Following the international conventions bureaus management model, the bureau is a nonprofit organization formed by numerous private initiatives in the Municipal Tourism Council. These actions are undertaken through combined efforts and financial contributions of agents associated with the bureau. The bureau focuses on the "business events" segment of tourism, seeking opportunities for attracting events compatible with the city vision. It is a major partner of the municipal government for integrating actions of government and private enterprise in a common direction.

In spite of the above, links between the local tourism sector and supporting industries in São Luís remain weak. Links with the international tourism sector, especially in aspects relating to cultural and ecotourism, should be further developed.

Priority Actions: Initial Recommendations

During the tourism cluster workshops in January 2008, cluster members identified two priorities for short-term action: developing and implementing a plan for tourism marketing and implementing training to enhance tourism capacities, in both the private and public sectors.

In following up on these recommendations, the Secretariat of Tourism recognized the need to pursue a more integrated approach. For example, for effective marketing, there is a need for better information on local tourism products and offerings, diagnosis of key market niches and areas of focus, and identification of the priority markets for initial efforts. The following short-term actions are therefore recommended. These are to be further refined through ongoing work by tourism experts and feedback from tourism cluster members.

- **Product inventory and diagnosis** should include:
  - *Drawing up an inventory of tourism products and offerings.* This would involve the mapping of major tourism assets, municipal services, and infrastructure related to tourism; hotels, and their classes and capacity; airport and air flight data; venues for cultural and business events; attractions (museums, cultural centers, and monuments) and events; internal transport; restaurants, bars, and entertainment; logistical matters; tours and package tours available; and other products under development.

  - *Diagnosis of current tourism products*, including existing products, services, and facilities and assessing tourism product inventory with regard to quality of facilities and services, including which products are ready for market and which need to be improved to meet minimum quality standards. The diagnosis should provide suggestions for short-, medium-, and long-term improvements in order for the products to become competitive. It should also include value chain analysis of the tourism products, and identify products at different stages (mature, developed, and developing).

- **Market research,** including market surveys to obtain insights of tourists' overall experience in São Luís, expenditure patterns, and evaluation of the quality of various tourism services (hotel, restaurants, destinations, and transportation). The research should study the source markets outside São Luís (primarily domestic markets) with residents who have been to São Luís and its environs, and those who have not. The study should conclude with a list of the priority markets for São Luís.

- **Tourism product improvement and expansion,** to address weaknesses identified by the product diagnosis and market research, in areas such as construction and renovation, training, improvements in maintenance, tour route improvement, and training to improve the quality of services. Some of the possible areas of focus, dependent on the results of the diagnosis, could be:
  - *Conserving cultural heritage*, through expansion and acceleration of ongoing historic conservation efforts, consolidation of partnerships with the public and private sectors, and strengthening urban planning and restoration guidelines to ensure the preservation of the historical characteristics of the UNESCO site.

- *Improving the quality of tourism facilities and services* (attractions, hotels, restaurants, tourist guides, and others), perhaps through establishing a certification system.
- *Strengthening the management of special events* (for example, key local festivals, or cultural experiences such as gastronomy and museums) to improve their quality, accompanied by aggressive marketing of these events.

- **Tourism promotion and marketing.** Based on good diagnosis and understanding of the tourism products and the market demands, a plan for tourism promotion and marketing can be developed and implemented, focusing primarily on the priority markets.

- **Action-oriented tourism cluster organization and implementation.** Based on the mapping of the tourism cluster, and the activities of collaboration already undertaken by the private and public cluster stakeholders, the tourism cluster organization should be formalized, with an agenda focused on undertaking joint actions to promote and develop the cluster. Because of the diversity of private and public sector entities involved, the Secretariat of Tourism would need to play a leadership role in organizing the cluster. However, it is crucial that private sector members be the main participants in the cluster. Ideally, over time, they will take over the leadership role of the cluster.

The cluster should be a key venue for all stakeholders to work closely with the tourism experts engaged by the municipal government in planning and implementing the key activities highlighted above. It would be important, in fact, to identify the responsibilities and participation of private and public stakeholders for actions to be proposed by the planning work.

Overall Strategy and Next Steps

São Luís is at a crossroads: Changes in recent years appear to favor the city, and these have led to improved infrastructure, positioning the city to play a leading role as a transportation hub. This already suggests a level of transformation that will be challenging from an urban management perspective. However, the opportunity to go beyond transportation into logistics, manufacturing, advanced services, and tourism appears within reach.

A framework is needed to convert goals into actions. This broader opportunity to diversify the economy significantly will require vision and changes to "the usual way" of doing things. Many projects, such as the industrial park adjacent to the port area, have been stalled for years, and a breakthrough in the city's way of handling such projects would have a significant impact on prospects for economic diversification. Similar experiences worldwide indicate that, given the limited resources of the government, such major changes are unlikely if they are a one-sided "push" by government—regions across the globe that have managed this transition in recent years have had far more success using public–private partnerships to accomplish these goals (Herzbert and Wright 2005).

There are a variety of methods for developing these partnerships—one such method is the cluster approach, outlined below in six key steps for the first year of launching the approach.

Step 1: Forming a Joint Public–Private Leadership Team

Often called "competitiveness councils," such leadership teams consist of the most influential and visionary public and private leaders in the region. While it is important to have key political figures committed to the venture, it is also recommended that private sector leaders, from a spectrum of large, medium, and small companies (along with bodies that represent them) form the largest "block" in the team. It is also important to include key figures from academe (usually university presidents), and any other community figures who are prominent and in a position to promote actions toward greater economic prosperity.

In the first year, such teams are ideally open to change and not formalized by legal statute or formal "slots" for representation or appointment. Such formalization often occurs in later years after the outlines of the initiative become more apparent—flexibility and rapid response are the most important qualities to foster in the first year. For this reason, it is often useful to use outside facilitation or sponsorship in this initial period to provide a neutral platform and ensure forward movement.

While this leadership team will be broadly representative of the stakeholders of the local economy, it is very helpful to have an institutional home—that is, a secretariat providing staff support, dealing with logistical issues, and providing analytical and implementation support. Generally, these matters are handled within a government department, although sometimes a chamber or university department can do them, and this approach may have some advantages given the institutional setup. A very important criterion in selecting a location for the secretariat is that its director is very capable, both in his or her understanding and direct experience of the economic issues, as well as in interpersonal and managerial skills. An inspiring and action-oriented individual in this crucial position can help overcome innumerable problems later on.

Step 2: Cluster Analysis and Benchmarking (Competitive Analysis)

São Luís has a favorable position geographically and economically, but it has direct competitors for its services. Other regions farther afield (such as Singapore and Hong Kong, China) provide valuable reference points for the role and evolutionary path of a transportation hub that evolves into a logistics, manufacturing, or advanced services and technology center. Careful evaluation of the key indicators of such competitors can be a valuable tool for understanding São Luís' position, as well as for helping create a sense of urgency for cluster participants.

The evaluation should also provide profiles of the three key clusters in São Luís—transportation, tourism, and manufacturing[3] appear to be three areas of importance—with a possible fourth area, services, that has potential, but could probably be covered as an integrated part of the other three at this stage. Some researchers might prefer a more fine-grained approach, disaggregating the clusters into 10 or more "microclusters." While this latter approach may have some methodological validity, we recommend staying initially with the broader groupings, partly because the economy is not yet highly differentiated, and partly because the resulting cluster working groups would be too small and too unconnected with the key existing drivers of the economy to mobilize change. There is always opportunity to form specific task forces or, at a later date, to diversify the clusters once institutional capacity has evolved to handle them.

There is often the temptation to overstudy the issues, devoting too much budget and time to a competitiveness analysis, merely postponing action and wasting time. Normally, a three-month study, relying mainly on existing studies and data sources, and outlining the areas where future more detailed studies can be useful, is sufficient.

The goal is to have a document whose key conclusions can be quickly absorbed by busy executives, rather than an exhaustive compendium that pleases academics and has an impressive thickness, but does not capture the interest or attention of key players in the economy. For this reason, we recommend an ongoing "analysis–action" approach shown below, where the initial diagnosis is sufficient to launch the process, and future analysis is conducted as needed in response to requirements of the leadership team or individual cluster working groups.

Step 3: Forming Cluster Working Groups

Within three months of launching the cluster initiative in São Luís, it should be possible to instigate three cluster working groups simultaneously. These would each consist of 10 to 20 business leaders, including key suppliers and related industries, as well as relevant government officials, specialized workforce providers, technology specialists, and marketing experts to provide a well-rounded group to evaluate the cluster.

The obvious starting point for a port-industrial cluster would be the top executives from all the ports, and the major shipping companies operating in them. However, what would make it a genuine cluster activity would be the inclusion of companies providing services to the ports, insurance providers, warehousing, and representatives of other modes (for example, railroads, highways, urban roads, and perhaps air cargo). Key researchers at the universities, marketing experts, trainers, labor unions and regulators would also be necessary. The leadership team would play a key role in helping identify the key participants and ensuring that they commit to participate, not just for one meeting (which is often inconclusive), but for the full four-meeting process (figure 5.5).

In the first cluster meeting, the concept of clusters would be introduced, and relevant examples from around Brazil and other countries presented. The composition of the cluster would be explored with the participants, generating a more detailed "cluster map," and key issues and challenges for the cluster would be identified. The aim of the second cluster meeting is to put more emphasis on developing a vision for the cluster's evolution, as well as the requirements for reaching that vision—the main outlines of a strategy. The third cluster meeting would elaborate strategies and identify specific actions.

Figure 5.5   Cluster Formation Process

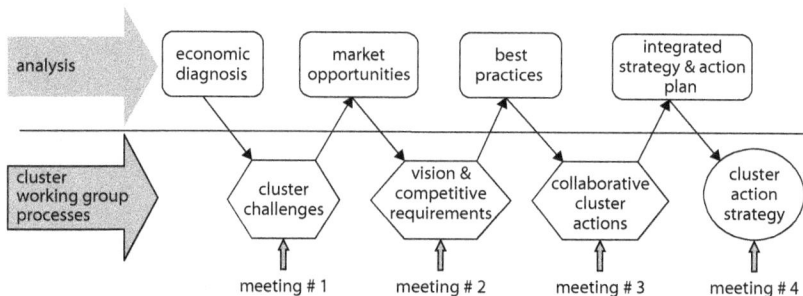

Source: Authors.

Step 4: Developing Integrated Strategy and Action Initiatives

The fourth meeting would bring all these elements together in an integrated action strategy for the cluster. Using this collaborative approach—with many smaller meetings for task forces on specific issues and initiatives between the second and fourth cluster meetings—a broad consensus can be reached, as well as ways of ensuring that each sector represented in the cluster has a role to play in implementation.

The benefits of this approach are not limited to the creation of an integrated action strategy—although this would be very valuable in itself. Companies begin to appreciate the wider context in which they operate, and generally become bolder in terms of their own strategies and ambitions for expansion. They begin to see more clearly the role that new technologies can play, the importance of marketing outside the region, and how skills development can assist in capitalizing on these opportunities. New networks are created, even among companies that already know each other but have not worked in such a relationship in the past.

Similarly, the quality of communication between companies and government can become far more constructive. Rather than operating in the earlier mode of lobbying on one side, and making decrees on the other, working together and forging more personal relationships can build trust, while the competitive context ensures that there is a common goal and that the best interests of the cluster are the result. Similarly, companies should find that they have a better understanding of the role that universities can play in upgrading the capabilities of the cluster.

Step 5: Communication and Outreach

Communication is an essential part of the process, as shown in figure 5.6. The majority of companies will not be able to participate in the cluster meetings (there would be too many participants), and overall public education on the economy is also important. Frequent, larger, "summit-style" meetings—giving cluster leaders an opportunity to present their initiatives to the wider community—can build support and bring in new leadership to the process.

Step 6: Organizing for Continuity

Also shown in figure 5.6 is the role of the leadership team, which needs to provide overall guidance to the process, and ensure that cross-cutting initiatives, which rise above the needs of individual clusters, are championed and implemented. As the overall initiative takes shape, the leadership

Figure 5.6   Full Organization of Cluster Initiative

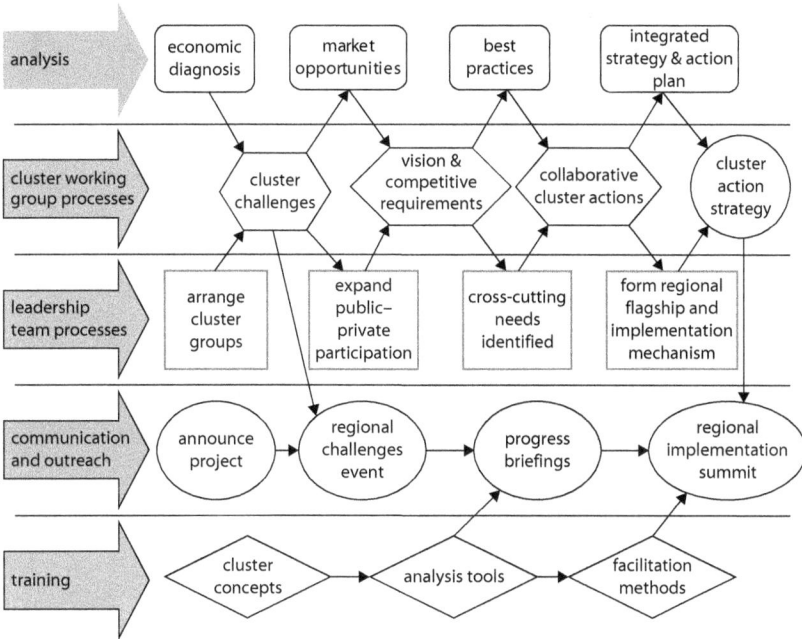

Source: Authors, based on work by the Economic Competitiveness Group.

group may evolve, bringing in new leaders, and the clusters may choose to continue as a cluster, or revert back to the constituent associations, chambers, and agencies that were there before—this tends to vary by individual cluster. However, having staff capability in the first year of the process (usually with the help of consultants) and continuing to support the entities during the implementation-intensive stages (second and third years) are essential, and provisions need to be made for training staff, and usually hiring one or two new staff with relevant experience.

Notes

1. The data used in this analysis come from RAIS, Ministry of Labor.

2. Such as the São Luís Convention and Visitors Bureau, Brazilian Association of the Hotel Industry in Maranhão, Association of Hotels and Bars in Maranhão, Association of Events Organizers of Maranhão, Association of Car Rental Companies of Maranhão, Association of Travel Agencies of Maranhão, and Association of Bars and Restaurants.

3. Manufacturing can be taken as one area or broken into light manufacturing (including food processing) and heavy or metals manufacturing.

References

Altenburg, Tilman, and Jörg Meyer-Stamer. 1999. "How to Promote Clusters: Policy Experiences from Latin America." *World Development* 27 (9): 1693–1713.

Amaral Filho, Jair, Tatiana T. Scipião, Lidiane A. Mateus, and H. H. S. Botão. 2006. *Subsídios para identificação de arranjos produtivos locais—APLs no Ceará.* Governo do estado do Ceará, Secretaria do Desenvolvimento Local e Regional. Fortaleza: Premius.

Amaral Filho, Jair, and Dayane Lima Rabelo de Souza. 2003. "Texto para Discussão No. 9, Arranjo Produtivo de Calçados do Cariri." Governo do Estado do Ceará, Secretaria do Planejamento e Coordenação, Instituto de Pesquisa e Estratégia Econômica do Ceará. Fortaleza.

Armstrong, H. W., and J. Taylor. 2000. *Regional Economics and Policy.* 2nd ed. Oxford: Blackwell.

Arthur, W. B. 1994. *Increasing Returns and Path Dependence in the Economy.* Ann Arbor: The University of Michigan Press.

Austrian, Ziona. 2000. "Cluster Case Studies: The Marriage of Quantitative and Qualitative Information for Action." *Economic Development Quarterly* 14 (1): 97–110.

Barro, R. J. and X. Sala-i-Martin. 2004. *Economic Growth.* 2nd ed. Cambridge, Mass.: MIT Press.

Bassanini, A., S. Scarpetta, and P. Hemmings. 2001. "Economic Growth: The Role of Policies and Institutions: Panel Data Evidence from OECD Countries." Economics Department Working Paper 283. OECD, Paris.

Begg, Ian. 1999. "Cities and Competitiveness." *Urban Studies* 36 (5/6): 785–810.

Bombay First–McKinsey. 2003. *Vision Mumbai: Transforming Mumbai into a World-Class City—A Summary of Recommendations.* New Delhi, India.

Brandão, F., and J. de A. Rosa. 1997. "A Indústria de Calçados no Rio Grande do Sul: Algumas Questões e Desafios que se Colocam para o seu Desenvolvimento." Núcleo Indústria, Documento Síntese, Indústria de Transformação. FEESEH/FPMR/Secretaria Estadual de Coordenação e Planejamento, Porto Alegre.

Brookings Institution. 2008. *MetroPolicy: Shaping a New Federal Partnership for a Metropolitan Nation.* http://www.brookings.edu/reports/2008/06_metropolicy.aspx.

Cabrero, Enrique, Isela Orihuela, and Alicia Ziccardi. 2003. "Ciudades Competitivas—Ciudades Cooperativas: Conceptos claves y construcción de un índice para ciudades mexicanas." CIDE. Proyecto de Trabajo 139. December.

Canova, F., and A. Marcet. 1995. "The Poor Stay Poor: Non-Convergence across Countries and Regions." CEPR Discussion Paper No. 1265.

Carvalho, A. S., S. V. Lall, and C. Timmins. 2008. "Regional Subsidies and Industrial Prospects of Lagging Regions." Policy Research Working Paper 3843. World Bank, Washington, DC.

Chandler, Billy Jaynes. 1984. *The Bandit King: Lampiao of Brazil.* Texas A&M University Press.

Chen, Tain-Jy. 2008. "The Emergence of Hsinchu Science Park as an IT Cluster." In *Growing Industrial Clusters in Asia: Serendipity and Science,* ed. Shahid Yusuf, K. Nabeshima, and S. Yamashita. Washington, DC: World Bank.

Cities Alliance. 2006. "Guide to City Development Strategies: Improving Urban Performance." Washington, DC.

———. 2007. "Understanding Your Local Economy: A Resource Guide for Cities." Washington, DC.

da Costa, Odorico de Morais Eloy. 2007. "O Arranjo Produtivo de Calçados em Juazeiro do Norte: Um Estudo de Caso para o Estado do Ceará." Doctoral dissertation submitted to Instituto de Economia of Universidade Federal do Rio de Janeiro.

da Mata, D., U. Deichmann, J. V. Henderson, S. V. Lall, and H. G. Wang. 2007. "Determinants of City Growth in Brazil." *Journal of Urban Economics* 62 (2): 252–272.

de Souza, Dayane Lima Rabelo. 2003. "Arranjo Produtivo de Calçados no Cariri." Master's thesis presented to Universidade Federal do Ceará, Faculdade de Economia, Administração, Atuária e Contabilidade, Fortaleza.

DIT (Department of Information Technology of India) and NCAER (National Council of Applied Economic Research). 2007. "India: E-readiness Assessment Report 2005." Annex I on Principal Component Analysis. January. www .mit.gov.in/download/ANNEX.PDF.

Dixon, R., and A. P. Thirlwall. 1975. "A Model of Regional Growth Rate Differences on Kaldorian Lines." *Oxford Economic Papers* 27: 201–14.

Djankov, S., R. La Porta, F. Lopez de Silanes, and A. Shleifer. 2002. "The Regulation of Entry." Working Paper 2661, World Bank, Washington, DC.

Dollar, D., A. Shi, S. Wang, and L. C. Xu. 2003. "Improving City Competitiveness through the Investment Climate: Ranking 23 Chinese Cities." World Bank, Washington, DC. www.worldbank.org.cn/english/content/23cities.pdf.

Eaton, J., and Z. Eckstein. 1997. "Cities and Growth: Theory and Evidence from France and Japan." Regional Science and Urban Economics 27: 443–74.

Easterly, W. 2002. *The Elusive Quest for Growth: Economists' Adventures and Misadventures in the Tropics.* Cambridge, Mass.: MIT Press.

Enright, M. J. 2000. "The Globalization of Competition and the Localization of Comparative Advantage: Policies toward Regional Clustering." In *The Globalization of Multinational Enterprise Activity and Economic Development,* ed. N. Hood and S. Young. London: Macmillan.

Feldman, M. P., and D. B. Audretsch. 1999. "Innovation in Cities: Science-Based Diversity, Specialisation and Localised Competition." *European Economic Review* 43: 409–29.

Feser, E. 2002. "The Relevance of Clusters for Innovation Policy in Latin America and the Caribbean." Background paper prepared for the World Bank, LAC Group. World Bank, Washington, DC.

Fujita, M., P. Krugman, and A. Venables. 1999. *The Spatial Economy: Cities, Regions, and International Trade.* Cambridge, Mass: MIT Press.

Glaeser, E. L. 2000. "The New Economics of Urban and Regional Growth." In *The Oxford Handbook of Economic Geography,* ed. G. L. Clark, M. P. Feldman, and M. S. Gertler. Oxford: Oxford University Press.

———. 2003. "Reinventing Boston: 1630–2003." *Journal of Economic Geography* 5: 119–153.

Glaeser, E. L., H. D. Kallal, J. A. Scheinkman, and A. Shleifer. 1992. "Growth in Cities." *Journal of Political Economy* 100: 1126–52.

Glaeser, E. L., J. A. Scheinkman, and A. Shleifer. 1995. "Economic Growth in a Cross-section of Cities." *Journal of Monetary Economics* 36 (1): 117–43.

Guasch, J. Luís. 2007. "Mainstreaming Export Competitiveness: How to Grow and Alleviate Poverty through Exports." Paper presented at the World Bank, Washington, DC.

Hansen, Alec. 2008. "Successful Factors for Cluster Development." Paper presented at the Cariri Footwear Cluster Strategic Planning Workshop, Juazeiro do Norte, January. Economic Competitiveness Group, Inc.

Hanson, G. H. 1997. "Increasing Returns, Trade and the Regional Structure of Wages." *Economic Journal* 107: 113–33.

Herzberg, Benjamin, and Andrew Wright. 2005. "Competitiveness Partnerships—Building and Maintaining Public–Private Dialogue to Improve the Investment Climate. A Resource Drawn from the Review of 40 Countries' Experiences." Policy Research Working Paper 3683. World Bank, Washington, DC.

Hill, Edward W., and John F. Brennan. 2000. "A Methodology for Identifying the Drivers of Industrial Clusters: The Foundation of Regional Competitive Advantage." *Economic Development Quarterly* 14 (1): 65–96.

HM Treasury. 2001. *Productivity in the UK, No. 3: The Regional Dimension.* London.

———. 2007. *Review of Sub-National Economic Development and Regeneration.* London.

Hotz-Hart, B. 2000. "Innovation Networks, Regions, and Globalization." In *The Oxford Handbook of Economic Geography*, ed. G. L. Clark, M. P. Feldman, and M. S. Gertler. Oxford: Oxford University Press.

IPEA (Instituto de Pesquisa Economica Aplicada), IBGE (Instituto Brasileiro de Geografia e Estatistica), and Universidade Estadual de Campinas). 2002. "Configuracao Atual e Tendencies da Rede Urbana." Serie Configuracao Atual e Tendencies da Rede Urbana. Brasilia.

International Finance Corporation. 2007. *Municipal Scorecard 2007.* Washington, DC.

Jacobs, S. 2003. "Keynote Address 1: The Importance of Institutions in Determining the Investment Environment." Paper presented at the South Asia FDI Roundtable, Maldives, 9–10 April. FIAS, World Bank.

Kaldor, N. 1970. "The Case for Regional Policies." *Scottish Journal of Political Economy* 17: 337–48.

Kleinhenz, Jack. 2000. "An Introduction to the Northeast Ohio Clusters Project." *Economic Development Quarterly* 14 (1): 63–64.

Klink, J. 2007. "City Regional Economic Restructuring with Weak Institutional Frameworks for Metropolitan Governance: Lessons from the ABC Region São Paulo." Paper presented at the Inter-American Development Bank (IADB), October 18.

Krueger, A. O. 2006. "Globalization and International Locational Competition." Paper presented at the Symposium in Honor of Herbert Giersch, Kiel, Germany.

Krugman, P. 1980. "Scale Economies, Product Differentiation, and the Pattern of Trade." *American Economic Review* 70: 950–59.

————. 1991a. "Increasing Returns and Economic Geography." *Journal of Political Economy* 99: 483–99.

————. 1991b. *Geography and Trade*. Cambridge, Mass: MIT Press.

————. 1996. *Pop Internationalism*. Cambridge, Mass: MIT Press.

Lucas, R. E. 1988. "On the Mechanics of Economic Development." *Journal of Monetary Economics* 22: 3–42.

McCombie, J. S. L., and A. P. Thirlwall. 1994. *Economic Growth and the Balance-of-Payments Constraint*. London: Macmillan.

Marshall, A. 1920. *Principles of Economics*. 8th ed. London: Macmillan.

Martin, P. 1998. "Can Regional Policies Affect Growth and Geography in Europe?" *The World Economy* 21: 757–74.

Martin, R., and P. Sunley. 2003. "Deconstructing Clusters: Chaotic Concept or Policy Panacea?" *Journal of Economic Geography* 3: 5–35.

National Governors Association. 2002. *A Governor's Guide to Cluster-Based Economic Development*. Washington, DC.

————. 2005. *Enhancing Competitiveness: Review of State Practices 2005*.

Nicoletti, G., and S. Scarpetta. 2003. "Regulation, Productivity, and Growth: OECD Evidence." World Bank Policy Research Working Paper 2944. World Bank, Washington, DC.

Nogueira, Cláudio André Gondim, and Daniel A. Feitosa Lopes. 2008. "A Dinâmica Econômica Setorial na Região Metropolitana do Cariri (RMC)." IPECE, Fortaleza, Ceará.

North, D. C. 1955. "Location Theory and Regional Economic Growth." *Journal of Political Economy* 63: 243–58.

OECD (Organisation for Economic Co-operation and Development). 2002. "OECD Territorial Reviews: Siena, Italy," p. 167.

————. 2003. *Entrepreneurship and Local Economic Development: Programme and Policy Recommendations*. Paris: OECD Publishing.

————. 2005. *Local Governance and the Drivers of Growth*. Paris: OECD Publishing.

————. 2006a. *Competitive Cities in the Global Economy*. Paris: OECD Publishing.

————. 2006b. *Skills Upgrading: New Policy Perspectives*. Paris: OECD Publishing.

Office of the Deputy Prime Minister. 2003. *Cities, Regions and Competitiveness*. London.

Oregon Business Plan. 2003. "Refocus Economic Development on Industry Clusters." Discussion Paper for Leadership Summit, http://www.oregonbusinessplan.org/pdf/EconDev(Cluster)Summit2003 DiscussionPaper.pdf (accessed May 20, 2008).

Palmade, Vincent. 2005. "Industrial Level Analysis: the Way to Identify the Binding Constraints to Economic Growth." Policy Research Working Paper 3551. World Bank, Washington, DC.

Porter, M. E. 1998. "Clusters and the New Economics of Competition." *Harvard Business Review* 76: 77–90.

———. 2000. "Location, Competition, and Economic Development: Local Clusters in a Global Economy." *Economic Development Quarterly* 14(1): 15–34.

———. 2002. *Clusters of Innovation: Regional Foundations of U.S. Competitiveness.* Washington, DC: Council on Competitiveness.

Porter, Michael, Xavier Sala-i-Martin, and Klaus Schwab. 2007. *The Global Competitiveness Report 2007–2008.* Geneva: World Economic Forum.

Prochnik, Victor. 2005. "Relatório Final de Pesquisa. Perfil do Setor de Calçados." Instituto de Economia da Universidade Federal do Rio de Janeiro.

Prud'homme, R, and C. Lee. 1999. "Size, Sprawl, Speed and the Efficiency of Cities." *Urban Studies* 36 (11): 1849–58.

Rauch, J. E. 1993. "Productivity Gains from Geographical Concentration of Human Capital: Evidence from the Cities." *Journal of Urban Economics* 34: 380–400.

Rice, P. G., A. J. Venables, and E. Pattachini. 2006. "Spatial Determinants of Productivity: Analysis for the UK Region." *Regional Science and Urban Economics* 36: 727–52.

Roberts, M. 2004. "The Growth Performances of the GB Counties: Some New Empirical Evidence for 1977–1993." *Regional Studies* 38: 149–65.

Roberts, M., and M. Setterfield. 2007. "Endogenous Regional Growth: A Critical Survey." Cambridge Centre for Economic and Public Policy Working Paper WP01-07. Department of Land Economy, University of Cambridge, UK.

Romer, P. M. 1986. "Increasing Returns and Long-Run Growth." *Journal of Political Economy* 94: 1002–37.

———. 1990. "Endogenous Technological Change." *Journal of Political Economy* 98: 71–101.

Rosenthal, S. S., and W. C. Strange. 2004. "Evidence on the Nature and Sources of Agglomeration Economies." In *Handbook of Urban and Regional Economics,* ed. V. Henderson and J. Thiesse. Amsterdam: Elsevier.

Rosselet-McCauley, Suzanne. 2006. "Methodology and Principles of Analysis." In *IMD World Competitiveness Yearbook 2006.* Lausanne, Switzerland: IMD.

Rowthorn, R. 2000. "Kalecki Centenary Lecture: The Political Economy of Full Employment in Modern Britain." *Oxford Bulletin of Economics and Statistics* 62: 139–73.

———. 2005. "Combined and Uneven Development: Reflections on the North-South Divide." Working Paper 305. Economic and Social Research Centre for Business Research, University of Cambridge.

Salone, Carlos. 2006. Presentation at International City Development Conference, Alexandria, Egypt, March.

Santos, Ângela Maria Medeiros M., Abidack R. Corrêa, Flávia M. Barreto Alexim, and Gabriel Barros Tavares Peixoto. 2002. "Deslocamento de Empresas para os Estados do Ceará e da Bahia: O Caso da Indústria Calçadista." BNDES Seotiral, no. 15. Rio de Janeiro. http://www.bndes.gov.br/conhecimento/bnset/set1503.pdf (accessed May 18, 2008).

Scaramuzzi, Elena. 2002. "Incubators in Developing Countries: Status and Development Perspectives." Report 26637. InfoDev Program, World Bank.

Schmitz, Herbert. 2005. *Value Chain Analysis for Policy-Makers and Practitioners.* International Labour Organization: Geneva.

Schmitz, H., and K. Nadvi. 1999. "Clustering and Industrialization: Introduction." *World Development* 27(9), 1503–14.

SETUR (Secretariat of Tourism). 2007. *Pesquisas Turismo Receptivo: Alta e Baixa Estação 2007.*

Simon, C. J., and C. Nardinelli. 1996. "The Talk of the Town: Human Capital, Information, and the Growth of English Cities, 1861 to 1961." *Explorations in Economic History* 33: 384–413.

Smith, Lindsay. 2002. "A Tutorial on Principal Components Analysis." http://csnet.otago.ac.nz/cosc453/student_tutorials/principal_components.pdf.

Solow, R. M. 1956. "A Contribution to the Theory of Economic Growth." *Quarterly Journal of Economics* 70: 65–94.

Straub, S. 2008. "Infrastructure and Development: A Critical Appraisal of the Macro Level Literature." Policy Research Working Paper 4590. World Bank, Washington, DC.

Swinburn, Gwen, Soraya Goga, and Fergus Murphy. 2006. "Local Economic Development: A Primer. Developing and Implementing Local Economic Development Strategies and Action Plans." World Bank, Washington, DC.

Swan, T. W. 1956. "Economic Growth and Capital Accumulation." *Economic Record* 32: 334–61.

Thirlwall, A.P. 1980. "Regional Problems Are 'Balance-of-Payments' Problems." *Regional Studies* 14: 419–25.

Une, Mauricio Yoshinori, and Victor Prochnik. 1999. "Desafios para a Nova cadeia de Calçados Nordestina." http://www.ie.ufrj.br/cadeiasprodutivas/pdfs/desafios_para_a_nova_cadeia_de_calcados_nordestinos.pdf (accessed May 15, 2008).

van der Linde, C. 2003. "The Demography of Clusters—Findings from the Cluster Meta-Study." In *Innovation Clusters and Interregional Competition*, ed. J. Bröcker, D. Dohse, and R. Soltwedel. Berlin: Heidelberg, and New York: Springer.

Van Stel, A. J., and H. R. Nieuwenhuijsen. 2004. "Knowledge Spillovers and Economic Growth: An Analysis Using Data of Dutch Regions in the Period 1987–1995." *Regional Studies* 38: 393–407.

Venables, A. J. 2006. "Shifts in Economic Geography and Their Causes." Paper presented at Jackson Hole Symposium, August 25. http://economistsview.typepad.com/economistsview/2006/08/ jackson_hole_sy.html.

Waits, Mary Jo. 2000. "The Added Value of the Industry Cluster Approach to Economic Analysis, Strategy Development, and Service Delivery." *Economic Development Quarterly* 14(1): 35–50.

World Bank. 2005. *Comparative Regional Development Initiatives: Lessons for Russia*. Washington, DC.

———. 2006. "Export Promotion Agencies: What Works and What Does Not." Trade Note 30. Washington, DC.

———. 2007. *Doing Business 2008*. Washington, DC.

———. 2008. *World Development Report 2009: Reshaping Economic Geography*. Washington, DC.

Yusuf, Shahid. 2003. *Innovative East Asia: The Future of Growth*. Washington, DC: World Bank.

Yusuf, Shahid, and Kaoru Nabeshima. 2006. *Postindustrial East Asian Cities: Innovation for Growth*. Palo Alto, CA: Stanford University Press, and Washington, DC: World Bank.

Zheng, Jianghuai, Yanyan Gao, and Xiaowen Hu. 2008. "Firm Concentration, Technology Promotion and Economic Performance: An Empirical Study on the Nature and Dynamics of Industrial Clusters in China's Development Zones along the Lower Reaches of Yangtze River." Discussion Paper, Industrial Economics Department, Nanjing University, China.

Index

Boxes, figures, notes, and tables are indicated by *b, f, n,* and *t,* respectively.

ECO-AUDIT
Environmental Benefits Statement

The World Bank is committed to preserving endangered forests and natural resources. The Office of the Publisher has chosen to print *Competitiveness and Growth in Brazilian Cities* on recycled paper with 30 percent post-consumer waste, in accordance with the recommended standards for paper usage set by the Green Press Initiative, a nonprofit program supporting publishers in using fiber that is not sourced from endangered forests. For more information, visit www.greenpressinitiative.org.

Saved:
- 8 trees
- 1 million British thermal units of total energy
- 413 pounds of net greenhouse gases (CO_2 equivalent)
- 1,990 gallons of waste water
- 121 pounds of solid waste

green press
INITIATIVE

www.ingramcontent.com/pod-product-compliance
Lightning Source LLC
Chambersburg PA
CBHW070910270326
41927CB00011B/2510